Marketing National Parks
for Sustainable Tourism

ASPECTS OF TOURISM

Series Editors: Chris Cooper *Oxford Brookes University, UK*, C. Michael Hall *University of Canterbury, New Zealand* and Dallen J. Timothy *Arizona State University, USA*

Aspects of Tourism is an innovative, multifaceted series, which comprises authoritative reference handbooks on global tourism regions, research volumes, texts and monographs. It is designed to provide readers with the latest thinking on tourism worldwide and push back the frontiers of tourism knowledge. The volumes are authoritative, readable and user-friendly, providing accessible sources for further research. Books in the series are commissioned to probe the relationship between tourism and cognate subject areas such as strategy, development, retailing, sport and environmental studies.

Full details of all the books in this series and of all our other publications can be found on http://www.channelviewpublications.com, or by writing to Channel View Publications, St Nicholas House, 31–34 High Street, Bristol BS1 2AW, UK.

ASPECTS OF TOURISM: 72

Marketing National Parks for Sustainable Tourism

Stephen L. Wearing, Stephen Schweinsberg and John Tower

CHANNEL VIEW PUBLICATIONS
Bristol • Buffalo • Toronto

Library of Congress Cataloging in Publication Data
Names: Wearing, Stephen, author.
Title: Marketing National Parks for Sustainable Tourism/Stephen L. Wearing, Stephen Schweinsberg and John Tower.
Description: Buffalo: Channel View Publications, 2016. | Series: Aspects of Tourism: 72 | Includes bibliographical references and index.
Identifiers: LCCN 2015033481 | ISBN 9781845415587 (hbk : alk. paper) | ISBN 9781845415570 (pbk : alk. paper) | ISBN 9781845415594 (ebook)
Subjects: LCSH: National parks and reserves—Management. | Sustainable tourism. | Tourism—Environmental aspects.
Classification: LCC SB486.M35 W43 2016 | DDC 363.6/8068—dc23 LC record available at http://lccn.loc.gov/2015033481

British Library Cataloguing in Publication Data
A catalogue entry for this book is available from the British Library.

ISBN-13: 978-1-84541-558-7 (hbk)
ISBN-13: 978-1-84541-557-0 (pbk)

Channel View Publications
UK: St Nicholas House, 31–34 High Street, Bristol BS1 2AW, UK.
USA: UTP, 2250 Military Road, Tonawanda, NY 14150, USA.
Canada: UTP, 5201 Dufferin Street, North York, Ontario M3H 5T8, Canada.

Website: www.channelviewpublications.com
Twitter: Channel_View
Facebook: https://www.facebook.com/channelviewpublications
Blog: www.channelviewpublications.wordpress.com

Copyright © 2016 Stephen L. Wearing, Stephen Schweinsberg and John Tower.

All rights reserved. No part of this work may be reproduced in any form or by any means without permission in writing from the publisher.

The policy of Multilingual Matters/Channel View Publications is to use papers that are natural, renewable and recyclable products, made from wood grown in sustainable forests. In the manufacturing process of our books, and to further support our policy, preference is given to printers that have FSC and PEFC Chain of Custody certification. The FSC and/or PEFC logos will appear on those books where full certification has been granted to the printer concerned.

Typeset by Techset Composition India (P) Ltd, Bangalore and Chennai, India.
Printed and bound in Great Britain by Short Run Press Ltd.

Contents

Case Studies		ix
Tables and Figures		xi

1 An Environmental Context for Sustainable National Park
    Marketing   1
    Introduction   1
    A Critical Reflection of Sustainable National Park Based
        Tourism Marketing   2
    Strategy and Marketing (as Practice), and Tourism
        in National Parks   5
    Principles of Marketing and its Application in
        National Parks   9
    A Model for National Park Marketing   11
    The Task of this Book   16

2 Mainstream to Alternative Tourism Marketing   25
    Introduction   25
    Sustainable Marketing and the Tree Model
        of Marketing Delivery   27
    Complementary Approaches to Marketing   33
    Summary of Marketing Strategies   51

3 Sustainable Tourism Marketing – A Wicked Policy
    Challenge for Park Managers   54
    Introduction   54
    The Dynamic and Wicked Business Environment   55

4 Approaches to Marketing Ephemeral Tourist Experiences   65
    Introduction   65
    Marketing a National Park Visitor Experience   66
    A Sacred Foundation to Visitor Perceptions of Parks   70
    Visitor Interpretations of Wilderness   73

      Marketing Authenticity in the National Park Experience   75
      National Park Interpretation   84
      Peak and Consumer Experiences of Nature on National
          Park Trails   87

5   The Multifaceted Rural, Power and the Marketing
     of Culture through Interpretation   98
     Introduction   98
     Cultural Legitimacy of Interpretation in a Multifaceted
        Rural Setting   100
     Halfacree's Three-Fold Model of Rural Place and Frisvoll's
        Power Extension   107
     Cultural Legitimacy of the Interpretive
        Message – Challenges for Park Managers   114

6   Tragedy of the Commons or Solution for the Commons   122

     References   130
     Index   154

"For the benefit and enjoyment of the people – Yellowstone National Park, created by an act of Congress, March 1, 1872"

(President Theodore Roosevelt)

Case Studies

Case Study 1: The strategic marketing plan for West Yellowstone   22

Case Study 2: Demarketing – Phillip Island Nature Park (Victoria)   53

Case Study 3: That wicked Quarantine Station (North Head National Park – Sydney)   61

Case Study 4: An ephemeral experience of John Muir   94

Case Study 5: North Yorkshire National Park – Mine or Moors?   119

Tables and Figures

Tables

Table 1.1	Guiding principles for the sustainable marketing of visitation in protected areas	12
Table 2.1	Framework for linking key issues with marketing approaches and guiding principles	34
Table 2.2	Traditional marketing principles	35
Table 2.3	Ecological marketing principles	38
Table 2.4	Social marketing principles	42
Table 2.5	Demarketing principles	43
Table 2.6	Cooperative promotion between parks and tourism operators	46
Table 2.7	Cooperative promotion between parks and state and national tourism organisations	48
Table 2.8	Objectives of parks managers and tourism operators in relation to parks and protected areas	50
Table 2.9	Relationship marketing principles	51
Table 2.10	Summary of marketing principles	52
Table 4.1	Common forms of interpretation	85

Figures

Figure 1.1	The 'Five Rs' framework for sustainable marketing of protected areas	12
Figure 1.2	Tree model of marketing delivery	17
Figure 3.1	The principle elements of a business organisation's environment	57
Figure 5.1	The three-fold model of rural space (after Halfacree, 2007)	110
Figure 5.2	Untangling power in the rural place (after Frisvoll, 2012)	112
Figure 5.3	Rural place legitimisation and a three-fold architecture of entangled rural power	115

1 An Environmental Context for Sustainable National Park Marketing

> *Handle the challenge of change well, and you can prosper greatly. Handle it poorly, and can put yourselves and others at risk*
> (Kotter & Rathgeber, 2006: 3)

Introduction

Since the World Commission on Environment and Development first proposed their iconic definition of sustainable development as 'development that meets the needs of the future without compromising the ability of future generations to meet their own needs' (World Commission on Environment and Development, 1990: 8); academia, the tourism industry, tourists and various other stakeholders have shown an innate fascination with exploring the processes and outcomes that are possible from the development of a sustainable global tourism industry. While the parameters of exactly what sustainable tourism does and does not encompass continue to be debated, a recurring theme in much of the published academic scholarship relates to the merging of a range of environmental, economic and social forces in particular destination settings.

Marketing represents the process through which economy is integrated into society to serve human needs (Drucker, 1958: 252 in Kotler, 2011: 135). Within mainstream marketing literature, Kotler (2011) recently advocated for a departure from a philosophy that sees marketing as having infinite resources to draw on and zero environmental impact. The marketing of tourism in sensitive environments of the world is not a zero sum game. Neoliberalist based strategic marketing decisions do inevitably have a range of social, cultural, experiential and ecological consequences for the environment in which they seek to operate. To this end Kotler (2011) suggests that companies need to give more consideration to the manner in which they balance and integrate their organisational growth targets with a range of other environmental targets.

In the present work we wish to explore the process of integration in an environment that for many is a quintessential part of tourism systems throughout the world, national parks. Since their initial inception, national parks have had a volatile relationship to the tourism industry. Because of their dual conservation/utilitarian management agendas, park managers, environmentalists and others are often quick to dismiss nature-based tourism as being yet another example of unrestrained travel based capitalism. In the present work we will aim to test this proposition, and ask two controversial questions of our readers in relation to national park based tourism marketing. Should marketing continue to be seen, as it so often is, as the quintessential exhibit of a neoliberalist based industry standing in direct opposition to environmental preservation? Or is it perhaps not better seen as a tool that can be used by park managers to advance their dominant environmental preservation agenda?

A Critical Reflection of Sustainable National Park Based Tourism Marketing

The development of a sustainable marketing orientation requires that one merge 'the conceptual principles of sustainable development with market orientation' (Mitchell *et al.*, 2010: 695). In doing so, one is forced to find a balance between supporting the continued growth of neoliberalist, profit oriented industries on the one hand; whilst simultaneously affording equal consideration to the more nuanced social forces in an organisation's operating environment. There are numerous mechanisms whereby this can be achieved. In Chapter 2 of the present work the authors will examine in detail a range of alternative marketing forms including: relationship marketing, ecological marketing etc. These and other forms of marketing are predicated on an idea from Belz and Peattie (2009 in Mitchell *et al.*, 2013: 698) 'that sustainable marketing responds to consumer needs and marketplace opportunities, [while] reflecting company values, [and being] ... well suited to company resources and capabilities'.

The companies to which we refer are the various protected area agencies that are responsible for the management of national parks and other protected areas throughout the world (see for example Griffin *et al.*, 2010b). These park managers, who form one of the main intended readerships of this book, are almost without exception committed to the preservation of the natural and social world. They are the custodians of a common resource that is important to people the world over, and are part of a noble lineage that can be traced back to the early environmental pioneers including John Muir and

Gifford Pinchot. John Muir once famously characterised himself as a man of many hats; 'I am a poetico –trampo – geologist – bot. and ornith – natural, etc. !!!' (MacFarlane – Introduction in Muir, 2007: vii). Far from diminishing Muir's legacy, the multiple faces of John Muir has allowed him to simultaneously unlock the geological secrets of the Yosemite Valley, whilst founding the modern conservation movement, and through his own prose, to draw an ever increasing number of readers into the innate beauty of the natural world. Change was a reality for Muir, just as it is for park managers today. In his lifetime he was forced to respond to competing stakeholder viewpoints over the sustainable management of a number of locations in the Californian wilderness including the Hetch Hetchy Valley and the Grand Canyon.

Some of Muir's advocacy endeavours were a success; others at the time were failures. The legacy that is inherited by park managers today is more than the preservation of particular plots of land. It is instead the 'widespread conviction that our national parks should be held inviolate' (Sierra Club, 2015). Exactly what it means to be held inviolate in the context of national park tourism management is just as vexed a question for park managers today as it was for Muir in the mid-19th century. In the course of describing his first avalanche, Muir makes an oblique reference to tourism's future potential noting that whilst others may say that 'steam has spiritualised travel; through unspiritual smells, smoke etc. … This flight in what could be called a milky way of snow-stars was the most spiritual and exhilarating of all modes of motion I have ever experienced' (Muir, 2007: xv–xvi). The notion that there is somehow something lacking in certain types of travel experiences, and simultaneously mysticism about others, draws the reader's attention to the case specificity of tourism development. Throughout this book we will draw attention to the long and evolving history of tourism in different national parks throughout the world. Drawing on the words which opened this chapter, from the influential organisational change and leadership theorist Professor John Kotter and his colleague Holger Rathgeber, we will argue that far from being at odds with the dominant national park conservation ethic; tourism, if planned correctly, can play an important part in ensuring a sustainable future for park ecosystems.

In order for tourism and conservation to achieve a symbiotic relationship of mutual dependence there is a necessity that both sides of the land-use fence realise their own unique, but also mutually reinforcing, histories. As Professor Tina Seelig from Stanford University has noted, it is through the reframing of problems that one can unlock innovation (see Seelig, 2012). When viewed from an organisational management perspective, innovation has been defined as the 'creation of either a new process (process innovation) or a new product or service (product/ service innovation) that has an impact on the way the organisation operates' (Clegg *et al.*, 2011b: 663). Over the last 100 to 150 years, innovation has become synonymous with modern business practice. Pioneers of business innovation including Henry Ford, along with waves of technology innovators including Steve Jobs and Bill Gates, have provided a fertile ground for academic inquiry, exemplified in iconic works including Clayton Christensen's *The Innovator's Dilemma* (Christensen, 2013).

Porter (1996 in Clegg *et al.*, 2011a: 183) defines the process of innovation as being connected to a firm's strategic priorities in the sense that 'strategy means being different, or doing different things'. The process whereby one sets one's self apart from ones rivals necessitates business seeing its position in a dynamic business environment made up of a diverse set of market and non-market forces. Sustainable tourism, which will be one of the major themes running through the present book, is not just about the preservation of an industry's position in an economically competitive travel market place; it is about the role that tourism has to protect the sociocultural and physical environment in which it is situated from unsustainable development. In this way we would argue, the strategy of nature-based tourism businesses must be situated in the context of practice (see Carter, 2013; Carter *et al.*, 2008a, 2008b; Jarzabkowski & Spee, 2009; Whittington, 1996 for a discussion of strategy as practice, 2007). Strategy as practice has been described by Clegg *et al.* (2011a: 27) as a 'network of scholars concerned with the everyday processes, practices and activities involved in the making of strategy'. Formed as a counterpoint to traditional strategy theorists, including Ansoff and Porter who had proposed a rationalist conceptualisation of strategy; strategy as practice theorists have proposed an *ad hoc* phenomena 'focussed on the processes and practices constituting the everyday activities of organisational life and relating to strategic outcomes' (Clegg *et al.*, 2011a: 27).

Evans (2009: 227) has noted that marketing constitutes one of the core strategic considerations of tourism firms, providing one of the primary mechanisms whereby businesses can seek to develop a competitive advantage over their rivals. As will be described further in the next section, mechanisms for strategic positioning including market segmentation and product placement are already established spheres of interest in many existing tourism marketing texts. In the present book we wish to expand on this existing body of knowledge and consider the theoretical underpinnings of concepts such as the ephemeral experience, a concept that is so fundamental to the marketing of iconic experiences in national parks but one that is also underpinned by a complex history of stakeholder interactions since the early years of the parks movement.

'A marketing strategy represents an internally integrated but externally focussed set of choices about how the firm addresses its customers in the context of a competitive environment' (Clegg *et al.*, 2011a: 150). Through the present book we will pursue a philosophy of pushing the boundaries of tourism marketing knowledge. In doing so, we will aim a new lens on many established marketing concepts, a lens which we acknowledge owes much of its development to the impact of fields including geography and sociology.

In the next section we will expand on some of the links between tourism marketing and business strategy.

Strategy and Marketing (as Practice), and Tourism in National Parks

In 1962 Alfred DuPont Chandler, Professor of Business History at John Hopkins University and the Harvard University Business School, wrote that organisational strategy [of which we would argue marketing is a core component (see Ruekert, 1992) is a product of environmental change; 'a response to the opportunities and needs created by changing population[s] and changing national income and by technological innovation' (Chandler, 1990: 15). The concept of environmental change affecting corporate practice has been a recurring theme throughout much of the literature on national parks and national park management. The world's first national park, Yellowstone National Park, was created in 1872 in part as a response to the opening up of the state of Montana to gold prospectors in the 1860s (Runte, 1997). Similarly, the 1916 *National Parks Service Organic Act*, which gave legislative provision to the creation of the United States National Park Service is said to have emerged from the confluence of a range of environmental forces – 'the religious naturalism of Thoreau and Emerson, romanticism in the arts and early nostalgia for what was obviously the end of untamed wilderness' (Sax, 1980: 7). Each of these iconic events is characteristic of what the present authors would describe as an increasing appreciation of symbiotic complexity; an appreciation amongst park managers that their concerns cannot simply be for the altruistic fulfilment of desired recreational experiences. Instead, through the signing of a range of legislative instruments (the 1973 Endangered Species Act, the 1979 Archaeological Resources Protection Act etc.), national park managers have shown an increasing appreciation of the complexities of ecological sustainability and the need to consider the future of industries like tourism in their broader environmental context.

Perhaps nowhere has the growing importance of ecologically sustainable park management been more evident than at the recently completed International Union for the Conservation of Nature (IUCN) World Parks Congress in Sydney Australia (November 2014). The Promise of Sydney Vision, which was endorsed by the more than 6000 conference participants from 160 countries, affirmed a promise to 'rebalance' the relationship between human society and nature. This was to be achieved in part through the promotion of sustainable land uses such as tourism. Marketing is a fundamental component of a competitive strategy for tourism destination development (see Evans, 2009) including in national parks. Encompassing the processes whereby buyers and sellers come together for the exchange of products and services; marketing has for many years formed a core component of a number of key tourism textbooks, monographs and journal papers (e.g. Buhalis, 2000; Clarke *et al.*, 2013; Dickman, 1999; Gilmore & Simmons, 2007; Hall, 2014; Heath & Wall, 1991; Krippendorf, 1987; Middleton, 1998; Pike, 2004; Witt & Moutinho, 1994). The recently published *Routledge Handbook of Tourism Marketing* has called for greater sophistication in the tourism industry's engagement with marketing topics to reflect the industry's growing importance in international business. Such a prioritisation is not without justification. Balmford *et al.* (2015) recently estimated that there are roughly 8 billion global visits to protected areas per year, visitation that provides approximately US$600 billion in direct in-country expenditure and a US$250 billion consumer surplus. At a more local scale, Wilton and Nickerson's (2006) showed that in 2001, 76% of travel expenditure in the US state of Montana was focused on the region's natural features, with the Glacier National Park being the most profitable site.

The aim of the present book is to contribute to scholarship on the interplay of sustainability principles and neoliberalist based service economies in national parks. What you will read is a departure from many traditional marketing texts that have tended to focus on the internal machinations of marketing delivery (i.e. the marketing mix, marketing operations and tactics, advertising sales and promotions etc.). For readers interested in exploring the machinations of marketing delivery, we would direct them to a range of works already in publication (e.g. Holloway, 2004; Lumsdon, 1997; Martin & Schouten, 2012; Middleton, 1998; Middleton & Clarke, 2012; Morrison, 2010; Pike, 2004, 2008; Seaton & Bennett, 1996; Witt & Moutinho, 1994). Rather than revisit this ground, the authors have chosen to leverage the work of Achrol and Kotler (2012: 44) who note that in addition to being about consumers and firms, 'marketing is about the economic, social and environmental sum of these contributions'. These issues present what Achrol and Kotler (2012: 44) describe as the superphenomena of marketing. Marketing they note must embrace 'a worldview commensurate with its vanguard role in the social and economic wellbeing of nations' (2012: 44).

In choosing to focus our attention on contextual issues rather than specific marketing tools and approaches, the authors are making a very specific statement about where we see the current state of tourism marketing in national parks. Specifically, we are suggesting that tourism marketing, however profitable it may be, should not be exclusively focused on the maximisation of tourism satisfaction and revenue. Rather, as Whitelaw *et al.* (2014) note, it should also extend to assisting park agencies achieve their broader organisational goals and missions. These missions have evolved over time as societal expectations on the value of preservation versus protection of natural assets has changed (see Sellars, 2009). While parks have always been fundamentally connected to the psyche and prestige of nations, their sustainable utilisation cannot be framed according to a set of indisputable scientific laws. Social attitudes evolve both temporally and geographically on the basis of a complex interplay of stakeholder viewpoints. Contemporary definitions of national parks by groups including the IUCN have been based around ideas including:

> Natural or near natural areas set aside to protect large-scale ecological processes, along with the complement of species and ecosystems characteristic of the area, which also provide a foundation for environmentally and culturally compatible spiritual, scientific, educational, recreational and visitor opportunities. (International Union for Conservation of Nature, 2014)

Definitions like this are built on the principles of ecological sustainability where social and economic processes are deferential to the maintenance of ecological processes. This places them in contrast to the historical views of wilderness activist and journalist Robert Sterling Yard, who in June 1916 penned the following statement for the article 'Making a Business of Scenery':

> We want our national parks developed. We want roads and trails like Switzerland's. We want hotels of all prices from lowest to highest. We want comfortable public camps in sufficient abundance to meet all demands. We want lodges and chalets at convenient intervals commanding the scenic possibilities of all our parks. We want the best and cheapest accommodations for pedestrians and motorists. We want sufficient and convenient transportation at reasonable rates. We want adequate facilities and supplies for camping out at lowest prices. We want good fishing. We want our wild animal life conserved and developed. We want special facilities for nature study. (Sellars, 2009: 28)

Robert Yard was not alone in proposing such utilitarian views. In the early years of the American National Park movement, the agency's inaugural director Stephen Mather had set out to promote visitation and promote the immodest goal of making national parks an American trademark in the competition for the world's travellers (Keiter, 2013). Marketing was a key element in the original agencies' strategic management planning, although this seems to have slowly been changed as the environment conservation philosophy came to predominate in later years and even now we find limited mention of marketing in the books on National Parks.

Whilst it would be simplistic to believe that the selection of isolated quotes from the IUCN and Robert Yard will provide us with a comprehensive appreciation of the value positions that different tourism stakeholders attach to the role of tourism in national parks; they do serve to illustrate the increasing trend towards seeing tourism as part of a larger system of sociocultural, environmental and other influences. Such trends are not immune to contestation. The Banff Bow Valley Round Table in the Canadian Rocky Mountains in the mid-1990s demonstrated the intractability of many stakeholder groups to in any way compromise their own values and ideology to accommodate people of different viewpoints. In seeking to manage the day-to-day contestation between environmentalist and human usage mandates in an environment like Banff, managers will often be forced to subscribe to a reality where strategic vision takes a back seat to control; 'controlling visitor impacts on the park, and controlling the park from an ecosystem management perspective that considers human presence and needs' (Eyre & Jamal, 2006: 194). This is an unfortunate state of affairs when one considers that in a corporate social responsibility context, adherence to the law is effective often at only holding people to the minimum standard of environmental behaviour. Rather than simply seeking to pursue strategies like demarketing in the hope that it will reduce the negative effects of tourism impacts, managers must also be conscious of the bigger picture and the possibility that demarketing may also 'increase the risk and likelihood of commercial failure, especially in view of the pursuit of sufficient revenue to fund remediation activities and park operations' (Whitelaw et al., 2014: 596).

The purpose of the present book is thus intended to provide for academics, students and park managers a comprehensive overview of some of the principles and challenges that can underpin tourism marketing in a national park context. In a recent paper focused on defining the 'Kuhnian shift' in the paradigm of marketing in the third millennium, Achrol and Kotler note that a more prosperous world 'magnifies the side effects of consumption societies on the ecology and resources of the world' (Achrol & Kotler, 2012: 50). Tourism has for many years had a contentious link with its environment, simultaneously being credited as a destroyer of social and environmental capital, whilst in other quarters being credited as a more environmentally sensitive utilisation of the natural world than many other industry alternatives. In a recent state of the art review on the state of academic research into sustainable tourism, Buckley (2012) notes that whilst sustainability has become something of a buzzword for tourism industries globally over the last few decades, the continued interest of policy makers and consumers has not been mirrored in an evolution of academic research interests in sustainable tourism. Within different research streams Buckley (2012) notes high levels of academic interest in protected area tourism, whilst simultaneously acknowledging what he describes as a low level of research progress into notions of cultural context, personal values and behaviours and responsibility. Whilst we are not asserting any definitive causative link between the different fields, Archer and Wearing (2002) have for a number of years been calling for sustainable tourism in parks to be achieved, not through the addressing of *ad hoc* on-site impacts, but rather through the addressing of broader causative issues including visitor behaviour, knowledge, awareness and attitude.

To achieve such outcomes, marketing scholarship must dispel with its universal preoccupation with the normative notions of the power of marketing management over consumers (Skålén & Hackley, 2011). While such mainstream marketing principles will play a role into the future, as evidenced in the definition of marketing of the American Marketing Association as a set of 'institutions, and processes for creating, communicating, delivering, and exchanging offerings that have value for customers, clients, partners, and society at large' (American Marketing Association, 2013); the expanding notion of marketing as practice, 'which sees consumers and producers as mutually constitutive phenomena' (Skålén & Hackley, 2011: 190) draws our attention to the need to think more critically of the process of marketing delivery. This is not a 'how to' marketing text but rather the focus is on issues that park managers must face as they address the need to manage their parks for the generations not yet born.

In Chapter 2 we will explore a range of alternative marketing strategies; ecological marketing, social marketing, etc., noting their theoretical constructs and the practicalities in applying them to the sustainable management of national park ecosystems. In the present chapter our aim is to lend an environmental context to these discussions, taking inspiration from the words of Shearman (1990 in Van Dam & Apeldoorn, 1996: 45) who noted that the 'implications of sustainability are to be found in the modifications and contradictions that become apparent when the consequences of sustainability are considered within a particular context'.

Principles of Marketing and its Application in National Parks

> *Marketing is merely a civilized form of warfare in which most battles are won with words, ideas, and disciplined thinking.*
> (Albert W. Emery)

Before we begin to discuss the challenges of reconciling conservation, tourism growth and park usage it is important to provide a fundamental overview of marketing principles that are used to guide the explanation of tourism marketing in national parks. To date, the body of literature that has sought to specifically canvas the links between national parks and tourism marketing is minimal (see Archer & Wearing, 2002; Audrey & Geoff, 2007; Beeton & Benfield, 2002; Deffner & Metaxas, 2009; Frank, 2008; Hogenauer, 2001; Kern, 2006; Lai *et al.*, 2009; Sharpley & Pearce, 2007; Watkins, 1990; Wearing, 2008a, 2008b; Worboys *et al.*, 2015). While authors including Crompton (1983) have been calling for decades for park agencies to reconsider their relationship to the corporate sector; Archer and Wearing (2002) identify that main-stream marketing principles have tended to be viewed with suspicion by many in the parks sector on account of their perceived orientation towards the principles of neoliberalism and the capitalisation of nature (see Himley, 2008). There is also, some would suggest, an element of park managers' poor understanding of marketing and how marketing principles could be applied in park settings (Marsh *et al.*, 2012).

Since the debt crisis of the late 1970s there has been an increasing preoccupation throughout the world with notions of privatisation, trade liberalisation, state reduction and currency devaluation as mechanisms for avoiding overdependence on the state. Power (2003: 9) has described the idea that the economy should have primacy over social norms as a 'religion in itself'. As a religion, the attractiveness of neoliberalism as an organising philosophy for tourism and other service based industries in protected areas is easy to appreciate. Eagles (2002) identified an underrepresentation of nature based tourism within the fiscal priorities of many governments who often prefer to concentrate on more easily discernible income generators such as mining and manufacturing. While recent scholarship by Deloitte Economics has positioned tourism as one of the top five growth areas of the Australian economy in the next 20 years (Deloitte Economics, 2013), the partially industrialised nature of the sector (see Leiper, 1990; Leiper *et al.*, 2008) combined with its small operator focus has continued to be seen by some as an impediment to its growth potential.

Throughout the world's national parks there are numerous examples of tourism development such as the Mawlands owned Quarantine Station in the Sydney Harbour National Park being used as an avenue for protected area development. While many scholars continue to debate the likely effects of such policies on conservation agendas (e.g. Büscher *et al.*, 2012; McElwee, 2012) and on societies in tourism destination regions (see Mullings, 2010), Archer and Wearing (2002) have suggested that perhaps there should be less of a focus on *ad hoc* responses to address the impacts of uncoordinated tourism development in parks. Instead they advocate that a greater level of attention needs to be given to addressing the strategic positioning and marketing of tourism industries as part of a broader process of sustainably managing park ecosystems.

The oft cited quote from Albert Emery, which opened this section, equated marketing with a form of warfare where the objectives of strategists is determined through persuasion rather than through violence. Since the 1920s, when Leverett Lyon introduced 'strategy' formally into the business vernacular, there has been an appreciation of strategy's link to marketing. As Sharma (1999: 73) notes, Lyon saw marketing managers 'using strategy holistically, within the economic-social order of our time (that is consideration of the external environment), and as integrally concerned with the diverse internal aspects of business including production and finance, consumer oriented, and having a sense of social responsibility'. Effective strategic marketing is complicated to achieve on the basis of the various relationships and values that exist among different stakeholder groups (Buhalis, 2000).

Theoretical constructs such as 'True Marketing' have been developed with a view to incorporating values constructs into marketing strategy, creating a hierarchical ladder that prioritises people ahead of financial profit based considerations (Mattsson, 2008). The first and most important principle of the personal level of True Marketing is being true to one's self; asking whether the action taken or being deliberated on is the right one for your organisation (Mattsson, 2008). The National Parks Service (ND-b) has characterised its values along such lines, asserting that their corporate values are a representation of who they are and what they stand for as an organisation. They are not something that is defined in relation to wider cultural norms or changes to market preferences (National Parks Service, ND-b). Throughout this book we will argue that the process of achieving sustainable strategic outcomes for tourism development within a national park is dependent upon a manager's ability to break down barriers between divergent value positions regarding the marketing of tourism products. It is this principle that is at the heart of our conceptual model, which we introduce in the next section.

A Model for National Park Marketing

In 1971, Kotler and Levy wrote a paper for the *Harvard Business Review* under the title 'De-marketing, yes demarketing'. By proposing that there are in effect limits on the environment's ability to fulfil consumer demand, Kotler and Levy were flying in the face of conventional wisdom at the time, which saw a two-fold role of marketing as finding customers for existing products and developing new products for as yet unmet customer wants (Kotler & Levy, 1971). Today, demarketing is an established response strategy in a range of protected area contexts as managers look to purposively redistribute tourist demand on the basis of ecological and social imperatives (Armstrong & Kern, 2011; Beeton, 2003; Beeton & Benfield, 2002; Clements, 1989; Deutsch & Liebermann, 1985; Groff, 1998; Kern, 2006; Quan, 2000). In developing the conceptual model of national park marketing that we will explore in this book, we have been guided by a series of core marketing principles, which we will introduce in this section.

These principles have been previously articulated in Wearing *et al.* (2001). In a report to the Sustainable Tourism Cooperative Research Centre it was identified that national park marketing should adhere to what the authors described as an 5R model of sustainable marketing (see Figure 1.1). The model in Figure 1.1 is predicated on a belief amongst the authors that sustainability in national parks is first and foremost about the protection of environmental integrity. However, the idea that the environment of a national park should be seen through a variety of lenses (physical, psychological, experiential, cultural, economic etc.) led to the conclusion that tourism is first and foremost about a series of direct and mediated relationships with, and in, the context of space/

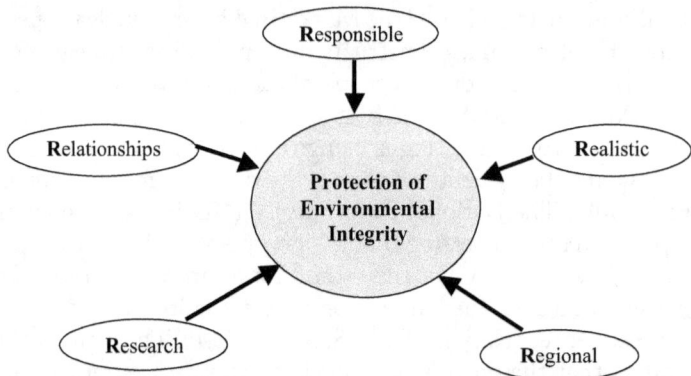

Figure 1.1 The 'Five Rs' framework for sustainable marketing of protected areas

place. Wearing *et al.* (2001) proposed a series of five independent variables; the 5Rs that attempt to articulate some of the values based determinants of environmentally sustainable marketing in national parks (see Table 1.1).

Notions of humankind's need to act **responsibly** towards their environment are not new. Gifford Pinchot, the inaugural head of the United States Forest Service and an early advocate for the sustainable utilisation of forest resources made the following observation at the beginning of the 19th century:

> Our forefathers bequeathed to us a land of marvellous resources still unexhausted. Shall we conserve these resources and in our turn transmit them, still unexhausted to our descendants (Pinchot, 1910: 2)

Table 1.1 Guiding principles for the sustainable marketing of visitation in protected areas

Principle	Description of Guiding Principle
Responsible	Sustainable marketing of protected areas should be designed and undertaken with conservation as a baseline and in an ethical manner.
Realistic	To be sustainable, marketing of protected areas should be done so in a manner that disseminates **realistic** images and information to existing and potential visitors.
Regional	Sustainable marketing of protected areas should be designed and used in a **regional** context.
Relationships	Cooperative **relationships** between relevant land management, industry and community stakeholders can benefit all.
Research	**Research** is a fundamental building block of sustainable marketing. The market environment provides a wealth of data that needs to inform market decisions.

Drawing on as yet largely minority held ideas such as intra-generational equity, Pinchot was posing questions that have remained largely unresolved over the ensuing century. His apparently simple, yet almost unresolvable conundrum that the United States is in possession of more than 4 million square miles of forested resources and now must consider its fate (see Pinchot, 1910) has parallels to current political debates in Australia over the continued categorisation of 74,000 hectares of forest in Tasmania as World Heritage listed. Debates over the correct utilisation of Tasmania's forest estates have been one of the defining characteristics of Australian political discourse over the last 30 years (Ajani, 2007; Dargavel, 2004; Lane, 1999). Decades long stakeholder conflicts in the island state of Tasmania that helped give birth to the creation of the world's first environment party, the Australian Greens (Lohrey, 2002) were only recently 'resolved' through the establishment of a peace deal between forestry unions, environmental activists and other stakeholders.

Following the September 2013 election, the Liberal National Commonwealth Government led by the former prime minister, the Right Honourable Tony Abbott MP, made representations to UNESCO for the delisting of more than 74,000 hectares of forests granted World Heritage (WH) status under the aforementioned agreement. The implications of this decision for the development of sustainable national park based tourism industries becomes clear when one notes that the World Heritage brand, in theory, 'signals property so irreplaceable to human kind that its values must be sustained in tact in perpetuity' (King & Halpenny, 2014: 768). A simple Google search yields evidence of a plethora of parks including Yellowstone, Kakadu etc. that have used WH standing as a mechanism for getting people to visit. Such marketing is in evidence not only in tourism operator brochures, but also through materials that are provided to visitors on the management of the site by the various governmental management agencies. To date, the success of the WH brand as a marketing tool is open to debate. One reason why this might be the case is alluded to by King and Halpenny (2014) when they discuss opportunities for future research around the notion of brand identity. Brand identity they note is 'the outward expression of a brand including its name, visual appearance and communication, reflecting how the owner wants the consumer to perceive the brand' (King & Halpenny, 2014: 783). Who is this owner to which they refer? UNESCO (2015) notes that upon inscription as a WH area 'the site [becomes] the property of the country on whose territory it is located, but it is considered in the interest of the international community to protect the site for future generations'. Commentary from the IUCN (2011 in Reggers *et al.*, 2013) has drawn attention to the notion that the sustainable management of protected areas is contingent on the active involvement of local people and other stakeholders in the planning process.

Co-management theory has been advanced as a governance approach that will facilitate the democratisation of protected area management, placing power increasingly in the hands of local people (Becken & Job, 2014). In pursuing co-management of protected areas around the world, policy makers have broadly been interested in pursuing an integrative approach to land management, drawing on both conservation and utilitarian traditions. How these forces are balanced is a source of contention. In the case of the aforementioned delisting of WH status in the Australian state of Tasmania, the former Australian prime minister Tony Abbott made the observation that national parks should not be considered a growth industry in Australia in the same way as forestry (Keenan, 2014). These comments from the Australian Prime minister have sparked a somewhat inevitable round of opinion pieces from academic and other commentators on the criteria for national park designation. The present authors support these discussions in the sense that authors such as Keenan (2014) have engaged in important deliberations over the extent to which many of the national parks in a country like Australia actually fulfil national and global protection targets. Where we would counsel caution, however, is with the possible outcome of these debates and specifically the potential marginalisation of the role of passive based ecotourism industries in the management of a nation's forests as neoliberal focused decision makers pursue quick fix economic opportunities and open up forests to extractive based industry sectors.

The present authors' justification for this plea is both ideological and pragmatic. National Parks represent one of the principle nature-based marketing drivers of tourism's contribution to GDP in many developed and developing nations. The Serengeti National Park in Tanzania by way of example is one of the main drawcards that have assisted the national tourism industry to earn US$1 billion in 2012–2013, nearly triple the GDP of the country's historical economic mainstay, the agricultural sector (Anon, 2013). Such figures fly in the face of Alfred Runte's national parks worthless lands hypothesis (see Runte, 1997) and also, in the Australian context, draw into question the implications for tourism of the Prime minister's statement that foresters are the true sustainability custodians of the nation's forests. In raising this issue we should note that we are not seeking to cast aspersions on the sustainability of other users (or potential users in the case of Tasmania's WH areas) of a nation's forest estate. Previous scholarship by Schweinsberg *et al.* (2012) has after all identified the important role of forest industries to the sustainable maintenance of forest estates in Australia's south eastern states. Instead, we are introducing this topic at this point to ask; what exactly are the characteristics of a **responsible** interaction of tourism (or indeed any other industry) with the ecological mechanisms and processes upon which all forest users are ultimately dependent? What constitutes **responsible** land use is an essentially values driven concept in the sense that how tourism firms seek to juggle economic growth imperatives with broader corporate social responsibility objectives to give something back to a community will depend on the establishment of **realistic** expectations amongst potential visitors. Simultaneously it will also depend on the provision of grounded and balanced information from park agencies and tourism service providers. This topic will be examined further in Chapter 4 when the authors will examine the ways that trail based interpretation may serve as a conduit for establishing greater environmental appreciation amongst national park visitors.

The **regional** and **relationships** components of the 5R marketing model are both predicated by notions of national park marketing initiatives being seen in the context of the stakeholder driven environment in which all national parks are ultimately situated. A central driving force behind the authors' push to develop the present book was a perceived need for **research** on the marketing of national parks to step away from a historical tendency to be seen in terms of a narrow relationship to the financing of park agencies (e.g. Eagles & McCool, 2002). In recent years, a range of monographs have been published charting the characteristics of tourism development in national parks (Bushell & Eagles, 2007; Frost & Hall, 2009). These works have been successful in positioning the growth of tourism in its multifaceted environmental context. As Allaby noted in the *Concise Oxford Dictionary of Ecology*, the environment is:

> The complete range of external conditions, physical and biological, in which an organism lives. Environment includes social, cultural and (for humans) economic and political considerations, as well as the more usually understood features such as soil, climate, and food supply. (Allaby, 1994: 138)

In developing this book, our aim has been to position tourism marketing similarly within its multifaceted operating environment. Traditional strategic business perspectives of tourism will of course continue to advocate notions of marketing tourism for competitive advantage (see Evans, 2009). We are not seeking to devalue such perspectives. Instead we are taking a leaf from the work of Morgan *et al.* (2003) who identified destination brands to be a representation of values; inciting a range of beliefs, inciting emotions and prompting particular behaviours. In Chapter 2 we will canvas the traditional 4Ps of marketing delivery (product, price, place and promotion) as we discuss the process whereby national parks deliver a product to consumers. Before this, however, we must recognise the existence of two further Ps of destination marketing – politics and paucity (Pride, 2002 in Morgan *et al.*, 2003).

Different national parks throughout the world are managed under a range of policy instruments including the *Organic Act 1916* (United States National Parks Service), and the *Environment Protection and Biodiversity Conservation Act 1999* (Parks Australia). These and other similar acts are responsible for legislating the dual conservation and human usage agendas of many protected area authorities. Eagles (2002: 1) has noted that the success of parks agencies and governments in treading the fine line between conservation and utilitarian interests is reliant on the presence of a 'mobilised constituency that actively supports government action in the field'. The increasing plurality of interests within this constituency often has the effect of complicating the ability of natural resource managers to respond to changing consumer demands. By way of example, the use of aerial drones in Yosemite National Park has increased in the park over recent years as more and more visitors use them to film above tree tops and film climbers accessing difficult climbing routes. In May 2014 the United States National Park Service moved to ban drones on the basis of the challenges they present for other visitor users including tourists, rescue personnel and local wildlife. Similar challenges with reconciling a plurality of stakeholder perceptions have been observed in the ongoing debate over the environmental and social benefits of hunting in national parks throughout the Australian high country.

National parks are social constructs; the consequence of the intersection of a range of historical and contemporary social forces including the democratisation of land access and concern for the utilitarian worth of land versus the value of land preserved in its natural state. Hogenauer (2001: 53) describes nationally protected areas as being based on the 'the enlightened withdrawal of lands and waters in the public interest'. When national parks are 'separated' from human activity, it is often the basis of market failures as industries struggle to operate efficiently in environments that are primarily seen as conservation reserves. The paucity of funds that exist for many public sector agencies to manage tourism's interaction with the natural world has in many instances led to strategies of demarketing. Since Clements (1989) completed the first tourism specific study on demarketing, a number of authors have identified the ways that demarketing could function as a deliberate policy response to discourage an objectionable tourist market segment (Benfield, 2000; Groff, 1998; Wearing & Neil, 2009). The mechanisms by which this can be achieved have often borrowed heavily from Kotler and Levy's original vision and include strategies such as restrictive pricing and restricting access (see Beeton & Benfield, 2002). At the present our interest is not with these mechanisms per se, but rather with introducing some of the environmental factors that give rise to their employment in a national park context.

The Task of this Book

The increasing involvement of protected area agencies in the marketing of national parks throughout the world necessitates academics formally integrating ethical, social and environmental values directly into the process of marketing strategy development. With this in mind, the arrangement of chapters throughout this book has been guided by the experiences of one of the authors and his work teaching marketing theory in a range of sport and recreational contexts at Victoria University. It is on the basis of this experience that John Tower has advocated the idea of a tree model for the delivery of sustainable marketing outcomes in national parks. The Tree Model of National Park marketing delivery is provided in Figure 1.2 below.

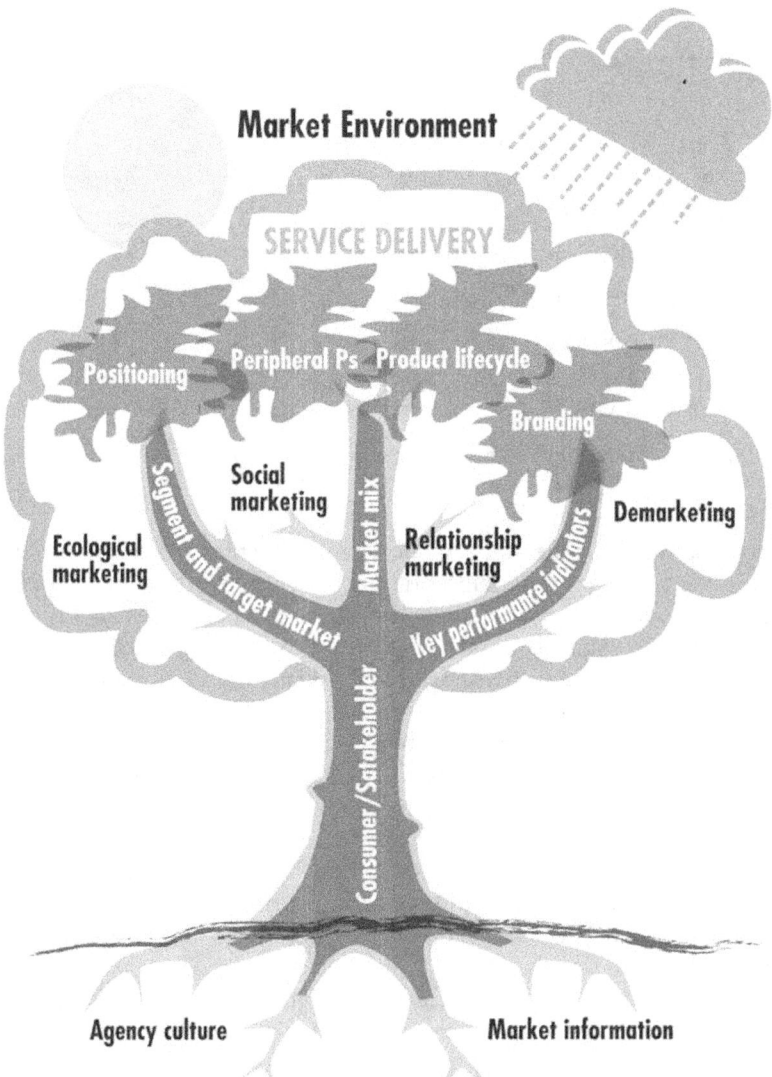

Figure 1.2 Tree model of marketing delivery

The tree model of national park marketing is predicated on the notion that a theory is a 'set of interrelated constructs (concepts), definitions and propositions that present a systematic view of phenomena by specifying relations among variables, with the purpose of explaining and predicting phenomena' (Kerlinger & Lee, 2000: 9). In the present book, the tree model serves both as a structure for the arrangement of chapters and as a statement of the author's belief as to the processes that facilitate sustainable tourism marketing in national parks.

As Joyce Kilmer once said in his evocative poem *Trees*:

> I THINK that I shall never see
> A poem lovely as a tree.
>
> A tree whose hungry mouth is prest
> Against the sweet earth's flowing breast;
>
> A tree that looks at God all day,
> And lifts her leafy arms to pray;
>
> A tree that may in summer wear
> A nest of robins in her hair;
>
> Upon whose bosom snow has lain;
> Who intimately lives with rain.
>
> Poems are made by fools like me,
> But only God can make a tree.

With these words Kilmer has provided something of a summary of many of the themes and ideas that will underpin this book. Firstly, in the opening stanza the poem affirms the authors' sincere belief in the merits of the national park movement. This is a belief that has been shared by many writers over the years. The United States National Park Service have acknowledged the work of the artist George Catlin as being one of the key early advocates for the development of large scale natural preservations for the people. Catlin was allegedly concerned about the negative effects of unplanned westward expansion in the Americas on the 19th century on flora, fauna and traditional Indian civilisations. To counter such trends he called for 'some great protecting policy of government ... in a magnificent park. ... a nation's park, containing man and beast, in all the wild[ness] and freshness of their nature's beauty!' (Harpers Ferry Center National Park Service, 2005). To this day, national parks are held up as being one pathway towards sustainable land management. Recognised as a separate category in the IUCN's protected area framework, national parks have been defined as:

> Large natural or near natural areas set aside to protect large-scale ecological processes, along with the complement of species and ecosystems

characteristic of the area, which also provide a foundation for environmentally and culturally compatible spiritual, scientific, educational, recreational and visitor opportunities. (International Union for Conservation of Nature, 2014)

Unlike other protected area categories that are 'strictly set aside to protect biodiversity' (International Union for Conservation of Nature, 2014); sustainability in a national park context is perceived according to a mixture of social, economic and ecological measures. Tourism and in particular tourism marketing has an important part to play in the reconciliation of debates over the primacy that should be afforded to different measures of sustainability. Runte (1997) notes that the iconic See America First marketing campaign, which was launched to draw Americans away from the established nature based tourism destinations of Europe, formed part of a process whereby environmentalists began to see tourism as an economic rationale for environmental preservation.

Although strictly speaking, proceeding the establishment of what could be termed organised tourism, John Muir, who will be discussed in more detail in Chapter 4 around the establishment of the Sierra Club, was an early campaigner for the myriad of benefits that Americans could gain from visiting national parks. Muir noted that:

> Thousands of tired, nerve shaken, over-civilised people are beginning to find out that going to the mountains is going home, that wilderness is a necessity, and that mountain parks and reservations are useful not only as fountains of timber and irrigating rivers, but as fountains of life (in Runte, 1997: 82)

As with any tourism destination region, national parks are typically blessed with a number of different ecological, social and other attributes. It is these attributes that will provide a justification for, as well as putting a constraint on tourism visitation (Thapa, 2012). Kilmer noted in stanza two of the poem that a tree has its hungry mouth pressed against the earth's sweet flowing breast. In the present work, we acknowledge the presence of these various destination-attributes. At the same time, however, we counsel caution over any attempt to view the natural and social features of a region as something that can be tapped to fill the altruistic needs of visitors. Instead, as we have suggested in Chapter 1 and will do again in Chapter 3 in the context of literature on wicked problems; there is an ever increasing need for park managers and marketers to embrace the contradictions and stakeholder defined complexities of the park space.

In the third and fourth stanzas of the poem *Trees*, Kilmer notes that it is in the context of its divine purpose that a tree 'may in summer wear a nest of robins in her hair'. From these stanzas, the authors have drawn inspiration for the discussion of park marketing at the intersection of macro and micro forces. We argue that it is on the basis of macro level insights, combined with information about its current users and stakeholders and market research data that park managers will choose relevant target markets, manage their market mix elements and determine key performance indicators. As Groff (1998) noted, demarketing strategies are a direct response to visitor demand. Consumers form the principal trunk of the tree model. The fact that tourists are not homogenous with respect to their degree of affinity for notions of conservation and natural processes (see Arnberger *et al.*, 2012) means that park managers must think critically as to how to engage visitors in sustainable consumptive practices. Dahl (1998 in Jones *et al.*, 2009: 817) defines sustainable consumption as 'staying within the global sustainability of resources'. Jackson (2006 in Jones *et al.*, 2009: 818) notes that sustainable consumption 'is to be achieved primarily through improvements in the efficiency with which resources are converted into economic goods'. With this in mind, in Chapter 2 the authors will engage with some of the central principles of traditional marketing and their possible application in national park management contexts. There are three main branches that provide the foundation of marketing concepts that will impact on how well the national park can meet the needs of its customers and stakeholders. These three branches, which will be explored in Chapter 2 are: (i) market segmentation and target markets (ii) the market mix (four Ps of product, price, place and promotion), and (iii) the key performance indicators that will determine how well the national park is meeting its objectives. In this chapter we will also seek to engage with the service delivery canopy, which in Tower's model articulates the range of marketing concepts that may be adopted by a national park agency to manage their marketing efforts. These complementary marketing concepts include peripheral market mix elements, positioning, product lifecycle, service orientation, social marketing and relationship marketing.

In discussing the various modes of marketing delivery in national parks the authors will emphasise that parks agencies can no longer see tourism, or indeed parks themselves, as homogeneous or monolithic. Rather, we suggest there is a need to consider both broader macro levels of process and structure (Chapters 1–3), as well as micro sites of the lived and the experiential. In Chapters 4 and 5 we will consider in detail the notion of ephemeral park experiences, and then the impact of culturally defined notions of power on the legitimacy of the message of different park management groups.

Our rationale for such an overt focus in Chapter 4 on the tourist (the trunk of the tree in the tree model) stems from the important role experience has played in iconic marketing campaigns including Brand Canada. Developed initially in 2005, Brand Canada was an attempt to reinvent a marketing brand that had become stuck in 'outdated and incomplete, reflecting only the beauty of the geography and the frontier life of the country's past' (Hudson & Ritchie, 2009). By encouraging tourists to in effect craft their own experiences, using the existing Canadian landscape as backdrop, Brand Canada was able to live up to its slogan 'Come to Canada: Create extra-ordinary stories of your own' (Hudson & Ritchie, 2009). The challenge that is created, however, from re-aligning marketing strategies to prioritise tourist concerns stems from the need for park managers to manage the juxtaposition of conservation and human usage concerns. Eagles (2014) has noted that social and political relevance is a prerequisite for park managers to be able to achieve conservation outcomes. 'How does one forge links with tourism, yet not be dominated [solely] by tourism's demands?' In Chapter 5 we will seek to answer this question with respect to the notion of culture as power and the legitimacy of different stakeholder viewpoints in the park management space.

Structures of power (and its imbalances – see reference to the effects of wind and rain in Kilmer's *Trees*) are important and largely marginalised aspects of current academic scholarship into park management. Almost since their inception, parks have come to be known as 'tourism platforms' that are influential in framing the way in which tourism is undertaken in the natural world. These platforms have been linked and studied from within broad social scientific disciplines, such as sociology and more directly management and marketing. Through the lens of the platform, tourism to parks can be regarded as being positive for the traveller and the destination because it encompasses respect for the social and environmental 'impacts'. In the past, these impacts have always been seen as objective and measurable – and hence potentially controllable for management of parks. In acknowledging the negative dimensions of tourism, many commentators sought to find alternative platforms or approaches that were adaptive rather than formulaic. From these polarizing and mediating platforms emerged approaches that were concerned with the knowledge's of tourism to parks – with understanding tourism in terms of such concerns as conflict, interaction, recreation, play and environmentalism. Perhaps the most influential of the knowledge-based platforms though, have been the studies of tourism that focused on the authenticity or otherwise of travel destinations such as nature and encounters in nature as a travel space. In Chapter 5 we will reflect on one such travel space, the multifaceted rural, as we discuss the cultural justification of power inherent in park interpretation strategies. Conclusions will then be offered in Chapter 6.

Before concluding this introduction one final word is in order. The tree model of marketing delivery represents the considered view of the authors of this book as to how the process of national park based tourism marketing may be conceptualised. Brydon-Miller *et al.* (2011: 389) noted in the context of participatory action research that 'theory is informed by practice and practice a reflection of theory'. In order for marketing to function as a practice based discipline there is a requirement that commentators give due consideration to the actions of marketers and the practices (symbolic, linguistic and material resources) they draw upon when they enact or perform marketing in organisations (Hackley *et al.*, 2008). As in the case of strategy as practice, the practices of marketing is specific to the circumstances of the sociocultural context in which it develops. For this reason we will close out each of the thematic chapters (1–5) in this book with an in-depth case study that explores some of the core theoretical concerns of the chapter in a particular geographical or temporal context.

Case Study 1: The strategic marketing plan for West Yellowstone

Throughout the present chapter an important theme has been with the way that marketing must be seen as part of the strategic focus of national park managers. The separation of tourism from conservation concerns we have argued has the effect of framing conservation and utilitarian interests as separate realities, rather than as mutually reinforcing perspectives that support the maintenance of a truly sustainable future for parks. Sustainability has long been recognised as a compilation of social, economic and environmental forces (Bartlemus, 2000; Beder, 1996; Diesendorf, 2000; Kirkpatrick & Lee, 1997; Krajnc & Glavic, 2005; McManus, 2000; United Nations, 1993, 2002). The development of a marketing plan for a sustainable tourism industry should not, we would suggest, be viewed as the same thing as the development of a marketing plan that allows tourism to contribute to sustainable development. With this conundrum in mind, we now turn to the first of our chapter case studies; an analysis of the 2014 marketing plan for West Yellowstone National Park.

The National Parks Service (2015) defines Yellowstone not only as the world's first national park, but also as a source of exemplary 'leadership for sustainability and climate change mitigation ... [outcomes which are achieved] by managing operations and adapting facilities ... to preserve our resources for this and future generations'. In 2014, the Montana Office of Tourism published a marketing plan for West Yellowstone (Montana Office of Tourism, 2014). In the paragraphs that follow, we will seek to make some observations on the degree to which this plan (on the basis of material written in the plan document only we might add) takes an integrated view of sustainability and focuses on developing a symbiotic relationship with Yellowstone Park management.

The first point that needs to be made about the plan is that it takes a very strategic approach, merging SWOT analysis principles with due consideration of the mission statement for Montana Tourism. Direct competitors and competitor routes are acknowledged, along with a range of tourist centred characteristics likely to affect demand including; negative press, inaccurate perceptions of access during winter and traveller frugality. Also recognised are the unique social and environmental assets of the region, which quite unashamedly are linked to resources provided by the park service including knowledgeable interpretive guides (further discussed in Chapter 5), interpretive centres, historic trails and the unique natural assets of Yellowstone. Identifying as a region that encapsulates the core characteristics of the Yellowstone national park more broadly; 'Yellowstone Plus' has become a catchy tag line for tourism marketing in the west Yellowstone region. The three goals of the plan, which say a lot about the objectives of its proponents, are:

(1) Attract visitors by communicating an image consistent with our long-term vision as a vacation destination and one that places high value on existing assets, amenities and natural resources of the region,
(2) continue to expand our market effectiveness by joining our efforts with those of marketing partners. Incorporate the Montana Brand pillars and initiatives wherever possible, and;
(3) continue to target our market as accurately as possible, to assure funding is used to reach an audience that asks for information, travels to West Yellowstone, and spends significant dollars.

The strategic focus on profit generation is understandable when one realises that in its most basic sense, the purpose of a marketing plan is to propose a strategy whereby a destination tourism organisation can seek to manage various supply and demand forces to achieve maximum profit generation over a specified time scale. A worrying trend we would argue is, however, the way that many marketing plans have tended to treat the national park environment itself as a blank canvas. In saying this, we should hasten to add we are not seeking to cast aspersions on the motivations of the Montana tourism office. Instead we are suggesting that future plans should talk positively of the ways in which tourism will not only use the Yellowstone environment as a backdrop to its economic activities, but more than this; will seek to instil in visitors the various national park values that has made the region the attractive proposition for travellers that it is today. Such a call is not just being made to tourism operators. A careful reading of the afore mentioned vision document for sustainability in Yellowstone national park

(continued)

> **Case Study 1:** The strategic marketing plan for
> West Yellowstone (*continued*)
>
> (National Parks Service, 2015) takes a fairly narrow, we would argue, perception of the links with tourism that can be facilitated to achieve sustainability objectives. While acknowledging that Yellowstone:
>
>> Preserves geologic wonders including the world's most extraordinary collection of geysers, hot springs and abundant and diverse wildlife, in one of the largest remaining intact temperate ecosystems on earth. It preserves an 11,000 year continuum of human history, including sites, structures, and events that reflect our shared heritage ...
>
> Simultaneously the vision document treats visitors as only a small influence on the region's sustainability potential. Strategies are proposed to allow visitors to become more energy efficient while in Yellowstone, to conserve water and to minimise the potentially negative impacts from onsite transportation activities. As we will show in Chapter 4, however, the links and motivations of people to travel in Yellowstone and other iconic parks are much more nuanced than a simple concern for minimising environmental impact. In many respects national parks represent an American legacy to the world and tourists, often following in the footsteps of colonial pioneers who view themselves as the current custodians of the rich cultural tapestry of the region. It would be nice, we would argue, to see such concerns given greater air time by managers on both sides of the tourism, park management fence.

2 Mainstream to Alternative Tourism Marketing

Introduction

The influential philosopher and pioneer of the field of political economics Adam Smith once noted that 'there is an intrinsic human propensity to truck, barter and exchange things – in other words to commodify the world through active engagement in markets' (Watts, 2009: 438–439). Belief in the benefits of free market enterprise did not begin in the 18th century with Smith's comments. Hudson (2004) has identified that widespread societal use of what we would identify as general purpose money dates back to the third millennium BC in southern Mesopotamia. Prior to this, what Hudson (2004: 99) terms 'archaic societies' employed a variety of compensatory mechanisms to give value to the various positive and negative experiences of the population. The rapid evolution of mass tourism, as well as various eclectic niche tourism products over the period since the end of the Second World War, has amplified society's need to understand the processes whereby the value in a product or service is communicated and sold to a consumer. Sir William (Billy) Butlin, the pioneer of a range of all-inclusive holiday camps in the United Kingdom in the 1930s was successful, in part, on the basis of his ability to identify often unusual customer interests (e.g. in beauty contests at his resorts) that could be cultivated and provided to a range of consumer groups (Middleton, 2010). Similarly AJ Hackett, the New Zealander widely credited with the export of bungee jumping to the world, was successful on account of his 'signing up' of a small group of flag bearers who could carry his message of bungee jumping to the wider population.

AJ Hackett's success was in part a product of his effective employment of vanguards and consumer movements to create buzz (see Dye, 2000 for a discussion of these and other approaches to strategic marketing). Such strategies have been employed to match consumer needs with product offerings in a never-ending number of tourism businesses throughout the world.

As Borden (1964) notes, the traditional focus of marketing practitioners has been in 'fashioning creatively a mix of marketing procedures and policies in an effort to produce a profitable enterprise'. Over time, however, the focus of tourism marketing has shifted. While technical issues such as the 8Ps of the marketing mix remain an important component of a range of introductory marketing texts (e.g. Morrison, 2010); gone are the days when tourism marketing is seen as a simple one way transaction process between buyer and seller. Instead, by taking a leaf out of Michael Porter's model of the 5 competitive forces that shape strategy (see Porter, 2008), Li and Petrick (2008) argue that tourists and tourism providers are in a marketing context co-creators and consumers of value.

To understand the process whereby sustainable marketing strategies may be developed therefore requires that we understand: (i) the nuanced and varied nature of tourist motivations and behaviour in protected areas (see Stanford, 2014), and (ii) the way these wants relate to current strategic management of park resources. This evidence is used to inform the understanding to guide marketing decisions. Middleton (1998) notes a range of instances where sustainability issues intersect with commercial marketing decisions. An examination of the issues Middleton (1998) identifies leads one to the conclusion that such relationships (a component of the previously cited 5Rs model) exist precisely because of the mutually assured destruction that would flow for both groups from damage to the natural world. When pursued sustainably, ecotourism is far more than a cynical marketing exercise. It is potentially an industry mechanism whereby responsible tourist behaviour to the natural world can be encouraged. Opportunities for encouraging tourist self-reflection are important on account of the fact that in most cases it is not fashionable or politically astute to preclude people from visiting national parks. Instead there is a need to remember Hardin's words in his seminal 1968 work *The Tragedy of the Commons*. Hardin (in Hall, 2014: 199) noted that measures to address a tragedy of the commons require 'a fundamental extension of morality'. For this to be achieved, Hall (2014) notes that one must consider their mutual responsibility to others in the tourism destination spectrum, responsibilities that extend to a variety of stakeholders (target markets) including non-users and the community at large.

For tourists to develop a more nuanced appreciation of their relationship to the natural world requires active and collaborative involvement of protected area planners and managers in tourist growth and development. In recent years, the authors have observed the limited uptake of such an ideal. Marsh *et al.* (2012) have identified something of a narrow understanding of marketing amongst park managers, which they ascribe to a lack of training and support from central management. Similarly Archer and Wearing (2002) note that marketing as a management idea has a relatively brief history in Australian park agencies and is often avoided out of a fear that the larger interests of the natural environment and host communities are at risk of being overwhelmed by market-place interests associated with the tourism industry. By expanding on the Tree Model of Marketing Delivery that was introduced in Chapter 1, we will discuss how alternative approaches to marketing such as ecological marketing, social marketing, demarketing and relationship marketing may offer the opportunity for the development of a sustainable marketing strategy in national parks.

Sustainable Marketing and the Tree Model of Marketing Delivery

Neoliberalism has been described loosely as a doctrine that 'argues for the desirability of a society organised around self-regulating markets, and free, to the extent possible, from social and political intervention' (Cypher & Dietz, 1997: 222–232 in Barnes, 2009: 497). Broadly developed as an antithesis of socialist and communist doctrines in the second half of the 20th century, neoliberalist mind-sets have come to be commonly accepted in a number of countries throughout the world. Tourism is often seen positively by neoliberalist proponents, being identified as an activity that can encourage human activity and enhance foreign investment opportunities (Palomino-Schalscha, 2012). Simultaneously, however, Harvey (2005) has noted the potential for neoliberalism to encourage the commodification of nature, a trend that Duffy and Moore (2010) have noted is particularly characteristic of ecotourism given the way that such sectors offer opportunities to open up new frontiers in nature to human consumption.

Kotler and Armstrong (2012) note that historically the strength of marketing and marketers has been their ability to determine the current needs and wants of consumers and to then fulfil those needs more effectively and efficiently than their competitors. As Kotler and Armstrong (2012) note, however, short-term gains for consumers can often be at odds with long-term benefits for consumers and societies at large. A good illustration of this fact can be seen in the changing societal attitudes towards smoking in the second half of the 20th century. Rojek (2005) notes that prior to the 1964 US Surgeon General's report, smoking was seen as a matter of individual choice and conscience. Throughout the first half of the 20th century numerous marketing campaigns targeting youth smokers were launched by groups including R.J. Reynolds, Chesterfield and Lucky Strike (Pierce & Gilpin, 1995). Following 1964 and the establishment of a clear causal link between smoking and increased rates of cancer and cardiovascular disease, the landscape of smoking changed with more questions being asked about the impact of smoking on non-smokers and the potential future costs of smoking related remedial health strategies on the wider community (Rojek, 2005). To counter such outcomes, various governments throughout the world have pursued demarketing strategies by providing anti-smoking information with a view to limiting the rates of smoking in the community (Shiu et al., 2009).

Sustainable marketing 'accepts the limits of market orientation and acknowledges the necessity of regulatory alterations to market mechanisms' (Belz & Peattie, 2009: 28) to foster corporate and collective commitment to sustainable development. When pursued correctly, we would argue that sustainable marketing offers an avenue to avoid many of the pitfalls of neoliberalist market mechanisms. Achrol and Kotler (2012) identify that the sustainability of a market initiative can be conceptualised both from supply and demand perspectives. Middleton et al. (2009) include market demand, product supply, transport infrastructure, destination organisations and travel organisers in this demand/supply mix. On the demand side, the consumers and sustainability in this sense relate to whether consumption rates are too high to allow comparable consumption rates between this generation and the next (Achrol & Kotler, 2012).

In the tree model, consumers/stakeholders represent the trunk of the tree and thus are the ultimate foundation for and beneficiary of any industry efforts to develop new product lines within national parks. The industry side of the marketing relationship where such product lines are formed is exhibited in the branches of the conceptual model (see Figure 1.1). The biological workings of a tree are characterised by the earth, trunk and branches working in a perfect symbiotic relationship.

The quality of the soil, the amount of rainfall, sunshine and other external factors will impact on the ability of the tree to fulfil its core functions. In much the same way in a tourism context, these external factors represent the impact of the external environment such as the economy, politics, legal requirements, demographic changes, social trends and technology (Shilbury et al., 2014). To be sustainable, Bramwell and Lane (1993 in Dinan, 2000: 1) note that 'one reduces the tensions and friction created by the complex interactions between the tourism industry, visitors, the environment and the communities that are host to holiday makers'. Tensions have manifested themselves in ongoing debates over the role of national park based tourism in the economic development of host communities (Mules, 2005) and the impact of tourism on the environmental resilience of park ecosystems (Arrowsmith & Inbakaran, 2002). Understanding such debates is important for understanding the capacity of park ecosystems to meet fluctuating levels of tourist demand. Insights from the external factors, combined with information about its current users and stakeholders and market research data will help the national park to choose relevant target markets, manage its market mix elements and be part of its key performance indicators (see Kotler & Armstrong, 2012 for a discussion of some of the systems available to marketers to source consumer insights and sync their product offerings to demand forces).

Returning to the tree model, we would argue that there are three main branches that provide the foundation for determining how well the national park can meet the needs of its customers and stakeholders. These three branches are (1) market segmentation and target markets; (2) the market mix (the four Ps of product, price, place and promotion) and (3) the key performance indicators that will determine how well the national park is meeting its objectives. The fulfilment of tourist needs is the generally accepted raison d'être for the development of tourism industries the world over. At its most basic level, tourism is a service-based industry that is focused on the provision of experiences. Whilst numerous works have been published over the last half century that are variously in support or critical of tourist motivations with respect to their relationship to different aspects of host culture (e.g. Ash & Turner, 1976; Cohen, 1979, 1988; MacCannell, 1976); tourism is still, we would argue, fundamentally focused on:

> The sum of the processes, activities and outcomes arising from the relationships and interactions amongst tourists, tourism suppliers, host governments, host communities, and surrounding environments that are involved in the attracting, transporting, hosting and management of tourists and other visitors. (Goeldner & Ritchie, 2012 in Weaver & Lawton, 2014)

The process of market segmentation and target marketing is fundamental to making sure the tourism locale is focused on market segments that fit within its broader operating goals and objectives. Arnberger *et al.* (2012) in a study of Gesaeuse National Park noted a positive correlation between tourist affinity to the park and support for the park's conservation agenda. The central premise of the current work is that since their inception national parks have operated with a dual conservation/human usage mandate, which have to be managed. Game hunting was a part of the early history of national parks in Australia including the Royal National Park south of Sydney. Recent scholarship by Jones and Lalley (2013) has, however, demonstrated the challenges in reconciling different forms of hunting with evolving interpretations of the ecotourism experience. In a study of game management in African national parks, Jones and Lalley (2013) draw attention to the multitude of land uses in national parks, along with the challenges in reconciling a relationship between ecotourism and hunting. Reflective of the notion that market segmentation is typically undertaken on the basis of a range of independent variables including geographic, demographic, psychographic and behavioral traits (Blamey & Braithwaite, 1997; Wade & Eagles, 2003); Jones and Lalley (2013) identified a number of differentiated market segments including factors based on nationality, gender and number of safari experiences. Similarly Jun *et al.* (2009) in a study of Cleveland metro parks identified a range of constraint variables including: other priorities (see Reis *et al.*, 2012; Veal *et al.*, 2013 for a discussion of the impact of time availability and other similar variables on leisure participation); setting elements, transport elements and social inhibitions that may inhibit access.

Better appreciation of market segments and target markets will assist parks to make better use of their promotion budgets. Agencies that do not make use of market segmentation in their outdoor recreation programmes spend more of their budgets on promotion than those organisations that focus on clear market segments (Zanon et al., 2014). Zanon et al. (2014) clearly demonstrate the value of understanding park market segments. Their large-scale sampling clearly identifies a range of viable market segments based on visitor activities and desired experiences. This potential commodification of the park experience demonstrates the capacity for a series of parks to deliver a range of relevant services and experiences to cater for diverse needs (Zanon et al., 2014). However, there is also a need to recognise the park's other stakeholders who may simply recognise the value of the heritage and environment and seek to protect the park for the very commodities that may be available to park users. Market segmentation and identification of target markets needs to incorporate the breadth of park stakeholders to guide the decisions about the management of the market mix (from a traditional perspective) or how the alternative marketing approaches may be applied.

It is understanding the range of stakeholders and the variables that influence the visitor experience that allows park managers to develop a better association with potential customer needs. The importance of understanding visitor experiences in national parks (see Armstrong & Weiler, 2003; Dorwart, 2007; Griffin & Vacaflores, 2004; Runnels, 2009; Russell & Russell, 2010; Tourism Australia, 2012; White, 2006) can be operationally linked, we would argue, to MacCannell's (1999 in Rojek, 2005: 114) theory of markers where he establishes that signs (see Chapter 4 on tourism interpretation) are not simply physical objects 'but symbolic systems'. In pointing out that 'signs narrate just as people narrate' (Rojek, 2005: 114) it is being established that human needs represent a tangible manifestation of tourists' attempts to exercise power in emergent tourism settings (see also Reed, 1997). Understanding these needs provides the foundation for managerial determinations of the nature of future strategically targeted landscape viewing opportunities, along with being a key driver in the push to provide appropriately trained park rangers capable of providing interpretation and outreach for visitors (Beh & Bruyere, 2007).

McCarville and McCarville (2002) notes the viability of a targeted market segment will be determined on the basis of a number of criteria, which can be related to national park contexts in the following ways:

- *Criteria 1*: Responsiveness – The level of interest a market segment shows to broader national park management agendas.
- *Criteria 2*: Identifiability – The ability to discern the boundaries of the market segment and separate them from the mainstream tourism population. Countries like Australia have sought to market national parks and

other protected areas to the experience seeker (see Tourism Australia, 2005). While experience seekers encapsulate a range of characteristics, including a quest for authenticity, which we will discuss further in Chapter 4; Waitt *et al.* (2003) have also noted that perceptions of nature are subject to individual constructions and that marketers play a key role in the perpetuation of pre-existing myths while also having the potential to support the dissemination of accurate portrayals of the complexities of a region's sociocultural and physical history.

- *Criteria 3*: Accessibility – The capacity of the national park to contact the market segment via its promotion and distribution methods. In a national park context Weaver (2011) has identified that accessibility will be underpinned by the need to undertake detailed market analysis, i.e. gaining the evidence to inform marketing decisions (see for example Weaver & Lawton, 2002), which is often beyond the financial means of most tourism small businesses.
- *Criteria 4*: Sustainability – McCarville and McCarville (2002) explains that sustainability in this context relates to the size of the market segment, which then leads to a determination as to whether it is important enough to warrant the attention of national park management. The present authors would concur with the notion that a greater level of understanding of the expectations, information requirements and desired experience of new visitor groups is central to the effective targeting of finite funds to relevant infrastructure/service provision and marketing strategies (Griffin *et al.*, 2010a, 2010b). Forming precise estimates of the size of the national park visitor group is complicated, however, by a lack of agreement on approach by different park agencies. In Australia, visitor data tends to be collected on an *ad hoc* basis with little regard for its integration into other park management tools or with its relevance/ usability amongst park agency staff (Darcy *et al.*, 2010). Where it is collected, agencies are often plagued by a number of cultural and technical issues relating to the robustness of visitor counts, lack of use of existing data and issues relating to staff training and capacity (Darcy *et al.*, 2010).

The second branch of the tree model refers to the marketing mix, which Kotler and Armstrong (2012) identify as being made up of the 4Ps of product, price, place and promotion. Product relates to the main service, commodity or idea that is consumed by the target market. The product needs to be managed to meet the needs or wants of the target market. The product provides benefits to the consumer or stakeholder; consumers purchase benefits rather than the actual product (Shilbury *et al.*, 2014).

Price includes both the monetary and the non-monetary costs that the target market will need to pay for the product. The monetary costs relate to direct expenses such as fees for park entrance or programme participation.

Monetary costs also include specialised equipment that may be necessary for particular activities, or the cost of travel to the national park. Non-monetary costs relate to the time, effort and association of being involved when consuming the park product. Time may relate to the travel time or the consumption time. Effort considers the expertise, skill level and the access to information associated with the product. Association relates to the image costs of being associated with a particular national park programme or activity (O'Sullivan, 1991). Price is one of the easier market mix elements to manage, but it needs to be set with a clear understanding of the financial considerations of providing the product and the environmental integrity of park usage. Price is often used to limit usage so only select market segments can access the service (refer to the demarketing explanation later in this chapter).

The decisions made by the national park regarding the accessibility of the product to the target market are covered by the place concept (see Kotler & Armstrong, 2012). The place of a national park is constrained by its pre-determined geographic location, but the park can decide its opening hours/seasons, and how it can be accessible to its target markets. Just as many museums now have outreach retail outlets and programmes, national parks could deliver programmes to different target markets such as schools by visiting classrooms rather than expecting all target markets to come to the geographic location. California state parks are changing their access by creating virtual park experiences that are designed to make the park more accessible to people via schools and specialised education programmes (Parks, 2014). Related to the concept of off-site interpretation, which will be canvassed in Chapter 4; parks often restrict access by limiting the number of visitors and requiring pre-bookings for different types of experiences. This type of 'demarketing' is explained later in this chapter.

Promotion is about how the national park communicates with its target market. The key to good communication is to not only make sure the message reaches the target market, but to also have mechanisms to listen to the target market to make sure their wants and needs are being met. Promotion covers all the media options such as advertising, publicity, special deals (sales promotion) and personal selling to communicate with target markets (Kotler & Armstrong, 2012). The capacity of websites and social media provide a range of communication opportunities that all national park managers should consider.

The third main branch of the marketing effort relates to having mechanisms to evaluate the marketing initiatives and having clear performance indicators of what the national park is trying to achieve. The key performance indicators (KPIs) provide information about how well the national park has achieved its marketing objectives. The KPIs should provide answers to a range of fundamental questions:

- How well is the national park reaching its target markets?
- Are the products providing the benefits that were designed to meet the needs of the target markets?
- Are the price elements effective and attractive to the target market?
- Are the products accessible to the target markets?
- Is the range of marketing promotions reaching the target markets and how are they responding to the messages?

The national park needs to establish data collection procedures that provide answers to these questions and any other aspects of the efforts to satisfy the needs of the target markets. O'Neil *et al.* (2010) note that to date 'little work has been undertaken aimed at defining the satisfaction construct in nature based settings and those forces that make a real difference in evaluating overall satisfaction and what influences the visitor's decision to revisit and/or recommend'. The systems to generate the KPIs need to be timely, effective and practical (see Bell & Morse, 2008). In saying this, we are guided by the notion that the national park environment is in a continual state of flux. Although marketing is primarily 'customer' driven, it is conducted within the context of the organisation's mission statement and goals. Because of this, it can also be used to improve relationships with agency visitors and other stakeholders. Traditional marketing principles can be applied to all park services, but new varieties of marketing including ecological marketing, social marketing, demarketing and relationship marketing (discussed below) can be used to complement the fundamental marketing principles. Importantly, each of these complementary marketing approaches can be applied usefully to management of visitors to national parks (see Table 2.1), and as will be seen, a number of researchers have already begun to examine and test the value and unique strengths that each approach can bring to managing this complex sustainability relationship. Examples of best practice are provided for each approach to alternative marketing.

Table 2.1 provides a framework for identifying how different marketing approaches can be used to respond to common issues in the park environment and also illustrates how the 5R frameworks for sustainability relate to these marketing approaches. It is clear that there is usually not one marketing approach, but a combination of approaches that the park manager needs to consider as they meet the needs of the park's consumers and stakeholders.

Complementary Approaches to Marketing

Although the principals of traditional marketing provide the foundation for satisfying the range of consumers and stakeholders, there is a range of alternative approaches to marketing that can also be used to take the

Table 2.1 Framework for linking key issues with marketing approaches and guiding principles

Issues	Marketing approaches used to address issue	Guiding principles
Lack of conservation messages in marketing and promotional materials	Ecological marketing Social marketing Relationship marketing	Responsible Realistic Relationship-based
Conflict between visitors groups and activities	Demarketing	Realistic Regional Research
Inequities in access to parks	Social marketing Demarketing	Responsible Research Regional
Crowding in parks	Demarketing	Regional Realistic Research
Lack of detailed visitor information	Traditional marketing Ecological marketing	Realistic Regional Relationship-based
Ineffective use of information brokers	Relationship marketing	Relationship-based
Confusion as to markets/promotes parks to current and potential visitors	Relationship marketing	Relationship-based Regional
Lack of control over mass and other media sources used by visitors	Relationship marketing	Relationship-based
Ensuring the protection of ecological integrity	Ecological marketing Demarketing Relationship marketing	Responsible Realistic Relationship-based
Ensuring the protection of cultural and historical heritage	Social marketing Relationship marketing	Responsible Relationship-based
Cultural and intellectual property implications of tourism, such as respect for sensitive information, copyright and use of images in marketing and promotion	Relationship marketing	Relationship-based Responsible Realistic
Expansion of economic and employment benefits of nature-based tourism in regional areas	Relationship marketing	Relationship-based Regional
Lack of cooperative partnerships and sponsorship programmes	Relationship marketing	Relationship-based Regional

Table 2.2 Traditional marketing principles

Marketing approach	Marketing principles				
Traditional marketing	Consumer/stakeholders provide the focus for marketing efforts	Impact of environment to provide evidence that informs marketing decisions	Market segmentation and target market selection	Market mix management of product, price, place and promotion	Evaluate marketing efforts through key performance indicators

marketing practices to a new level. These alternatives provide additional value and perspective to enhance marketing's capacity to deliver more positive outcomes for sustainable tourism. The foundation principles of traditional marketing are provided in Table 2.2. These marketing principles need to be applied in all marketing activities and these principles provide a foundation that enables the alternative approaches to add unique value.

Ecological marketing

The *Dictionary of Sustainable Management* defines ecological marketing in the following terms:

> Developed in the 1990s, a marketing approach to highlight products and production methods that improve environmental performance, further ecological causes, or solve environmental problems. Marketing products and services on these effects is growing but not all environmental claims are accurate. Some might be examples of green-washing. Ecological marketing works well with some groups of users, in particular "True-Blue Greens" or other groups oriented toward ecological causes. Commonly referred to claims include "non-toxic" and "bio-degradable." However, these claims may turn-off other customers who are sceptical of environmental claims. (Anon, 2012)

Ecological marketing is ideally suited to the marketing of national parks precisely because of its focus on ensuring positive ecological outcomes for environmentally conscious consumers. Nearly 30 years ago, the now departed Professor Jost Krippendorf identified that the tourism industry will need to become more environmentally oriented if it is to fulfil the desired outcomes of visitors and safeguard its prospects for growth into the 21st century (Krippendorf, 1987). Over the ensuing years there has been considerable uptake of environmental preservation approaches in tourism industries worldwide. The growth in green consumerism (see Peattie, 2001) has manifested itself in the development of a range of eco/green accreditation programmes (e.g. Green Globe, Ecotourism Australia's Eco Certification programme), which in addition to focusing tourism industry attention on the importance of environmentally sensitive operations, are aligning themselves with evolving consumer sentiment.

Environmentally sustainable marketing is not just the domain for national parks. Increasingly businesses, particularly those that provide products for nature-based activities, are embracing environmentally sustainable marketing practices. These companies are adopting policies that are designed to generate profits but also striving to help the planet (Kotler & Armstrong, 2012). The focus on ecologically responsibility is getting more support because it is good for business. It is what consumers want and expect from responsible business. National parks should consider the ecological values and practices of their partners when entering into partnerships to provide services in the park sector. The matching of values and shared goals is more likely to lead to better collaboration. This will be discussed further in the section about relationship marketing.

The development of environmentally focused marketing in national parks has cognitive, affective and conative aspects. On the cognitive level there is an expectation that operators working in a national park will offer sufficient information to allow tourists to make an accurate prediction of environmental impacts (Neagu, 2011). Beyond the provision of information, there is also a requirement that the communicated knowledge will create in the visitor some real feelings about the environmental issues. Finally, there is the requirement that pro-environmental behaviour will be encouraged from the visitors (Neagu, 2011). Each of these levels can be illustrated with respect to the history of tourists climbing Uluru (Ayers Rock) within the Uluru – Kata Tjuta National Park.

Tourists climbing Uluru has been a reality since the 1950s when the site was excised from a large Aboriginal reserve (James, 2007). Because of Uluru's dual role as an Aboriginal cultural site, and as the geographical heart of modern European Australia, there remains to this day an expectation amongst many foreign visitors that climbing is central to the fulfilment of their Australian tourism experience. James (2007: 402) notes that the overarching theme of tourism marketing is the opportunity to experience Central Australia 'as a space of the natural and cultural other'. The ability of tourists to, in a sense, separate their experiences from the expectations of the Aboriginal other was connected in part to a lack of information pre-visit, as well as the somewhat neutral stance taken by a number of tourism operators.

Uluru forms the centrepiece of Australia's red centre national landscape and for this reason is an important tourism drawcard for Australia. In order to ensure that as much as possible the right kinds of tourists are visiting Uluru, Tourism Australia has drawn a close connection between its experience seeker target market and the types of experiences that are communicated. In order to ensure that carrying capacity is not breached, there is a real focus on authentic experiences that will see tourists engaging with the whole natural and social landscape. A result of ecological based marketing of an environment like Uluru is that for many tourism operators, particularly those with a fixed asset (such as the Yulara Resort near Uluru), there is an incentive to operate their business with due consideration for not only their own business viability, but also for the surrounding areas of Uluru and Kata Tjuta which are subject to impacts from tourists staying at the resort. Consideration of the effects of ecological marketing on business viability requires due consideration of relevant local and national environmental legislation. Around Uluru, the Voyages Hotels and Resorts conduct comprehensive environmental impact assessments of all developments, along with continual monitoring of environmental management systems and environmental management plans.

Over recent years there has been a renaissance of tourist interest in notions of wilderness and self-discovery of nature. Such sentiments were characteristic of early national park visitors:

> When the tourist of an early time came to the parks, he (sic) inevitably left the city far behind him (sic). He (sic) may not have been a backpacker or a mountain climber, but he was genuinely immersed in a natural setting. He (sic) may only have strolled around the area near his hotel, but he (sic) was in a place where the sounds of birds ruled rather than the sounds of motors, where the crowds gave way to rural densities, and where planned entertainments disappeared in favour of place with nothing to do but what the visitor discovered by himself (sic). (Herremans & Reid, 2006: 181)

Progressively however, the rise of mass tourism led to a level of scepticism amongst early tourism pioneers over the type of tourism being developed and marketed in national parks throughout the United States:

> In addition to serving the drive through visitor, Yosemite accommodates those who wish to stop over, providing campsites, cabins and a hotel in Yosemite village. At times the valley which contains this village and attracts most of the visitors becomes an off-shoot of Los Angeles, complete with traffic jams and smog conditions – the very conditions tourists are trying to escape. (Murphy, 1985: 41 in Holden, 2007: 178–179)

Implicit within ecological marketing is the notion that if an activity is environmentally harmful, it should be discouraged. Examples of how park agencies have practiced ecological marketing are provided by Island Escape Tours & Sealink Tours at Kangaroo Island South Australia and Hanauma Bay in Hawaii. Visitors to Kangaroo Island need to use the Sealink ferry to get to

Table 2.3 Ecological marketing principles

Marketing approach	Marketing principles				
	Target market are environmentally conscious consumers	Affiliated (where possible) with green accreditation programmes	Provides information to:		
Ecological marketing			Inform visitors about environmental impacts	Create feelings about environmental issues	Encourage pro-environment behaviour

the island. Messages in the Sealink ferry and Island Escape Tours provide information about the environmental sensitivity of Kangaroo Island and the need for visitors to leave no trace of their visit (Wearing, 2008b). Similarly, Hanauma Bay Nature Preserve in Hawaii provides compulsory visitor briefings, including a video about the environmental sensitivity of the area and the need to protect the park environment before the visitors can enter the park (Hanauma Bay Nature Preserve, 2014). Pre-visit information and education of visitors will assist appropriate behaviours by park visitors so the environmental integrity of the park is maintained.

Table 2.3 provides a summary of the marketing principles that underpin the ecological marketing approach. It builds on traditional marketing by incorporating the specific target market that has ecologically inclined values and responds to their needs by providing information and services that meet their needs.

Social marketing

The National Social Marketing Centre defines social marketing as:

> An approach used to develop activities aimed at changing or maintaining people's behaviour for their benefit. Whereas marketing in the commercial world ultimately seeks to influence consumer behaviour for profit, social marketing encourages behaviours that provide benefit for individuals and society as a whole. (National Social Marketing Centre cited by Hall, 2014)

Social marketing strategies attempt to influence the behaviour of target markets through the application of marketing ideas and principles that promote a social cause, and activities that have outcomes beyond simply the satisfaction of individual desires. Hall (2014) suggests there are two approaches for the application of social marketing. First, there is the 'traditionalist' marketing approach that uses the traditional marketing tools to be applied in a social context to benefit the social cause. Alternatively, the 'convergent' marketing approach uses tools that go beyond the traditional marketing approach

(Hall, 2014). (Both approaches are explained throughout this book). The traditionalist approach is effective because it is relatively simple and it has a capacity to help park managers to begin to understand and apply marketing principles. However, there is also value in the convergent approach because it provides wider range of marketing principles and practices that may be more beneficial when addressing particular marketing challenges.

At the time of writing there are numerous examples of successful social marketing campaigns in the areas of climate change, and further back in time around issues such as HIV/AIDS prevention. In a national park context, it is frequently linked to ecological marketing on the basis of the need to encourage tourists to protect the park's environmental estate. The Trail of the Great Bear is an example of an ecosystem-based approach to tourism, focusing on creating awareness of the region's natural and cultural heritage. The Trail of the Great Bear is a touring route covering 2000 miles of the Rockies that link Yellowstone in the United States with Banff and Jasper in Canada. As a geographical concept, the Trail links the major habitats of the grizzly bear. As a tourism initiative, the Trail is committed to the well-being of the region's communities, by promoting a greater understanding and awareness of the resources upon which it is based (Notzke, 2004). Aboriginal North America constitutes an important aspect of the Trail's sense of place. The Trail offers unique travel products including learning and enrichment programmes, special interest group tours, customised self-drive itineraries, guiding services and brand merchandising. A partner consortium of over 350 organisations addresses the social marketing initiatives to ensure the protection of cultural and historical heritage (Wearing *et al.*, 2007).

In order to illustrate the importance of social marketing for national park based tourism industries, this section will be focused on trekking in Nepal that is synonymous with international tourism, national parks and social injustice. It is our view that social injustice and the repression of the rights of local workers are directly connected to a failure of many tourism marketers to pursue a social justice based marketing agenda.

Since Nepal was first opened up to international travellers in the 1950s it has become synonymous with human endeavours to conquer some of the most spectacular natural terrain in the world. The Himalayas, which contain eight of the world's ten highest peaks, includes the Sagamartha National Park which is the target of mountain climbers and trekkers from across the world. Tourism marketing in the region has historically concentrated on the visual grandeur of the Himalayan mountain range:

> Traverse through the Great Himalayan Range and appreciate the sheer geographic diversity – from the verdant, forested valleys and tropical jungles of Arunachal having amazing wildlife and the flowering meadows carpeted with rare orchids, to the rugged terrain of the Trans Himalaya that extends to the Tibetan plateau. (Travel Himalayas, 2006)

The perpetuation of traditional approaches to tourism marketing, which focuses on the market driven sale of a tourism product (the Himalayas) to international travellers, has led to a situation where the tourism industry has tended to either deliberately or inadvertently ignore the conditions experienced by porters in the Himalayas. The perpetuation of somewhat romanticised notions of the strength of the Himalayan Sherpa, as portrayed in their exploits in support of the late Sir Edmund Hillary, is a useful selling point for tourism providers.

By emphasising the Sherpas' helpfulness, resilience and strength, the tourism industry is able to market tourism experiences based around mental relaxation and calmness in what would normally be a very challenging natural environment. By promoting accessible experiences to ever increasing tourist markets, tourism operators in Nepal are able to achieve their own economically driven organisational objectives. However, what is potentially compromised is their ability to instil in their visitors a sense of motivation to protect the rights of local workers and other aspects of Nepalese society. Trekking brings tourists into direct contact with local people, thus forcing the tourism consumer to consider the local relationships behind the product they are consuming. In spite of this, there remains a tendency in Nepalese tourism circles to present an idealised representation of porters.

Determining a social marketing strategy for an environment like the Himalayas requires tourism operators to give greater consideration to identifying target markets that are likely to be inclined to adopt sustainable behaviours. Trekkers throughout the world are often not homogenous with respect to their attitude to local people and conditions. A study of climbers of Uluru by McKercher *et al.* (2008) found that there were a number of distinct climbing groups. Firstly those 'that reject the Aboriginality of place; those with different value sets that who see nothing inherently wrong with their actions; and a large group who is aware that its actions may be inappropriate and therefore need to invoke some form of neutralisation technique to justify their actions' (McKercher *et al.*, 2008: 369). The variable concerns of visitors are a problem for park managers who are tasked with preserving environmental integrity, whilst encouraging increased visitor access to capitalise on the tourist dollar. Pursuing a sense of ownership and environmental stewardship amongst visitors is one way in which this may be achieved (Lai *et al.*, 2009). The challenge for Himalaya tourism operators is to find the balance between the target market of their programmes and services, with the needs and integrity of the local residents, especially the Sherpas. Social marketing provides a framework for finding this balance.

To understand trekkers' interest in environmental stewardship we must consider the tourists' destination image. The construction of marketing strategies for an area is reliant upon the development of images, which are deemed acceptable by visitors. From a postcolonial perspective, destination image can be seen as the impressions an individual has about a particular locality

(Echtner & Ritchie, 2003) that can enable the perpetuation of the neocolonialist representation of trekking. Crompton (1978: 18) defines destination images as 'a sum of beliefs, ideas and impressions that a person has of a destination'. Limited empirical research has been undertaken on the motivations of Nepalese trekkers, making it difficult to develop a comprehensive picture of a trekker's destination image. Holden and Sparrowhawk (2002) do, however, note that in many respects trekkers' exhibit motivations similar to that of other ecotourists. Over 95% of respondents in their study of trekkers in the Annapurna region of Nepal indicated that they were motivated by a desire to enjoy nature (Holden & Sparrowhawk, 2002). It is this desire to experience nature, which is typically the inspiration for marketing strategies that are targeted at the segment who have different value sets and see nothing inherently wrong with their actions in the Himalayas. There is the potential for Nepalese tourist services to move towards a sustainable marketing goal that appreciates tourism's links to the natural environment, and advocates for the rights of Nepalese workers who are frequently marginalised and idealised in traditional marketing strategies.

Operators in national parks and other wilderness areas may focus beyond the economic indicators of corporate success to address social and environmental priorities. Social marketing encourages tourist operators to be proactive in determining the relative social benefits and costs of a tourism journey. Local people, such as Nepalese porters, generally represent one relatively powerless entity. It has been found that they are usually the last to benefit from economic neoliberalism in development (Timothy & Tosun, 2003). This idea is supported in social impact assessment literature where it is noted that the social impacts of development (e.g. tourism) are primarily felt by individuals at a local scale, while the economic benefits are accrued by more regional stakeholders (Howitt, 2002). A body of sustainable tourism literature and case examples suggest that the development of a triple bottom line conscious tourism industry in national parks requires that a broad spectrum of stakeholders be involved in the consideration of destination areas. Social marketing provides a focus that takes the consideration of a wider range of stakeholders into account to provide benefits to both the individual consumers and society as a whole (Hall, 2014). This issue will be considered further in Chapter 5. Table 2.4 provides a summary of the key social marketing principles.

Demarketing

Demarketing refers to the systematic restriction of the public use of a tourism asset and the provision of information on the reasons for the restriction through various marketing mediums (Inglis *et al.*, 2005). First proposed by Kotler and Levy (see 1971); demarketing has been applied in a number of tourism contexts including nationwide strategies in Bermuda

Table 2.4 Social marketing principles

Marketing approach	Marketing principles			
Social marketing	Often applies the traditional marketing principles but with a focus on wider social issues rather than just meeting consumer needs			
	Provides benefits for society and individuals	Target markets are selected because they are inclined to social issues	Provides information to:	
			Raise awareness of relevant social, cultural, heritage and social justice issues	Illustrate social causes

(where mass tourism is discouraged in favour of high spending niche markets) and in promotional campaigns run in Cyprus to discourage visitation by the youth package holiday market (Weaver, 2011). Through a combination of measures including price increases and the elimination of tourism products that may attract undesirable visitors, demarketing acts as a complementary approach to target marketing whereby particular target markets are discouraged (see Weaver & Lawton, 2014) and may function to reduce visitor interest in environmentally sensitive parts of the natural environment.

A good example of demarketing is provided by Parks Canada. Ecological integrity is at the core of Parks Canada's mandate. It was necessary to mitigate the stresses and impacts of habitat loss and fragmentation, pollution, pesticides, loss of fauna and flora, introduction of exotic species and human over-use. Parks Canada (2000) shifted its marketing strategy away from a product focus based on parks as tourist destinations, to a demarketing and social marketing approach aimed at appropriate target markets with messages emphasising the ecological integrity of the parks. Not only did Parks Canada change its own marketing strategy, but it also worked with regional and provincial tourism marketing organisations to educate them about the ecological integrity of the parks. These partnerships (see the next section about relationship marketing) were able to encourage Parks Canada's partners to include ecological integrity messages in their marketing programmes and promotional materials (Wearing et al., 2007).

Kern (2006) examined the notion of demarketing in the context of the Blue Mountains National Park west of Sydney. Kern (2006) noted that a number of factors influenced the use and effectiveness of demarketing strategies:

- Pragmatic considerations, resource considerations and stakeholder considerations include the feasibility and effectiveness of certain demarketing measures, which are influenced by the specific context of the national park.

- Resource considerations relate to financial, human and temporal resources and the findings suggest that a lack of resources can influence, and at times, inhibit the use of demarketing measures. It was also found that various stakeholders have a profound influence on the use of demarketing measures. The stakeholder groups have diverse interests and therefore influence the use of demarketing in different ways by supporting or impeding certain measures.

Throughout various national park and marine park jurisdictions there is increasing concern over the rate of tourism growth. A recent paper by Cunningham *et al.* (2011) drew attention to the rapid expansion of whale watching industries globally from 9 million in 2001 to 13 million in 2009. Whale watching currently contributes in excess of US$2 billion to national economies (Cunningham *et al.*, 2011), but at what cost? The amount of tourism development that can be supported in a protected area is governed by its carrying capacity. Weaver (2011: 106) defines carrying capacity as the amount of activity that can be accommodated at a site without incurring (some form of) unsustainable impact. Within a national park sustainability context, carrying capacity has a number of economic, environmental, social and psychological components. The need to control tourism's effect on any or all of these fronts can be the rationale for the establishment of demarketing strategies.

Demarketing is a set of principles that clearly complement the intentions of ecological marketing and social marketing. The distinctive difference for demarketing is the emphasis on discouraging particular target markets that do not appreciate the sustainability goals of national parks. Table 2.5 provides a summary of the main principles of demarketing.

Table 2.5 Demarketing principles

Marketing approach	Marketing principles				
	Applies the traditional marketing principles but the focus is on restricting usage, especially of undesirable target markets				
Demarketing	Minimises product options to cater for limited range of target markets	Manipulates price to discourage particular groups	Limits access (place) to minimise the number of visitors	Provides information to explain reasons for the limited access	Introduces technology, e.g. green screen, to provide environmentally acceptable encounters with wildlife

Relationship marketing

Relationship marketing (RM) emerged in the early 1980s to complement new and evolving organisational forms. Bitner (1995) credits Berry in 1983 as the first publication to use the term 'relationship marketing' to describe how service firms work with their customers. Since that time, the relationship marketing literature has evolved to become a new marketing paradigm that focuses on relationships rather than transactions (Berry, 1995; Sheth & Parvatiyar, 1995b). There has been some debate regarding the application of RM in consumer markets, but there are clear applications of the potential benefits of RM when working within inter-organisational relationships (IORs). Resource dependency theory (Pfeffer & Salancik, 2003) has been used to inform the research about IORs (Oliver, 1990). IORs have been used to critically analyse a range of relationships in the sport and community leisure services (Frisby et al., 2004; Thibault & Harvey, 1997) but there has been limited research of RM or IORs in the park management context.

The value of RM in park management is its capacity to guide the management of relationships. Tower et al. (2006) defined RM as a shift from traditional marketing, with its focus on managing the marketing mix, to a focus on relationships whereby the organization concentrates on managing relationships that bring value based on collaboration and cooperation. They identified 28 constructs that were likely to influence how organisations manage their relationships (Tower et al., 2006). These constructs range from commitment, cooperation, communication and control to leadership, shared goals and trust. Further research identified eight constructs that were most important in the management of relationships (Tower et al., 2010). Effective management of relationships can be achieved by focusing on (1) communication, (2) trust, (3) facility, (4) leadership, (5) shared goals/values, (6) cooperation, (7) commitment and (8) quality (Tower et al., 2010).

Park managers need to focus on the following questions regarding how they manage their relationships with all their key stakeholders:

- Is there potential to work with relevant stakeholders with whom a value-adding relationship can be established?
  - How can the collaboration generate positive outcomes that neither organisation could achieve on their own?
- If a new relationship is pursued, are their conscious efforts to:
  - Manage the communication processes in the relationship?
  - Build trust among the partners?
  - Understand the facility needs of all the stakeholders?
  - Practice the leadership principles of motivation, commitment, enthusiasm, vision, patience, open mindedness and perseverance?
  - Identify shared goals/vision among the partners?

- Develop cooperative actions by all partners to achieve mutual outcomes?
- Be committed to the relationship by providing resources, effort and time to support the relationship?
- Generate quality outcomes from the relationship based on quality processes of service delivery?

Park managers that put effort into these points will be more effective in the management of their relationships. As mentioned earlier, park managers have the potential to establish partnerships with businesses and other organisations that reflect their values of ecological sustainability alongside meeting specific target markets' (including all the stakeholders) needs.

National park agency interest in relationship marketing has developed as a response to the evolving make-up of the national park stakeholder set. While national park agencies in Australia are legislated to carry out conservation agendas; the presence of an increasingly powerful collection of stakeholders including tourism operators and coal seam gas providers who wish to use national parks for their own purposes has necessitated conservation agencies to mobilise their own political support (Buckley, 2003). Relationship marketing is therefore a market-led, partner oriented concept aimed at forming and sustaining profitable, mutually beneficial relationships by bringing together the necessary parties and resources to deliver the best possible value proposition for all the partners. The 'collaborative' foundation on which relationship marketing is based holds considerable value for the sustainable management of protected areas. The most visible aspects of relationship marketing are the promotion materials that are produced by partners in a relationship. Tables 2.6 and 2.7 (previously published in Wearing *et al.*, 2007) illustrate best practice examples of how collaborative promotion may be achieved by State and National Tourism Organisations, national park agencies and tour operators. The cooperation among the stakeholders enables a range of important messages from the partners to be provided to the customers in a more cohesive manner. Not only does the collaboration generate more effective messages but it also makes better use of the limited promotion resources.

The examples in these tables illustrate how park and tourism organisations can share resources and materials to deliver more cohesive promotion packages. Promotion is the visible side of the relationship but the cooperation and commitment is based on the shared values/goals and functions because of trust that is developed between organisations and their desire to deliver quality outcomes. These examples demonstrate the value of adopting strategies to generate positive outcomes for all the relationship partners.

One of the best illustrations of cooperation within relationship marketing practices is Australia's national parks and protected areas National Eco Certification Program. Originally developed in 1996, the Program was an

Table 2.6 Cooperative promotion between parks and tourism operators

Success Factor	Examples
(1) Operators educating potential visitors regarding appropriate environmental behaviour within marketing and promotional literature.	The cooperation between service providers in South Australia's Kangaroo Island illustrates how cooperation can deliver complementary messages. Island Escape Tour brochure, Island Escape Tours, includes conservation messages in its holiday brochures – *'At Island Escape Tours we are aware that some of the environments we visit are fragile. It is important to us to protect these precious areas. You can be assured that every effort is made to leave no trace of your visit. Small group sizes help us to achieve this goal. This allows the sensitive Tasmanian environment to be enjoyed by all including its permanent residents – the unique wildlife'.* *Sealink Kangaroo Island* The brochures for Sealink Kangaroo Island include the following message: *'Kangaroo Island is a special place with a delicate environment. We are all very proud of it and ask you to tread lightly and be very careful to leave it exactly as you found it. Use the rubbish bins provided or preferably bring out everything that you take in. Take nothing but photos, leave nothing but footprints'.*
(2) Tour operators providing visitor information and interpretation in parks thus improving dissemination of this information.	*Kings Canyon Resort* A consortium consisting of Voyages Hotel and Resorts, Centre Corporation, Indigenous Business Australia, and the Ngurrutjuta Association developed this resort. Although the land on which the resort is located on has been excised from the national park, the property is wholly encompassed within the park. The resort provides the same visitor information services that in other parks is provided by park-managed visitor centres. This has enabled park management to focus on the core business of land management. The resort has become the de facto face of the park. Parks staff provides education services about the park to new employees at the resort through the resort's induction programme (Department of Industry, Tourism and Resources, June 2003).

Table 2.6 (*continued*)

Success Factor	Examples
(3) The promotion of park names or qualities that provide a 'point of difference' and/or quality stamp for tourism companies to reach customers.	*Aries Tours Natural Bridge Glow Worm Tour* The tour operator benefits from access to a World Heritage Listed area creating a higher valued tour package with participants receiving a World Heritage Visitation Certificate, featuring the official World Heritage logo (Department of Industry, Tourism and Resources, June 2003).
(4) Operators provide realistic images and information to ensure accurate expectations by visitors.	*Great Barrier Reef Marine Park* An image library is available to operators to source accurate and realistic images for promotion initiatives. Informal advice is also provided on how best to present and interpret their product. Proof reading of brochures can be undertaken upon request of operators and proactively (i.e. picking up brochures opportunistically and checking content) to ensure accuracy and currency.

industry initiative that was developed in response to a recognised need for a system to identify genuine nature tourism and ecotourism products in Australia. Ecotourism and nature tourism certification programmes provide industry, protected area managers, local communities and travellers with an assurance that a certified product is backed by a commitment to best practice ecological sustainability, natural area management and the provision of quality ecotourism experiences. The benefits of this Program are that it provides an umbrella for the tourism industry and parks agencies to integrate and align their marketing and promotion messages, and that the ecological integrity of the tourism product is communicated accurately. This Program gives operators a competitive advantage in marketing products, while improving practices, leading to fewer negative environmental impacts as well as a more efficient use of parks and greater control for parks agencies. Specific promotion assistance, which is provided to accredited operators, includes representation at national and international trade shows and media referrals. Further information on the Eco Certification Program can be found at http://www.ecotourism.org.au/eco_certification.asp.

For initiatives such as the National Eco Certification Program and other forms of relationship marketing to be successful there needs to be an appreciation of the diverse range of stakeholder vision and goals in national parks. The partners must have shared goals/vision or the relationship is destined to fail. Partners that have shared goals/visions are likely to be able to

Table 2.7 Cooperative promotion between parks and state and national tourism organisations

Success Factor	Examples
(1) Joint promotion through travel brochures.	*South Australia Secrets brochure* The South Australian Department of Environment and Heritage (SADEH) works closely with the South Australia Tourism Commission (SATC) in the 'Secrets' Campaign and pages that are dedicated to National parks are contained in these tourist brochures. SADEH is gradually refining the information to focus more on activities that can be undertaken and also information and messages about conservation and the work of parks that they would like to get out to the world.
(2) Linking destinations and providing information and access.	*South Australia Desert Parks Pass* This pass is provided for travellers visiting the northern parts of South Australia. It comes as a kit with a handbook, park maps, tourism brochures and wildlife information. People visiting any one of the Desert Parks are required to purchase this pass for entry and therefore find out about the other parks in the region as well. The pass is distributed through the Royal Automobile Club, the South Australian Tourist Commission and commercial outlets as well as National parks offices.
(3) Providing a national portal for electronic distribution of information about parks and other heritage experiences.	*Heritage Places and Routes Online* This initiative will provide a major national tool to link information about natural and cultural heritage places online for international and domestic travellers. The mechanism for delivery of the tool would be the Australian Tourism Data Warehouse (ATDW). It is the national tourism data management system supported by all State and Territory governments and the Australian Government who use the system to manage data for existing national and state tourism websites, www.australia.com and www.seeaustralia.com. The tool will enable travellers to comprehensively search for places or heritage trails, tracks and travel routes of interest to them either by searching geographically, by theme or by text search.

collaborate so they generate additional value that would not be possible in a traditional exchange arrangement. To understand the breadth of these objectives requires an appreciation of the personalised meaning and histories of each stakeholder group's relationship to the national park environment. Schweinsberg et al. (2012) have noted that 'over recent years "place" theories have become more and more a central idea in environmental management debates'. For the tourism industry, the focus will typically be on commercial advantage (increasing market share and making a profit) while for park agencies, the goals will be community and environment related (e.g. conservation of a heritage site). It is important that both parties recognise that they operate under very different legal, social, economic and environmental constraints. Tourism bodies including national tourism bodies, state tourist organisations, regional and local tourism organisations are also involved. Each organisation has specific objectives that are determined by government to promote tourism destinations. Partners also need to be clear that the audience they are targeting in any joint promotion is appropriate for all stakeholders.

The following summary (Table 2.8) was produced drawing on a similar table in the Australian Government's 'Pursuing Common Goals' report published in 2003. It summarises the key objectives of protected area managers, tourism operators and tourism organisations. The interests of non-participant stakeholders should also be taken into account (e.g. in the development of training courses). The list of shared objectives illustrates the potential for relationship marketing principles to be pursued.

The common objective of both conservation agencies and tourism stakeholders is to maximise the quality of the visitor experience in national parks, while protecting the inherent natural and cultural heritage values of these highly significant areas. Bramwell and Lane (2000) suggest that partnerships are likely to be particularly significant in future attempts to achieve sustainable tourism practices. The private sector is likely to have significant levels of information relating to demand, and well-established marketing techniques, while the public sector tends to be more aware of acceptable levels of tourism impacts and have the ability to apply necessary sanctions when they relate to agreed resource capacities.

A relationship marketing approach is likely to provide tourism businesses with access to new or more diverse visitor markets. For example, attractions in relative proximity to each other or of a similar nature commonly attract more visitors through joint marketing initiatives. The provision of packages incorporating the total holiday experience is facilitated by cooperation among the various suppliers involved in providing the total visitor experience. Relationship marketing approaches also spread the costs associated with promotion across a number of organisations, allowing them to embark on more ambitious promotional campaigns through the support of 'pooled' resources.

Table 2.8 Objectives of parks managers and tourism operators in relation to parks and protected areas

Objectives of protected area managers	Objectives of tourism operators	Objectives of tourism organisations
Help with conservation of ecosystems, biodiversity and heritage values	Sustainability of the physical and business environment underpinning their operations	To encourage visitation to the area
Better visitor management	To secure access to Protected Areas for operations, preferably exclusive of other commercial operators	To increase the contribution of tourism to the economy
To achieve environmental outcomes through planning and regulation	Provide suitable infrastructure for visitors to ensure satisfaction	To assist in the development of the tourism industry through promotion, industry development and sound government policies
Visitor and community enjoyment, understanding and support	Opportunities for product development or improved service delivery	To support tourism operators and government programmes
An environment that attracts visitors and enhances their product	Minimal bureaucracy and streamlined systems. low overhead costs, commercial viability and profits	
Additional income for management and projects	Flexibility to cope with changing circumstances and demand	
Help with research		

(Source: Adapted from Department of Industry, Tourism and Resources, 2003).

The establishment of relationships with other community groups provides the park agencies with opportunities to reach target markets that they may not normally be able to contact. Devine (2012) explains how partnerships with disability-specific organisations will help to develop more inclusive services. A partnership between a national park and disability-specific organisations will assist the national park to address goals related to inclusion that it would not likely to be able to achieve on its own. On a broader context Marsh *et al.* (2012) recommend parks establish partnerships with health organisations to develop the delivery of physical activity programmes and services in parks. Relationship marketing provides the framework and tools to guide park managers to establish partnerships with a range of strategic partners. These partnerships can incorporate joint marketing and programme delivery that may include joint promotion,

Table 2.9 Relationship marketing principles

Marketing approach	Marketing principles				
	Introduces strategies to guide collaboration with partners				
Relationship marketing	Focus on value-added relationship with strategic partners	Identifies shared goals/values to guide relationship outcomes	Manages communication to understand partners' needs and to build trust	Commits to cooperative activities to achieve mutual outcomes	Adopts quality processes to generate collaborative outcomes

collaborative programme development, and access to specific target markets. To be successful, however, it must be recognised that partnerships exist in a dynamic environment that is composed 'a host of variables such as political and legal forces, economic considerations, technology and competition' (Crompton & Howard, 1980: 332). The agency cannot control these variables, therefore it must adapt to them. These issues will be discussed further in Chapter 3.

Relationship marketing provides a framework to guide approaches for working with like-minded partners to achieve shared and complementary goals. Table 2.9 provides a summary of the key relationship marketing principles.

Summary of Marketing Strategies

This chapter has explained a range of marketing strategies that can be used to guide park managers. The principles of the Tree Model of Marketing Delivery provide the foundation for the alternative marketing approaches. There is no substitute for having evidence to guide the marketing decisions, making strategic decisions regarding target markets, managing the market mix elements and knowing how the KPIs will be used to analyse the effectiveness of the marketing strategy. The traditional marketing principles are complemented by alternative marketing approaches that offer a more refined set of principles that are acutely in tune with the sustainability goals of national parks.

Table 2.10 provides a summary of the marketing principles for each of the options discussed here. Park managers need to be aware of these options as they grapple with the complexity of balancing tourism developments while maintaining their sustainability requirements. It is likely that no individual market strategy group will be sufficient to meet every circumstance. However, park managers' awareness of a range of alternative marketing principles will assist them to select relevant principles to guide their activities to meet the needs of all their stakeholders.

Table 2.10 Summary of marketing principles

Marketing approach	Marketing principles				
Traditional marketing	Consumer/stakeholders provide the focus for marketing efforts	Impact of environment to provide evidence that informs marketing decisions	Market segmentation and target market selection	Market mix management of product, price, place and promotion	Evaluate marketing efforts through key performance indicators
Ecological marketing	Target market are environmentally conscious consumers	Affiliated (where possible) with green accreditation programmes	Provides information to:		
			Inform visitors about environmental impacts	Create feelings about environmental issues	Encourage pro-environment behaviour
Social marketing	Often applies the traditional marketing principles but with a focus on wider social issues rather than just meeting consumer needs				
	Provides benefits for society and individuals	Target markets are selected because they are inclined to social issues	Provides information to:		
			Raise awareness of relevant social, cultural, heritage and social justice issues	Illustrate social causes	
Demarketing	Applies the traditional marketing principles but the focus is on restricting usage, especially of undesirable target markets				
	Minimises product options to cater for limited range of target markets	Manipulates price to discourage particular groups	Limits access (place) to minimise the number of visitors	Provides information to explain reasons for the limited access	Introduces technology, e.g. green screen, to provide environmentally acceptable encounters with wildlife
Relationship marketing	Introduces strategies to guide collaboration with partners				
	Focus on value-added relationship with strategic partners	Identifies shared goals/values to guide relationship outcomes	Manages communication to understand partners' needs and to build trust	Commits to cooperative activities to achieve mutual outcomes	Adopts quality processes to generate collaborative outcomes

Case Study 2: Demarketing – Phillip Island Nature Park (Victoria)

The penguin parade on Phillip Island's Summerland Peninsula represents one of the mainstays of Victoria's tourism industry. With over 500,000 people braving the arctic winds from Bass Strait each year, the Penguin Parade regularly returns over US$96 million per year to the local and broader domestic tourism economies. Over 100 jobs are provided by the not-for-profit Phillip Island Nature Park, which also has responsibilities other for nearby attractions including the Koala Conservation Centre and Churchill Island Heritage Farm. Whilst penguin viewing is a mainstay of the island economically, penguin viewing has a chequered history with respect to its impacts on the natural environment of the area. Following the establishment of informal penguin viewing in the 1920s by a group of local entrepreneurs, extensive damage was experienced to penguin burrows and breeding sites due to tourist eagerness to fulfil their psychological needs.

In the 1960s visitor management strategies were pursued in order to protect the last remaining penguin colony on the island. Land that was developed into residential housing on the nearby hinterland was re-purchased and rehabilitated; a 4000 seat viewing platform and boardwalks were established to control visitor movement and a large interpretive centre was developed. The ongoing development of sustainable tourism operations on Phillip Island has necessitated the use of a number of overt and subtle demarketing strategies to control visitor expectations. Online marketing through websites and other mediums places an emphasis on the responsible management of the world's smallest penguin species (http://www.penguins.org.au/). While there are no attempts to deliberately exclude certain visitors, tourists have it emphasised to them through the use of various onsite interpretive mechanisms (see Chapter 4 for a further discussion of national park based interpretation) that they are in the penguin's habitat and for this reason photography is banned on the beach and there is no opportunity for any physical contact between penguins and visitors. The use of green screen technology to provide virtual experiences with penguins is provided at the visitors centre. Crowd control measures brought in to protect penguin populations have been criticised on the basis that they restricts visitor movement and thus may lead to conflict. Others have also raised the possibility that demarketing does not in fact go far enough and have drawn attention to the fundamental question of whether humankind should encourage ecological outcomes through the full-scale commodification of penguin habitats. This brings us back to the conservation versus human usage debates which are wicked problems at the core of this book, which will be formally canvassed in Chapter 3.

Source: Wearing et al. (2001).

3 Sustainable Tourism Marketing – A Wicked Policy Challenge for Park Managers

Introduction

The concept of wicked problems was first introduced by Rittel and Webber (1973) in an article for the journal *Policy Sciences*. Writing in the context of dilemmas in urban planning, Rittel and Webber posed the notion that many policy problems cannot be described in positivist, measurable scientific terms. Instead, on account of their social construction they possess a range of intractable characteristics that characterise them as 'wicked'. In the four decades since the introduction of the term, wicked problems have become a common topic of inquiry for commentators in business journals such as *Harvard Business Review*, as well as a term that provides a neat dumping ground for policy makers wrestling with the many complex challenges facing society. Challenges including climate change, food security, sustainable development itself and poverty are often described as 'wicked' on account of their definitional ambiguity, their basis in human values, interrelationships with other wicked problems, and lack of a single perfect policy solution (Camillus, 2008).

Wicked problems exist within a complex stakeholder defined system, which for the rest of this chapter will be termed the dynamic business environment. Such systems see the processes of tourism product delivery (marketing, distribution, human resource management etc.) as being situated within a multifaceted array of social, political/regulatory, demographic and other forces. The confluence of such forces has exercised an increasing impact on the direction of tourism marketing since the 1960s, with Clarke *et al.* (2013) citing the publication of works including Rachel Carson's *Silent Spring*, the Club of Rome's *Limits to Growth* and *Our Common Future* as key drivers of the trend towards formal recognition of the importance of triple bottom line approaches to marketing by groups including the American Marketing

Association. In Chapter 2, the authors outlined some of the central characteristics of alternative marketing forms including ecological marketing, social marketing etc., which have made them well suited to alignment with sustainability doctrines. Within each of these marketing approaches lies an implicit expectation that marketing agencies would 'take a wider view of their role and consider not only their own welfare and development, but also that of the society in which they are based' (Dinan, 2000: 3).

Seeing beyond one's own self-interest, values and perceptions is an essential requirement for effective management of tourism resources in reserve regions, which are subject to competing conservation and human usage mantras. As Baker (1992: 164 in Clarke & Clegg, 2000: 47) notes; 'You manage within a paradigm. You lead between paradigms'. Paradigms, which were initially described by Thomas Kuhn as 'a constellation of beliefs, values and techniques, and so on shared by the members of a given community' (Kuhn, 2012: 175) will vary across the myriad of stakeholders that make up the dynamic national park business environment. By unpacking some of these value positions in this chapter, we will lay the groundwork for a detailed examination of the value positions of tourist consumer groups in Chapter 4 when we consider the processes whereby tourism marketers deliver ephemeral visitor experiences in national parks.

The Dynamic and Wicked Business Environment

Peter Drucker, who was recently identified as the 'father of modern management' by *Forbes* magazine wrote that 'marketing is ... the process through which the economy is integrated into society to serve human needs' (Drucker, 1958: 258). For the present authors, such a definition is important on account of its ability to identify that while marketing will likely always retain traditional consumer elements including needs, wants, market based exchanges etc. (Kotler & Armstrong, 2013); simultaneously there is an expectation that the outcomes of marketing must stretch beyond market based forces to embrace the full range of stakeholders. Societal outcomes from producer-consumer exchanges are an important outcome for social and other alternative marketing forms. Hall (2014) identifies the role of social marketing as being to promote a re-evaluation of consumer values and thus effect a positive change in behaviours to achieve positive outcomes for communities.

At their most basic level, human values can be defined as a 'belief pertaining to desirable end states or modes of conduct; that transcends specific situations; guides selection or evaluation of behaviour, people, and events; and is ordered by importance relative to other values to form a system of value priorities' (Schwartz, 1994). Open to revision and replacement over time (see Schweinsberg *et al.*, 2012); human values go far beyond the product value created for consumers by producers in traditional ethnocentric approaches to marketing (Balabanis *et al.*, 2002). Instead, values encompass a range of abstract and intangible beliefs that govern the epistemological position individual stakeholders apply to different circumstances in business management. Kotler and Keller (2007) explain that sociocultural values include, but are not limited to, peoples' views of themselves, views of other, views of society and views of nature etc.

Local level concerns such as those referenced by Kotler and Keller (2007) form an important part of sustainable regional development in which national park based tourism industries are situated. Ravetz defines regional sustainable development to be:

> a goal led model of structural transformation towards ecologically sustainable development, which is implemented at region level [sic], in parallel with local and global levels. (Ravetz, 2004: x in McManus, 2008: 1277)

On account of this local level complexity, throughout the rest of this chapter the authors will advocate that the dynamic business environment for national park based ecotourism sector is 'a values focused' stakeholder defined entity. Wearing *et al.* (2010) have previously described tourism as a form of embodied social interaction where the individual tourist will constantly seek to construe the personal on the basis of changing societal interactions. These societal interactions are, we would argue, subject to the impact of evolving host community and other stakeholder views on the role of tourism in regional sustainable development.

The model that the authors will employ to illustrate the idea of a complex, stakeholder defined dynamic business environment is represented in Figure 3.1. At the centre of Figure 3.1 are the various components of a company's internal business processes. This central section comprises the extraction, production and development and promotion components of Michael Porter's traditional value chain model (Porter, 1987). These internal business machinations of national park based nature/ecotourism industries have already been covered elsewhere in a range of industry specific sectoral case studies, and thus will not form a major part of the present chapter. Instead we wish to focus on select elements of tourism's micro and macro business environment. In regard to Figure 1.1, these elements would be in the soil, the air and general environment in the tree model of market delivery. Traditionally tourism systems theorists (Leiper, 1990; Mill & Morrison, 2002) have defined tourism as an essentially 'open' system, on account of their interactions with the environment, in which they exist (Skyttner, 2001). Jacobides (2010) has drawn parallels between notions of open systems and strategy, identifying that ambiguity in a firm's environmental context necessitates seeing strategy as a combination of narratives, which are defined by different stakeholder groups.

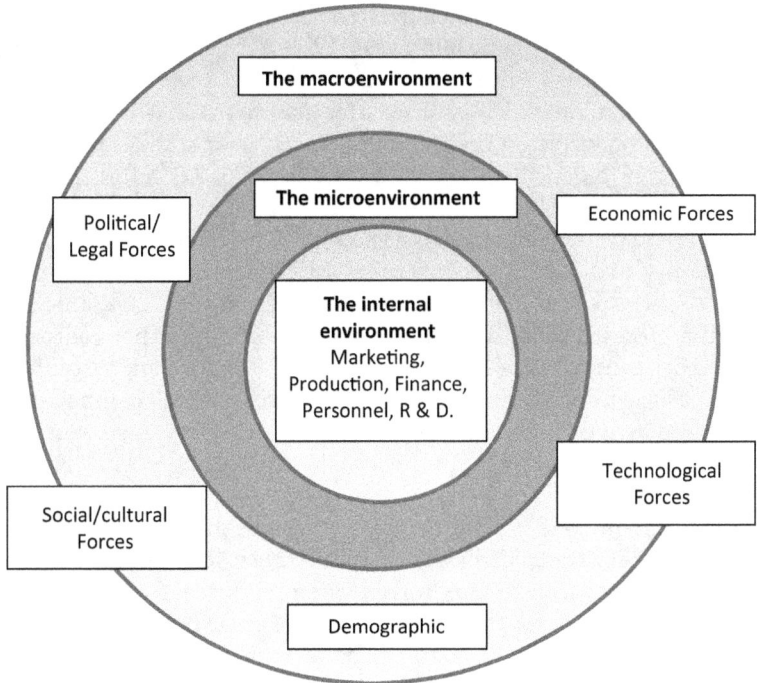

Figure 3.1 The principle elements of a business organisation's environment
Source: University of Technology Sydney (2013).

In order to draw together a never ending number of evolving stakeholder defined narratives, Kotler *et al.* (2010) have defined five essential characteristics of good strategy:

(1) it has an integrated aspect, in other words it relates to overarching areas/parts of the company;
(2) it is intentional on the part of decision makers;
(3) it is activity formulated with a focus on direct action;
(4) it is comprehensible to third parties, and;
(5) it pursues the long-term achievement of objectives.

Strategy of the type that Kotler *et al.* (2010) describe is related to marketing in the sense that firms strategically draw on their environment 'to replace obsolete products/markets with new ones which offer higher potential for future profits' (Ansoff *et al.*, 1990: 42). These profits may not be economic, but address social or environmental benefits that are valued by the stakeholders. For a firm to develop appropriate marketing capabilities in a mixed land use environment like a national park requires in the first instance that marketing strategies be integrated in to the broader environmental management remit of park managers. Budowski (1976) defined nature-based or ecotourism as an industry with considerable potential to work symbiotically with conservation forces. Whilst the latter may sometimes view the former with a degree of suspicion on account of often poor standards in tourism planning; when pursued correctly Budowski (1976: 27) notes there is the potential for a partnership that 'can contribute greatly to development—the right kind of development involving the right kind of change—leading to a better quality of life for all concerned'. In the nearly four decades since Budowski uttered these prophetic words, the authors have anecdotally observed a growing realisation amongst commentators that tourism as a land use that cannot be marginalised in the search for park sustainability. Instead we have noticed an increasing acceptance that well planned tourism is recognised as providing real opportunities for tourists to be educated on the ecological value of a region whilst also contributing positively to local communities. Striking the balance between growth and development is a challenge for marketers. Carter et al. (2008a) note that market penetration and development strategies have historically been founded on approaches whereby producers seek to maximise economies of scale. Whilst undoubtedly a useful approach for those seeking to maximise profit generation, it is often in contrast to rationale comprehensive approaches to planning where strategists will seek to consider the full range of stakeholder views before arriving at a decision. It is this recognition of the range of stakeholders (target markets) that complicates the decision making process but also contributes to the overall benefit of the decisions for all the stakeholders. The wicked problem, nonetheless, may mean that all the stakeholders will not be satisfied with the decisions.

Middleton and Hawkins (1998 in Clarke *et al.*, 2013) note that there are a range of rationales including regulatory compliance and consumer perception that can help explain the growing interest of many tourism operators in socially and environmentally responsible corporate practice. In seeking to pursue corporate social responsibility approaches to business practice, tourism providers must realise that the 'internal competencies or external pressures inherent in the industry create a "specialization" of social interests' (Griffin & Mahone, 1997: 10 in Inoue & Lee, 2011: 791). Understanding what those interests may be requires us, as Clarke *et al.* (2013) note, to wrestle with the notion of the dominant social paradigms and their impact on levels of environmental concern amongst tourism operators. Dominant social paradigms have been defined by Milbrath (1989: 116) as 'society's belief structure that organises the way people perceive and interpret the functioning of the world around them'. Drawing on a range of theoretical constructs relating to liberal democracy and the liberal economic principles of free markets and individual enterprise; Kilbourne *et al.* (2002: 202) note that belief in such principles often negatively impacts on an individual's level of environmental concern. The present authors would not dispute this notion. We would, however, suggest that tourism operators within national parks should place greater emphasis on interpretation and environmental education as a way of merging the competing agendas of economic growth and environmental consciousness. This issue will be discussed further in Chapter 4.

Kotler (2011) has identified that it is increasingly common for firms to attempt to resist the short-term pull of the economic imperative by seeking to tap into growing consumer interest in a firm's sustainability credentials. So called green consumerism (see Bergin-Seers & Mair, 2009; Miller, 2003) has formed a core marketing message for a range of ecotourism firms in protected areas throughout the world. Green marketing, Polonsky and Rosenberger III (2001: 21) note, is successful when firms take a holistic and integrated approach to its implementation; making marketing part of the 'cultural fabric that binds an organisation together, flowing from the spirit of the firm into its strategic approach and on to its tactical implementation'. Such holisticity is particularly important in national park environments on account of their public good characteristics (Mitchell & Carson, 1989).

Public goods are frequently characterised as such on account of their being non-rival and non-excludable. The provision of open access for all was a defining characteristic of early national parks in Australia. Lucas (1879 in Pettigrew & Lyons, 1979: 86) notes that early legislators aimed through the provision of spaces for public recreation 'to ensure [the development] of a healthy and consequently vigorous and intelligent community'. A recurring theme in the present volume is the idea that in the more than 140 years since the creation of Yellowstone in 1872, there has been something of a stakeholder re-evaluation of the role of tourism in the future of the parks movement. Instead of being seen as the primary purpose of park legislators, tourism and recreation should now only be provided where it is environmentally and culturally compatible with the broader sustainability of park ecosystems.

Public policy represents the specific actions (positions, strategies, actions etc.) of governmental decision makers as they respond to localised contests of opinions between different ideas, values and interests (Dredge & Jenkins, 2007). In the context of a discussion of public policy formation in the Yellowstone National Park area, it has been suggested that public policy formation is itself a wicked problem (McBeth & Shanahan, 2004). The absence of universal stakeholder acceptance in the merits of positivist frameworks for addressing environmental problems or for advancing economic benefits as the sole determinant of the need for environmental protection has meant that policy officers have been forced to engage with a range of often intangible cultural and spiritual values (see also Borrie *et al.*, 1998). Perhaps nowhere has this situation been more noticeable than in the now iconic campaign to preserve the Lake Pedder region of South Western Tasmania in the 1960s.

Today, the Lake Pedder region of Tasmania is home to the Franklin-Gordon Wild Rivers National Park. Declared in 1908, the park has been the site for some of the most concerted environmental campaigns in history. For a region that was described as having the potential to become Australia's own Ruhr Valley in the 1930s, initiatives were put in place in the mid-20th century to dam sections of the river to provide for the power needs of the expanding Tasmanian population. Opposition to the proposals has seen the creation of the Wilderness Society, High Court Challenges, the launch of political careers and political parties (Lohrey, 2002) and ultimately the crystallisation of an environmental philosophy that has resonated through land use disputes in other parts of the country including Terania Creek in northern New South Wales, Queensland's Fraser Island and the wild northern coast line of Western Australia (Dovers, 2003; Hickey & Brown, 2003; Law, 2001; Sewell et al., 1989). Each of these localities forms an important component of the marketing strategies for Australia's wild regions. The wilderness of Tasmania forms an important part of Tourism Australia's *National Landscape* programme. Lake Pedder itself, if it hadn't been dammed in the late 1960s, has been identified by the environmental historian Peter Hay as an environment that 'would have the same sort of status in Australian mythology as other landscape icons like Uluru and Kakadu and the Great Barrier Reef ... It was a place of immense symbolic importance' (Australian Broadcasting Corporation, 2007).

Sustainable national park marketing strategies are those that are targeted at tourists in a manner where the actions of both marketer and market place are focused on the protection of the environment ahead of their own personal interests. Achieving such an outcome is complicated by the fact that within a non-rival and non-excludible public environment such as a national park; 'both marketers and consumers [must] face the challenge of determining which activities are truly green enough to serve the long-term best interests of both the environment and its inhabitants' (Shultz & Holbrook, 1999). The achievement of long-term or intergenerational objectives is a core component of Kotler et al.'s (2010) characteristics of good strategy. How one sets about achieving this objective and promoting sustainable consumption practices that are ethical with respect to their dealings with local cultures (see Manoochehri, 2001) is complicated by the before mentioned diversity and intractability of stakeholder values and perceptions. As with sustainable development itself, which is not 'a fixed state of harmony' but rather process that is negotiated against a range of technological and institutional circumstances (World Commission on Environment and Development, 1987), the development of effective park marketing strategies must also focus on not only businesses 'responding to the rapid pace of technological [and other forms of environmental] innovation' (Chandler, 1977: 12 in Carter et al., 2008b: 20); but also making appropriate changes to their organisational structure to allow for sustainable relations with the afore mentioned environmental forces to be pursued.

What makes the development of sustainable relations with the business environment complex is the idea that the business environment is in a constant state of flux. This is particularly evident in the evolution of transportation options both to and in national parks. Since the very earliest years of the National Parks movement the railways have formed an important marketing strategy for railway companies and associated industry sectors. Campaigns including 'See America first' (Shaffer, 1996) were predicated on an archaic notion of the need to 'convince middle- and upper-class Americans to consume the region's natural and cultural wonders' (Wyckoff & Dilsaver, 1997: 1). Today, the transportation of people both to and within national parks has become one of the most pressing management issues facing park managers. Rapid escalations in the degree of private automobile use (White, 2007) from the 1920s to the present became more complex with the passing in 1969 of the National Environmental Policy Act and the formal integration of the American public into the environmental approval assessment process (Johnson, 2012).

In seeking to draw the largest possible range of stakeholders into the environmental assessment process, the managers of national parks such as Yosemite have progressively found themselves confronted by a wicked management problem. What right tourists, local residents and others have to use parks and the degree to which government has the right to enforce variable levels of access through management campaigns? For example, the implementation of the Yosemite Area Regional Transportation System (or YARTS – see Herremans & Reid, 2006) cannot be undertaken in a manner that will be universally acceptable to all (a common characteristic of wicked problems). In addition, the vagaries surrounding the precise level of contact with other tourists that are needed to affect a downturn in experience mean that there will not be universal acceptance of the need to develop new transportation management strategies. YARTS was developed on the basis of major traffic jams in Yosemite in the 1990s and whilst the literal clogging of the region's roads represented to many the thin end of the wedge and an 'obvious' threat to the carrying capacity of the region; the imposition of new transport controls carries with it the potential to put park managers at odds with the original principles of open access that have defined the history of tourist interactions with the national park movement. In the next chapter, the authors will seek to delve into these issues in more detail as we consider some of the complexities for marketing ephemeral experiences in national parks.

Case Study 3: That wicked Quarantine Station (North Head National Park – Sydney)

Located in what is now the North Head National Park, the North Head Quarantine Station was in operation from 1928 to 1984. Developed

(continued)

Case Study 3: That wicked Quarantine Station
(North Head National Park – Sydney) (*continued*)

originally to facilitate the isolation of immigrants to Australia who either were carrying, or were suspected of carrying, an infectious disease, the site has in recent years been run as an upmarket tourism boutique by Mawland Hotel Management Pty Ltd.

The North Head Quarantine station site covers 31 hectares and includes 67 heritage buildings (New South Wales Government, 2003) on the north head of Sydney Harbour. From 1984 when the site stopped being used for the purpose of disease control it had been run by the NSW National Parks and Wildlife Service (NPWS). Recognising their responsibilities to maintain the site's cultural and environmental significance the NPWS had since the mid-1980s sought to encourage small scale commercial utilisation in the form of conferences, interpretive tours etc. (Wearing & Darcy, 1999).

Limitations imposed by current state government funding arrangements necessitated the NSW Government in the early 2000s, putting the site out to commercial tender, a process that led to the awarding of a 21-year-lease to the group Mawland Hotel Management Pty Ltd in 2006. Within the tender process, there is clear evidence of Mawlands being forced to recognise its role in a public private partnership arrangement with the government:

> Mawland's proposed adaptive reuse of the site has been designed to generate sufficient wealth to better conserve the site and increase public access, interpretation and marketing. The Proposal will also return a profit share to the National Parks and Wildlife Service for the conservation of other cultural heritage sites within Sydney Harbour National Park. The Environmental Impact Assessment of the Proposal required Mawland's consultants to identify the condition of the site, past spending on conservation, public access and interpretation, and the economic impacts resulting from the Proposal. This exercise should provide some ideas and lessons to enhance the economic management of other heritage sites. (McArthur, 2001: 130 in Darcy & Wearing, 2009)

The final Mawland's proposal involved the adaptive reuse and restoration of the site for cultural tourism purposes. Uses included: a visitor centre and museum; guided tours; a restaurant; accommodation; facilities for functions and conferences; and an environmental and cultural study centre. The proposal involved physical changes to the site, including the buildings and the landscape. It involved the restoration of a number of heritage buildings on the site that had been previously closed to the public as they were deemed unsafe for public access. It also included an expansion in visitor numbers from 30,000 to approximately 100,000 per year (New South Wales Government, 2003). Approximately 230 conditions were applied to this approval, establishing one of the most challenging operating environments for any tourism activity in Australia. Redevelopment of the site and restoration of the heritage buildings was essentially completed in 2008. The site has been operating as commercial resort since that time

While the natural environment and cultural resources of the site were keys to the conservation of the site and the development of a public private partnership for its ongoing management, it also has significant impact on the marketing of the site. Mawland not only provides resort style accommodation, but also has a number of other activities that it promotes. The heritage of the site is promoted using historical tours, education programmes and ghost tours of the site, all of which can be combined with restaurant meals or accommodation (Brown & Weber, 2011). Additionally the natural resources of the site are promoted for special events such as weddings and conferences. Marketing sells an overall experience of beautiful natural landscapes coupled with professional event spaces and service.

For all its potential as a site of conservation/tourism partnership, for years the Quarantine station redevelopment has been clouded by stakeholder contestation over its future. Reflecting something of a NIMBY (not in my backyard) philosophy, over 1340 written submissions were received in a public inquiry in the late 1990s. A range of stakeholder groups can be identified for the Quarantine Station including the self-entitled Friends of the Quarantine Station (FOQS), the Manly Greens, Friends and Residents of Manly and the National Parks Association of NSW. The mission statement of the FOQS is:

> To raise public awareness of the rich heritage that exists at Manly Quarantine Station, to campaign to reverse the current privatisation plans of the National Parks and Wildlife Service and to work towards a sustainable management structure for the Manly Quarantine Station which would preserve the station intact for this and future generations.

With these aims, we have encapsulated the wickedness of the Quarantine station debate; when we have a range of stakeholders that

(continued)

> **Case Study 3:** That wicked Quarantine Station
> (North Head National Park – Sydney) (*continued*)
>
> are all in their own way committed to the conservation of the park site, how can one manage such diametrically opposing viewpoints for the benefit of all. Literature on wicked problems tells us that just as there is no immediate and ultimate test of a wicked problem, so too is every solution a one shot operation. There is no opportunity for managers to learn from trial and error. The consequences of an incorrect call are also huge. In spite of the task being essentially impossible, planners have to stand by their decisions. They have no right to be wrong (see Rittel & Webber, 1973).

4 Approaches to Marketing Ephemeral Tourist Experiences

> *Experience is individually enacted even as it is collectively, structurally and organisationally shaped, if only because people rarely make histories in circumstances of their own choosing*
> (S. Clegg & Baumeler, 2010: 1719)

Introduction

Since the creation of the world's first national park at Yellowstone in Wyoming, USA in 1872, opportunities have existed for iconic immersive experiences with pristine natural and sociocultural environments. Trekking in the Sagamartha National Park, Nepal offers visitors the chance to step in the footprint of colonial pioneers whilst experiencing the visual grandeur of the Himalayan Mountain Ranges (Wearing *et al.*, 2007). Iconic tracks, such as the Overland Track, in the Cradle Mountain National Park in Western Tasmania provide the back drop for '360 degree views of Cradle Mountain ... Just trees and peaks, rocks and glacial valleys, and shining tarns under a blue sky' (Sharpe *et al.*, 1994). Similarly, in the United States and Canada, the Chilkoot Trail offers visitors the chance to walk in the footsteps of 'stampeders' who once participated in the Klondike Gold Rushes.

Ephemeral trail based tourism experiences provide one *raison d'être* for the existence of national parks; justifying 'in economic terms the retention of relatively undisturbed natural areas' (Armstrong & Kern, 2011: 22) against the encroachment of various extractive based primary industries. The title of this chapter 'Approaches to Marketing Ephemeral Tourist Experiences' was chosen specifically on the basis of the characteristics of ephemeral pools that exist in national parks throughout the United States and elsewhere. Ephemeral pools represent naturally occurring basins where rain water and wind-blown sediment collect, attracting a range of inhabitants including 'aquatic opportunists, species that occupy both temporary and permanent waters, and specialists with precise adaptations for living in temporary aquatic environments' (Graham, 2002). The idea that ephemeral pools offer a site of refuge for an eclectic mix of species taps into the escapist characteristics that underpin the varied motivations of many national park visitors. Common tourist inhabitants of ephemeral national park environments include urban opportunists, who are keen to find respite from their day-to-day existence, but who have little affinity with the environment they are entering beyond a desire for passive engagement with pristine natural settings. In contrast, one also has groups including trail bike, snow mobile and horse riders. These groups seek various degrees of active engagement with natural settings, supported by various temporary and/or permanent national park infrastructures. Finally, one has hard-core ecotourists, seekers of immersive experiences that involve adapting themselves to the ecological situation of their nature experience.

The presence of an eclectic mix of visitor types and motivations within a defined national park boundary presents challenges for tourism marketers and protected area managers in equal measure. While national parks serve as a magnet for rural tourism development in many parts of the world (Urry, 1995); tourism marketers must reconcile a plurality of tourist views relating to the acceptability of cultural and environmental commodification of the national park tourism destination region. Pike (2008: 177) has identified commodification to be an emerging issue in the marketing of tourism destinations, noting that while 'an effective brand strategy can provide the means for successful [product differentiation] ... too many brands drift aimlessly and appear to stand for nothing in particular'. Strong brands such as the World Heritage trademark carry with them reputations for enhancement of the biodiversity of any protected area they are affiliated with (King & Prideaux, 2010).

In order for the effect of marketing brands to be enhanced, park agencies must provide infrastructure (including interpretation infrastructure, visitation infrastructure etc.) to facilitate visitor access in a manner that is in line with visitor expectations and within the accepted limits for development of the park's conservation designation. At the conclusion of the present chapter, the authors will canvas the potential role of interpretation on park trails as a facilitator of peak tourist experiences.

Marketing a National Park Visitor Experience

The aim of marketing in a national park is to create a link between people and the environment, working to instil realistic expectations in the minds of visitors (Wearing & Archer, 2001) and managing expectations in light of conservation realities. In the Australian context, campaigns such as the 2006 National Landscape Initiative were strategic marketing partnerships between tourism and conservation interests; partnerships that were developed with the specific aim of meeting tourism needs that were consistent with the natural and cultural conservation outcomes of the protected locality in which they were situated. The dissemination of these dual messages we argue must occur prior to a tourist visiting and whilst they are on site, hence our focus on onsite interpretation at the conclusion of this chapter.

How does one, however, market a national park based tourist experience to an increasingly discerning market place? Fritsch and Johannsen (2004) have noted that the first stage in the process is to make potential visitors feel dissatisfied with their current situation and eager for an experience that will satisfy their unique personal needs. Success with this objective is conditional on appropriate market segmentation, which itself is dependent upon recognition of the psychographic and other personal motivational variables that may underpin a tourist's decision making processes. While national park based ecotourism theoretically appeals to higher level needs including self-actualisation; also central to the development of sustainable national park marketing strategies is the synergies that are created between the demand and supply sides of the marketing mix (see Eagles & McCool, 2002; Wearing & Neil, 2009). Havitz (1988) notes that marketing of park based tourism serves an end for protected area agencies in that it allows them to target conservation messages more effectively than would be achieved by directionless marketing to the general public. The question of how this could be achieved will be explored in the next chapter when the authors investigate the contribution that onsite trail based interpretation may make to the socio-ecological education of visitors. While authors including Pearce and Moscardo (1998) have identified the presence of a role for interpretation, both as an precursor to visitor satisfaction, and as a tool for promoting learning and appreciation of the natural assets of a site; what is still largely under researched is the way that the synergies between interpretation and experience marketing can be operationalised. Before this, however, we will unpack the notion of park based experience marketing in more detail.

Over the last half century there has been a growing level of academic interest in the notion of the countryside as a locale of consumption. In the Australian context, Veal (2003) talks of the increasing preoccupation of policy makers to encourage participation in outdoor recreation and to encourage equality of access across the social spectrum. In the state of Queensland, a recent report for the Queensland Outdoor Recreation Federation identified a direct US$2 billion impact from outdoor recreation on the state's gross domestic product (Synergies Economic Consulting, 2012). In the early years of the United States National Parks movement, the patronage of outdoor recreationalists has been identified as inherent to the very survival of the movement against the competing interests of pastoralists who saw conservation as the outcome of the locking away of otherwise profitable agricultural land (Shaw & Williams, 2002). Access to national parks and other protected area designations affords a range of user and non-user benefits for tourists and society at large. Shultis (2003) talks of benefit categories as including psychological, personal development, psychophysiological, economic, environmental and sociocultural.

The juxtaposition of tangible versus intangible benefits in Shultis's categorisations presents a difficult balancing act for resource managers and marketers. As was stated in Chapter 1, there are currently a range of protected area designations being employed by groups such as the International Union for the Conservation of Nature. Different designations provide for variable levels of human engagement with nature. At the summit of the protected area hierarchy are the World Heritage Areas (WHA), which were recently identified by James Purtill (former head of the Queensland Parks Service) as the 'jewels in the crown' of Australia's protected area tourism inventory (Putrill, 2013). Even WHAs are not, however, immune from the impact of competing valuations of nature. At the time of writing, the Great Barrier Reef, which is perhaps the most well-known of Australia's WHAs and the recipient of 1.99 million visitor nights in the year ending December 2012, has come under scrutiny over the potential effects of the dumping of dredged material as part of the Abbotts Point Coal Terminal redevelopment. The idea that this development could eventually lead to the delisting of the reef from the global World Heritage register has sparked a flurry of consternation from a range of stakeholder groups seeking to highlight the potential impacts on Australia's international reputation and tourism marketing potential.

It is easy to draw a direct correlation between an increased primary industry presence in protected areas such as the Great Barrier Reef and a possible decline in an area's tourism marketing potential. There is, after all, a mixture of situational components in the 4Ps marketing mix, which interact with identified tourist market segments to fulfil the needs of the visitor. But what are those needs? Urry (2002) notes that the rural areas in which so much of the world's protected area inventory is based have grown in popularity on the basis of a general disillusionment with the pace and direction of urban development post World War II. Whilst often viewed as a positive antithesis to uncontrolled urban expansion, not all aspects of rurality are said to be consistent with an individual tourist's ideal landscape. Urry (2002: 88) notes that perspectives of nature represent 'individualist ways of seeing' Having made this statement, however, Urry then goes on to say that landscape implies an inherent separation of utilitarian interests and natural setting; 'the countryside is there to be gazed upon, and ideally one should not be gazing upon other people, whether workers or other tourists' (2002: 88). The truth, or not, of this statement requires one to grapple with the notion of authenticity as it applies to nature. Cohen (1988) identifies that authenticity, which we will revisit later in this chapter, is a subjective and modern idea. It has emerged as a subject of scholarly inquiry on the basis of 'the impact of modernity upon the unity of social existence' (1988: 373). Stronza (2001) asserts that the quest for authentic tourism experiences is underpinned by an aim to 'reconnect with the pristine, the primitive, and the natural, that which is as yet untouched by modernity'. There is, within this statement, a level of recognition of the cultural component of the national park product offering. Throughout the world's protected regions cultures clash on the basis of differing perspectives on the subjective concepts of wilderness and conservation. Due acknowledgement of the importance of such complexities was recognised by Aldo Leopold (1989: 204) who noted that a land ethic requires human beings to shift from being the 'conqueror of the land community to plain member and citizen of it. It implies respect for his (sic) fellow members and also respect for the community as such'.

Through our conceptual model, which was introduced in Chapter 1, the authors are asserting that the sustainability of tourist marketing initiatives is predicated on the health of the environment in which the tourism industry is situated. In Chapter 1, the authors canvassed a range of historical issues relating to the evolution of this environment including the evolution of the culture of many park agencies to recognise the potential for mutual reinforcement of values that can flow from more symbiotic relations with tourism industry stakeholders. In this chapter, we will open by revisiting some of this history, but this time framing the debate in terms of the influence of evolving stakeholder interpretations on the value of nature on the subsequent evolution of marketing strategies. In this way we will take a leaf from the work of Vargo (2011) who argued in the context of service dominated logic that 'markets are characterised by mutual value propositions, and service provision, governed by socially constructed institutions'. We will open with a discussion of perhaps the most fundamental of values a tourist can associate, the opportunity for a religious experience. Cronon (1996) offers the following by way of illustration, drawing on the words of William Wordsworth in *The Prelude:*

> The immeasurable height
> Of woods decaying, never to be decayed,
> The stationary blasts of waterfalls,
> And in the narrow rent at every turn
> Winds thwarting winds, bewildered and forlorn,
> The torrents shooting from the clear blue sky,
> The rocks that muttered close upon our ears,
> Black drizzling crags that spake by the way-side
> As if a voice were in them, the sick sight
> And giddy prospect of the raving stream,
> The unfettered clouds and region of the Heavens,
> Tumult and peace, the darkness and the light

> Were all like workings of one mind, the features
> Of the same face, blossoms upon one tree;
> Characters of the great Apocalypse,
> The types and symbols of Eternity,
> Of first, and last, and midst, and without end

A Sacred Foundation to Visitor Perceptions of Parks

National parks and their various socio-environmental properties are considered sacred by many communities throughout the world. The former Australian politician and founder of the Australian Greens, Bob Brown, wrote in a preface to a work on female forest activists in Australia's South East that 'forests give us beauty, inspiration and adventure. We resonate with their wild and complex mystery' (Broder et al., 2006: 7). Ramakrishnan (2003) wrote of the symbiotic interconnectedness between biophysical and sociocultural components of the sacred forest. Citing examples from various eastern religious traditions, Ramakrishnan (2003) identifies that many sacred natural features such as Mount Mani Mahesh in the Indian state of Himachal Pradesh are essentially viewed as common pool resources by a range of cultural groups. Mani Mahesh is the site of a significant religious pilgrimage that is completed by more than 700,000 pilgrims annually (Singh & Sharma, 2010). Miles-Watson and Miles-Watson (2011) note the potential for conflict to develop between different groups of Mani Mahesh pilgrims on the basis of their own critical self-appraisal of the impacts of 'competing' groups on the natural environment. The pilgrimage environment (i.e. the mountain) is identified as having to be a 'loving wife to some and virgin seductress to others ... [and] the contrasting nature of these conversations with the mountain leaves its trace' (Miles-Watson & Miles-Watson, 2011: 331). Privette (1983) has identified occasions of sexual love as one of the most common triggers for peak experience, which we will discuss in detail later in this chapter in the context of park trails.

The demarcation of wilderness areas as sacred is not confined to eastern traditions. In 2006, the United States Senator Dianne Feinstein penned a letter to the director of the national parks movement in response to proposed changes to management policies. In this letter the Senator referred to national parks as 'America's cathedrals' (Feinstein, 2006). The notion that national parks may provide the 'colonies' of the United States with a natural foundation to rival the established built religious histories of Europe has been articulated by a number of authors (Runte, 1977; Turner, 2002). Such sentiments are influential in a marketing context as they provide a means for establishing an appropriate marketing segmentation framework for national parks where product offerings are linked to visitor motivations for experiencing various forms of recreation, spiritual enlightenment, cultural immersion etc. Over the course of the history of America's national parks movement the nature of society's connection to wilderness has changed from one of fear, to exploitation, to reverence (Manning, 1989). The latter of these phases has been characterised by what Adams and Mulligan (2003 in Johnston, 2009) describe as a form of fortress conservation where wilderness landscapes are protected from all forms of human incursion.

The evolving nature of society's connection to wilderness has led to an uneasy relationship between conservationist and utilitarian perspectives on best practice in park management. The early years of national parks in the United States were characterised by conflict between the utilitarian conservationist doctrines of Gifford Pinchot on the one hand, and the aesthetic preservationists represented by John Muir on the other (Sharpe et al., 1994). Utilitarian philosophies amongst the early national park managers have led to the development of profitable nature based tourism industries in many of the world's iconic national parks (Ma et al., 2009: 21). Stankey (1989) notes that it was possible to manage such conflicts in the early years due to the relatively small number of visitors to parks. In recent years however, the increasing number and diversity of visitors to the world's iconic parks has grown considerably. Between 1873 and 1877, 500 people visited Yellowstone National Park (Sharpe et al., 1994). In 2010, 3.64 million people visited Yellowstone National Park, spending US$334 million dollars in surrounding communities and supporting 4,900 local jobs (Travel Montana, 2012). Abbey (1968 in Herremans & Reid, 2006: 161) writing on the increasing diversification of trail users to include motorised vehicles notes that such trends should be discouraged on the basis that 'we should treat our national parks with the same deference [as other sanctums of our culture], for they too are holy places'.

In Australia, a recent article completed for the *Conversation* sought to highlight the damage that is being caused to Australia's pristine ecosystems by unrestrained tourism development and the variable impacts of grazing and pest animal control (Ritchie et al., 2013). This article in a sense supported the previously mentioned notion of a fortress conservation approach to forest management, arguing laudably that:

> A return to the out-dated views of the 19th century – when parks were little more than playgrounds for city dwellers to escape the urban *malaise* - would run counter to everything that Australians have learnt about environmental conservation in the last 150 years. (Ritchie et al., 2013)

Australia's early national parks were founded on the basis of the need to provide respite for urban populations. Whether this was respite in the form of tourism opportunities in the Fish River Jenolan Caves region in the 1860s, or respite from the negative health impacts of Sydney's industrial expansion, which was offered by the creation of the Royal National Park south of Sydney in the 1870s; Australia's national parks have always had a strong utilitarian agenda (see Hall, 1988). The ability of national park managers to find a balance between utilitarian and conservation agendas rests ultimately with the adherence of tourism industries to the principles of sustainability. Gilmore and Simmons (2007) have established that one of the principle national park based sustainability debates relates to the need to preserve the resources on which the industry is ultimately founded. Debates over the relative merits of applying strong versus weak interpretations of sustainability (Hunter, 1997) have led to a range of marketing responses as park managers attempt to integrate tourist experiences into the broader fabric of the reserve environment. Proponents of a conservationist perspective have often gone as far as to promote demarketing as a means of managing tourism's impacts. Armstrong and Kern (2011: 22) discuss demarketing as a mechanism for managing demand for a product through the management of 'visitor levels, visitor types, behaviour and expectations'. As explained in Chapter 2, often demarketing is managed through the manipulation of price and access (place). The management of price usually makes the parks available to only those who can afford it. Whereas, the management of access is more utilitarian through the use of ballot systems for access to national parks such as Wilson's Promontory National Park during the summer season, or access systems such as the restrictions to get to places like Hanauma Bay Nature Preserve. Underpinning arguments in favour of demarketing is the disputed notion that the quality of nature is directly proportional to the level of human contact with the land. Other authors such as Chase (1996 in Rettie *et al.*, 2009: 411) have noted in contrast that 'natural areas are not made less natural by human presence ... the world of nature and culture overlap'. National parks offer unique opportunities for national tourism offices to market a distinctive utilitarian imagery to the world; one that in the case of Canada supports notions of nationalism and democracy in respect to access for all (Kopas, 2007).

Gilmore and Simmons (2007: 199) establish that 'marketing can be utilised to raise awareness of the unique benefits of national parks'. Marketing strategies such as Brand Kakadu in Australia's Northern Territory have successfully struck a balance between consumerism and conservation by reaching out to a variety of tourists that will be respectful of Aboriginal societal traditions and its extensive World Heritage assets (TTF Australia: Tourism and Transport Forum, 2007). Historically, Wearing and McDonald (2002) note that tourists will often possess unequal power relations with local people, an occurrence which they note will lead to a marginalisation of local people to a position of 'other' in the framing of tourist experiences. While such an occurrence is obviously best avoided, one must still look to actively involve tourists in the creation of experiences in a natural wilderness setting (Eagles & McCool, 2002).

The tourism industry was actively engaged in the creation of Brand Kakadu, working collaboratively with traditional owner, Parks Australia and the Northern Territory Government. Such a participatory approach to the creation of a marketing brand is important in the sense that 'our collective understanding of nature is produced by social and cultural processes and practices involving the interventions of all kinds of produces' (Markwell, 2004: 19). Hall and Cole (2012) identify that components of experience include both active and passive engagement with nature, opportunities for solitude and opportunities for social interaction. Because experience can be both active and passive one may draw a connection here to an idea from Wattchow and Brown (2011: xxi) that a protected area visitor's conceptualisation of 'place is influenced by both the imaginative and physical reality of a location and its people'. Over time, the precise framing of this experience in a trail environment may vary. By way of illustration Ord (2013) notes that since a team from the Tasmanian Government's Tourist Bureau first trekked the Overland Track in the 1930s there has been over 8000 overlanders who have completed the walk. Gone are the days, however, of 'blundering through some of nature's wildest terrain, an environment infested with leeches ... all the while battling Tasmania's notoriously unpredictable weather' (Ord, 2013: 20). Today trekkers 'sit inside cosy huts, sipping red wine by firelight, warm and snug after their hot showers, barely sore from the day's tramp having lugged only backpacks' (Ord, 2013: 20). Whilst such experiences on the track today are appealing in the sense that they provide an ease of access to nature that can be enjoyed and marketed to an increasing diversity of user groups, do they really provide instances of transcendent experience where tourists will experience a 'sense of union, power [and] timelessness engagement with nature' (Williams & Harvey, 2001: 250)? At the beginning of this section, the authors identified that national parks have an inherent sacred element, which is a fundamental underpinning of experience. The sacred element does not always have to result in positive experiences for those involved. The Scottish Physician Alexander Hunter wrote that 'it is natural for men [sic] to feel an awful and religious terror when placed in the middle of a thick wood' (Williams & Harvey, 2001: 250). While trails offer a form of direction to visitors, reducing their need to create informal tracks of their own (Dragovich & Bajpai, 2012), the acceptability of the experience will ultimately depend on the visitor's interpretation of the wilderness setting in which the trail is situated.

Visitor Interpretations of Wilderness

Gill (1999) identifies wilderness to be a multifaceted phenomenon with characteristics that are anchored in complex sociocultural discourses stretching back to antiquity. While Johnston (2009: 810) defines wilderness generally as a 'condition, usually applied to a landscape of being wild, out of human control, uncultivated and uninhabited'; Gill (1999) identifies wilderness as a social as much as a physical phenomenon imbued with a range of colonialist, religious and other influences. Throughout history wilderness as a generic concept has variously been perceived as a site of foreboding, untapped opportunity and renewal. Literary works such as Joseph Conrad's *Heart of Darkness* paint a picture of the all-encompassing, inherent evilness of wilderness in the context of European colonial expansion in the African Congo in the 19th century:

> And outside, the silent wilderness surrounding this cleared speck on the earth struck me as something great and invincible, like evil or truth, waiting patiently for the passing away of this fantastic invasion. (Conrad, 1995)

Throughout *Heart of Darkness* the reader is exposed to a fascinating juxtaposition of metaphors of European technological superiority (paddle steamers, Winchester rifles) in conflict with the eternal uncompromising wilderness, which would eventually see the company man Mr Kurtz proclaim of 'the horror, the horror' with his last breath. Questions as to whether wilderness of the African Congo could be conquered were not solely a literary device employed by Conrad to examine the consequence of acquiring knowledge of the unknown. They were also designed to articulate a struggle, which Conrad describes as characteristic 'of our time' and with lessons that could be applied positively to ongoing 'civilising works in Africa' (Levenson, 1985).

Perhaps more than anything, the metaphor of darkness, which imbues Conrad's novel, can be acquainted with the equally chilling notion of the unknown. The very wilderness, which today offers urban travellers a psychiatric refuge from the ills of western civilisation (see Fletcher, 2009) was, in the early days of the environmental movement, something to be preserved and by implication conquered. By engaging with a white interpretation of wilderness, the early colonialist pioneers including Carleton Watkins and John Muir were seeking to pursue policies that saw traditional native inhabitants as impediments to a nation's true destiny (DeLuca & Demo, 2001). An early Yosemite National Park advocate summed up the attitude of many at the time when he made the following statement regarding indigenous inhabitants of the American West, a region today that is home to noteworthy tourism sites including the Yosemite falls, Cathedral Peak and Mono Lake:

> We know that they are not our equals ... we know that our right to the soil, as a race capable of its superior improvement is beyond theirs, [therefore] let us act directly and openly in faith ... Let us say to [the Indian] ... you are our ward, the victim of our destiny, ours to displace, ours to protect. (Bowles in De Luca & Demo, 2001: 544)

Such views on the role of indigenous peoples in park management invoke notions of top down autocratic land management, an idea that is to many the antitheses of modern ideals of participatory sustainable development in park management. It is not our intention in this chapter to argue against the injustices suffered by many indigenous populations worldwide, as they were artificially incorporated into western concepts of conservation. Instead, in the next section we will seek to grapple with the notion that authenticity as it applies to the marketing is a social construct. Tourists, Laing and Crouch (2005) note, are increasingly seeking to engage with the frontier of civilisation, participating in a range of extreme wilderness experiences with the aim of exacting a level of prestige amongst their peers. Circumnavigation of the globe by balloon or boat, the development of space tourism by Virgin Galactic and skiing across Antarctica are all cited as examples of such experiences today. We say today because as Laing and Crouch (2005) note the boundaries of civilisation, and we would argue by implication wilderness, are constantly changing. As we strive for marketing authentic experiences, be it in a national park or elsewhere we must examine both our evolving human perception of the appropriateness of the experience and the idea that the wilderness locality itself is evolving and influencing the way society perceives its ideal management.

Marketing Authenticity in the National Park Experience

The tourist experience is simultaneously one of the most studied and least agreed on fields in the academic lexicon. Seminal academic works including MacCannell's *The Tourist* have received over 5000 Google Scholar citations since being published in the 1980s. Tourism agencies the world over have engaged in segmentation studies of the tourist marketplace with the aim of matching tourism market segments with the unique product offerings in different geographical localities. Marketing strategies, including New Zealand Tourism's 100% Middle-earth and 100% New Zealand campaigns, have been designed to tap into the potential for movie lovers to experience fantasy of J.R.R. Tolkien's Middle-earth in the reality of New Zealand. Within each of these successful marketing strategies there is evidence of an innate ability of marketing professionals to create synergies between the values of the brand and the translation of such values 'into a suitably emotionally appealing personality and the targeted and efficient delivery of that message to visitors' (Morgan *et al.*, 2002: 336). Peaslee (2011: 45) talks of a 'parallel between the intrepid Hobbits and those who would make the physically and economically arduous flight Down Under to discover Middle Earth'. Weaver and Lawton (2014) critique whether the experience of a film set can ever be considered to be authentic, noting the apparent correlation in the minds of some travellers between the identities of Middle-earth and New Zealand, as well as alluding to the idea from Buchmann *et al.* (2010 in Weaver & Lawton, 2014) that authenticity should perhaps best be viewed as a longing for immersive myths that offer an antidote to reality.

Cochrane (2006) identifies that the tourism industry will often use myths as a means of establishing a marketable sense of place in destination regions. In a locality like a national park, the composition of such myths will frequently flow from the region's pioneering history and will be presented in such a way that it is more likely to appeal to common market segments (see Bandyopadhyay & Morais, 2005). It becomes easier to satisfy visitors' experiences in a manner that is acceptable to the other stakeholder groups that inhabit the destination region when the visitors are attuned to the environmental and sociocultural context of the destination. Backhaus (2003) notes that while certain ecotourism segments may perceive authenticity as tied to the maintenance of ecological values, the same cannot necessarily be said for more mainstream mass tourism sectors where the increasing commoditisation of international tourism has in many instances 'dissolved the boundaries between a place centred view of authenticity and an aesthetic illusion' (Hughes, 1995). In a generic sense authenticity has been described as 'the genuineness, trustworthiness, and accuracy of an object or account' (Johnson, 2009: 43).

The application of theories of authenticity to the study of tourism has a history dating back to the 1960s. The writings of Boorstin (1964) began the trend, calling into question the ability (or indeed intention) of hedonistic tourists to seek out anything beyond the inauthentic and contrived in the rapidly growing mass tourism sectors. Over the ensuing years there has been something of an evolution in the academic study of tourism authenticity. Gone are the days when authenticity was seen solely in objective terms relating to measurable characteristics of the toured object (see MacCannell, 1973, 1976). Instead, in a trend that is based partly on Cohen's assertion that 'there is no single tourist as such but a variety of tourist types or modes of tourist experience' (in Urry, 2002: 8); authors including Wang (1999) have moved to portray authenticity as a combination of existential and object related forces.

The idea that visitors may articulate their own definition of authenticity is fundamental to the success of a range of quintessential national park (or wilderness) consumer groups. The Sierra Club, by way of example, was incorporated as a legal entity in 1892 under the auspices of its founder John Muir (see www.sierraclub.org/history/origins/ for a history of the organisation). The organisation, which was founded around a mixture of human usage and conservationist agendas, has been fundamental in ensuring the gazettal and ongoing management of Yosemite National Park in the US state of California and now has grass roots chapters throughout a number of states. The environmentalist agendas of the Sierra Club are widely respected, with members of the group involved in a range of direct action protests against developments such as the Keystone XL tar sands pipeline. Simultaneously however, authors including Luke (1997) have drawn attention to the uneasy relationship between utilitarian and conservationist forces in the Sierra Club's history. If one examines the original charter of the club the following aims are articulated:

> To explore, enjoy and render accessible the mountain regions of the Pacific Coast; to publish authentic information concerning them; to enlist the support and co-operation of the people and government in preserving the forests and other features of the Sierra Nevada Mountains. (Le Conte in Gilliam, 1979: 44)

These aims of the Sierra Club express an apparent symbiosis in the minds of its proponents between human enjoyment/recreation and environmental preservation. Such links are not confined to the United States. In 1914 Miles Dunphy established the Mountain Trails Club in Australia with the aim of identifying land of high conservation value, an initiative that would assist in the gazettal of large tracks of land as national parks throughout the Blue Mountains and Australia's Alpine regions (Slattery, 2009). Both the Mountain Trails Club and the Sierra Club can be said to be illustrative of Wang's (1999) belief that existential authenticity is the greater determinant of authenticity. Slattery (2009: 1) has drawn attention to the increasing critique of bushwalkers over the need to be more 'responsive to landscape and to culture, and less to the experience of self'. The Sierra Club was founded on ideals, which saw authenticity connected to a narrow, middle to upper class, white interpretation of wilderness. De Luca and Demo (2001) illustrate how Muir was able to use emotive, almost religious, imagery of the power of nature to marginalise the exotic features of the landscape including indigenous populations, and promote an authentic experience that would be accessible in the homes of suburbanites.

The ability of travel writers such as John Muir to market a vision for a national park stems, we would argue, from their ability to tap into the sensibilities of the listening public. Robinson and Andersen (2002) talk of literature as being simultaneously an object or culture and a mechanism whereby culture may be created. Travel writing in mediums, including poetry and popular magazines, has the ability to inspire people to visit national parks. In this regard, Urry (1995) talks of the influence of poets such as Coleridge and Wordsworth on visitor interest in England's Lakes District. Similarly the environmental historian Runte (2002) talks eloquently of the ways in which in magazines including *Life* and the *Saturday Evening Post* provided a source of inspiration for his mother to visit national parks. Runte (200: 70) identifies that the result of her eventual visit was a renewed commitment to life that stemmed, she believed, from her exposure to a 'country as magnificent as it was healing'. The ability of a national park experience to provide such a source of fulfilment (perhaps a peak experience?) to a visitor(s) is dependent upon the visitor's own travel ontology and the degree to which the objective world is in sync with human being's perceptions of it. Woodard and Jones III (2000) note that advances in post structuralism have seen a tendency in academic fields such as geography for ontology to be viewed less as a series of binary distinctions, but instead as a concept that must be critiqued on the basis of personal epistemological constructs, which are 'mired in cultural, political and, most importantly, linguistic and discursive imaginaries' (Woodard & Jones III, 2000: 512). The variability of perception that this situation encourages has links to the writings of Wang on the quest for authenticity in experience where it is asserted that existential authenticity is the greater determinant of authenticity on the basis that tourists will concern themselves 'less with the authenticity of toured objects but rather search for their own authentic selves with the aid of these activities' (1999: 3). The following quote from a Presidential Address to the Royal Geographical Society by the celebrity traveller and society president Michael Palin is offered as an example of this phenomenon:

> I am not a scientist nor have I any specialist expertise, but geography underlies everything I'm interested in as a traveller, which is (sic) by and large the people I meet. Geography helps me understand who they are, where they are, and why they are the way they are. I enjoy the solitude of great deserts and mountain ranges, but I didn't travel to the Sahara or across the Himalaya to get away from people. I travelled to the Sahara and the Himalaya to find them. Many live on the edge of the wilderness, and I'm fascinated to see how they survive where others would be destroyed. And not merely to tick them off on a list of anthropological curiosities – been there, done that – but to learn something from them that might just possibly help me to live better. (Palin, 2011)

Himalayan Tourism of the type that Palin experienced has played to its strengths for a number of years, positioning its marketing efforts to capitalise on the market preferences of visitors. Authors including Holden (2003) and Holden and Sparrowhawk (2002) have reported that visitors to the Annapurna region of Nepal were motivated by a desire to enjoy nature. Marketing groups such as Himalayan Tourism have tapped into these preferences, designing marketing syntax with the intent of 'sparking the imagination to the point where the actual experience may be anticlimactic' (Buck, 1977: 199):

> East Himalaya provides a wide potential in tourism that has yet largely remained unexploited. The perennially snow-capped mountains, lush green tropical and temperate forests, gurgling streams and the rich flora and fauna – a true Shangrila or 'Nye-mae-el' which simply means

'heaven'. Situated in North East India, just south of Sikkim, Darjeeling provides the perfect ambiance of a hill resort with its mild climate and laid back charm. Its verdant hills and valleys are steeped in colour, and are interspersed with vast stretches of rolling green tea gardens. Presiding over all this is Mt. Kangchenjunga, the third highest mountain on Earth, looming over the northern horizon, giving a magical aura to the land that leaves one's senses intoxicated. (Himalayan Tourism, 2012)

From this quote, it can be seen that the natural environment in a locality like the Himalayas forms an important component of place. Place, Tuohino and Pitkanen (2004) note, represents security, space in contrast represents freedom. The brilliant simplicity of this argument synthesises in four words many of the challenges in developing marketing strategies that are simultaneously tourist and context centred. Principally, it places the notion of tourism wants at the centre of place formation. Service-based economies such as tourism have for a number of years placed a premium on the fulfilment of a tourists' wants and desires; recognising that this variable is fundamental for the development of a positive destination brand (Crompton, 1979). While authors such as Urry (1990) have taken it to the extreme by contending that places die when they cease to possess the capacity to provide for human consumption, or alternatively, when they become inhospitable for human habitation; there is, nonetheless, a general acceptance that the economic sustainability of the industry is first and foremost based around the development of product lines or commodities that will allow for effective product definition and differentiation.

Over the last 20 or so years, there has been a general acceptance of the centrality of the tourism product to the formation of the 8Ps of the tourism marketing mix. In its most basic form a tourism product represents the 'range of available goods and services, their quality and warranty and after sale service' (Weaver & Lawton, 2014: 208). Over recent years, there has been debate over exactly what the product encompasses (Smith, 1994), which has stemmed from broader debates over partial industrialisation and the constituent components of the tourism industry itself (Leiper, 1990a; Leiper et al., 2008). In the paragraphs that follow, we will not seek to contribute to these discussions directly, except to say that there may be considerable challenges presented to tourism marketers who wish to arbitrarily characterise enterprises such as national parks as tourism when, as Robertson (1988) notes 'their ultimate product is perhaps [not the provision of experience] but rather the insurance that future generations will have the opportunity to understand and experience the natural environment in settings which, for the most part, are unsullied by the industrial activities of mankind'. Campbell (1996) defines sustainable planning as the process of managing the inherent tension between environmental protection, social equity and economic development. To illustrate the difficulties in this process we will deviate briefly from our discussion of national parks and consider another related typology of protected area; the botanic garden[1].

Botanic gardens have been defined as 'institutions holding documented collections of living plants for the purposes of scientific research, conservation, display and education' (Botanic Gardens Conservation International, n.d.). While the history of gardens as localities for the study of plants dates back to antiquity; by the 19th century the focus of gardens had shifted from the 'abstract contemplation of God's wondrous creation, to economic and ... scientific laboratories where botanists brought the natural world under rational scrutiny and attempted to provide new products for colonial economies' (Ginn, 2009). Visitor motivations to spend time in botanic gardens have been identified as stemming from opportunities for education, passive and active recreation (Ballantyne et al., 2009). In the same way as national parks represent wicked problems for policy makers, botanic gardens similarly suffer from an unsettled confluence of human values that has led in many instances to conflict over their future direction. A recent example of such conflict has been the public debate over the future of the Royal Botanic Gardens in Sydney, Australia.

Sydney's Royal Botanic Gardens are located on the southern shores of Port Jackson and were formally declared a botanic garden by Governor Macquarie in 1816. Prior to this designation, the area had served as a private reserve for the governors of New South Wales since the establishment of the colony in the 1780s. Before this they formed part of the ancestral home of the Cadigal people of the Eora Nation. On Sunday April 6 2014, the Royal Botanic Gardens and Domain Trust in Sydney Australia released a draft master plan for public comment and consultation. The master plan was spruiked as the first such planning initiative in the nearly 200 year history of the park, and an opportunity to ensure the site's future:

> This is not only in terms of history place and character but importantly, the master plan will create the means to continue our role in scientific research and in promoting appreciation, understanding and knowledge of plant life. (Royal Botanic Gardens and Domain Trust, 2014)

In the weeks that followed, the announcement, the details of the plan (including the proposed hotel development on the site of the nearby Sydney Domain car park, enhanced visitor amenities at Mrs Macquarie's Chair, adaptive re-use of historic buildings as function space etc.) have been variously lauded or lambasted by a range of prominent stakeholder groups. The Australian Tourism and Transport Forum[2] recognised the economic importance of the nearly 8 million visitors to the site each year, and the importance of strategic, as opposed to *ad hoc* initiatives to ensure that acceptable experiences are offered, which will minimise the size of the developmental footprint on the local area (TTF Australia, 2014). In contrast, former Australian

Prime Minister Paul Keating sought to demonise the 'greedy and crass tourism industry' along with the Art Gallery of NSW Board and others for seeking to attack the city's 'hallowed open spaces' (Keating, 2014).

Chiesura (2004) has identified the importance of parks and their associated public spaces to the maintenance of quality of life for urban populations. In the early years of the Sydney colony, the description of the Botanic Gardens as 'public' was largely erroneous, as evidenced in the oppressive restrictions placed on access to the site by Governor Macquarie. Endersby (Endersby, 2000: 316) quotes an edition of the *Sydney Gazette* which stated that access was to be restricted to 'the respectable class of inhabitants' who would be admitted 'for innocent recreation during the day time'. In this way the Sydney Botanic Gardens were, in their early years, representative of the late-19th century pleasure park (see Henty, 1988) with their characteristics of elitist engagement with nature and scientific endeavour. Moves to broaden the scope of recreational offerings in the area did not come quickly. In the 1830s the one time curator of the gardens Allan Cunningham was said to approve of access to the park for the elite, if for no other reason than it helped on public use grounds to justify the considerable cost associated with the park's creation and upkeep. Ballantyne *et al.* (2007) has emphasised the myriad of motivations including recreation and tourism that underpin contemporary public interest in urban parklands. In subsequent sections, of this chapter the authors will explore peak and supporting consumer experiences, along with the ability of park managers to use interpretive education mechanisms to ensure a synergy between visitor motivations and the authentic characteristics of 'place' in the destination region. To achieve this objective we must first, however, consider the idea of the authenticity of the toured object as it has evolved on the basis of changing societal norms. This is an idea that has been largely absent from recent academic commentary on the tourist experience.

As we have stated previously, throughout much of the recent literature on the authenticity of tourism there is a tendency to see authenticity as an amalgam of objective and existential forces. The former is portrayed as locked and measurable against absolute and objective criteria (Reisinger & Steiner, 2006). In contrast, constructivist notions of authenticity, which have underpinned the trend towards considering existentialism in tourism studies (see Kim & Jamal, 2007; Wang, 1999) have tended to see authenticity as transient, negotiable and context specific (Steiner & Reisinger, 2006). The present authors do not object to the increased academic focus on the transient nature of existential authenticity. It is within the power of tourists to variously seek out authentic or inauthentic experiences on the basis of their mood moment to moment. Visitor experiences cannot, however, exist in a sustainability vacuum, divorced from the environmental and sociocultural context of their host environment. To be truly sustainable, there is a requirement that a balance be struck between the promotion of human enjoyment and the maintenance of the full range of stakeholder values within a heterogeneous park locale. One of many challenges for park managers in this regard is the evolving nature of stakeholder defined social norms regarding the role of the indigenous voice and communities in environmental land management.

A community may be defined as 'a group of people who share common culture, values and/ or interests, based on social identity and/ or territory, and who have some means of recognising and (inter)acting upon, these commonalities' (Anon, 2009). Themes of indigenous culture play a major role in the marketing of tourism in countries such as Australia where in the 2010 calendar year, indigenous tourism generated US$3.8 billion for the national economy (Tourism Research Australia, 2010). While such industries serve as an important marketing theme of national parks; the renowned Aboriginal scholar Professor Marcia Langton cautioned against the removal of interests and viewpoints from the management of the environment, arguing against what she sees as a redneck attitude amongst many in the environmental movement (Langton, 1996). While there are synergies between so called sustainable tourism sectors such as ecotourism and indigenous interests in the provision of opportunities for nature based viewing and education of examples of indigenous culture; for many years academics have wrestled with the question of whether ecotourism should be seen as a panacea for the ills of marginalised indigenous cultures or as a threat to their existence (Fritsch & Johannsen, 2004; Johnston, 2000). Since the creation of the world's first national parks in Yosemite and Yellowstone, western conservation agendas have frequently clashed with the concerns of indigenous populations. Colonialist interpretations of wilderness, which sought to equate wilderness with notions of primitive naturalness led to a 'dichotomization of nature from culture' (Lannoy, 2012) and the marginalisation and displacement of many indigenous community groups from their ancestral homes.

The 1975 publication of the Kinshasa Resolution marked the start of a renewed focus amongst protected area agencies including the World National Parks Congress to recognise the rights of indigenous populations (Colchester, 2004). This in turn has led groups such as the United States National Parks Service and Parks Canada to establish American Indian Liaison Officers and the Aboriginal Affairs Secretariat to formally integrate indigenous interests into park planning processes. Kakadu National Park in the Australian Northern Territory is often praised for its formalised partnerships between government, tourism and indigenous interests (Director of National Parks, 2007). It was the first national park in the world to deviate from what Haynes (2009) defines as the Yellowstone model where park land is owned by the state. By giving indigenous people a formal voice on the park management board it has been possible to ensure that Aboriginal interests are recognised with respect to determining the pace of development and nature of tourism development in the region.

In the introduction to an article on the role of indigenous methodologies in geographic research, Louis (2007) identifies an increasing push for equality of power relations in the 'western' study of indigenous populations. Gone are the days when indigenous epistemologies could be deemed as culturally deficient to western knowledge systems (see Louis, 2007). Instead there has been a call for greater recognition of Aboriginal ontologies with their associated blending of nature and society (Howitt & Suchet-Pearson, 2006). One mechanism through which this may be achieved is through hodology, which Turnbull (2007) describes as the conceptualisation of trails as embodiments of socially constructed space based performance. Iconic indigenous trails such as the Lurujarri Heritage Trail and the Bundian Way provide opportunities for the visitors to experience an evolving sense of place as traditional pre-colonial Aboriginal campsites exist side by side with living histories of early European settlement in Australia. The significance of hodology to the present discussion stems from Turnbull's (2007: 142) observation that 'the act of tracking, of moving through the environment ... and reading the signs, creates a complex of intellectual and cognitive connections and, at the same time, a physical trail'.

A perfect example of the juxtaposition of real and imagined trail experiences can be seen in Muir's description of an anonymous tree top decent in the Sierra's for the work *The Mountains of California*. In Chapter 8 of the aforementioned work, Muir describes tourists as one of a succession of groups that have come to admire the Yosemite Park over the first few decades of its existence. Following in the footsteps of naturalists, agriculturalists (sheepmen) and miners; 'thousands of admiring tourists passed through sections of the lower and middle zones on their way to that wonderful park, and gained fine glimpses of the Sugar Pines and Silver Firs along the edges of dusty trails and roads' (Muir, 1894). A review of the website, the Yosemite Experience, illustrates the durability of such themes to the present day. In visiting Yosemite, tourists are variously encouraged to 'take in soaring valley views and first-class stargazing from a 3200 foot perch' at Glacier Point or 'feel tiny beside giant sequoias, the planet's largest living organisms' at Mariposa Grove (Yosemite and Maripossa Country Tourism Bureau, n.d.). Whilst representing quintessential national park experiences, Muir goes on to assert that there are limits to the transformative potential of parks for such visitors. Continuing from *The Mountains of California* Muir noted:

> But few indeed, strong and free with eyes undimmed with care, have gone far enough and lived long enough with the trees to gain anything like a loving conception of their grandeur and significance as manifested in the harmonies of their distribution and varying aspects throughout the seasons, as they stand arrayed in their winter garb rejoicing in storms, putting forth their fresh leaves in the spring while steaming with resiny fragrance. (Muir, 1894)

The implication of these words is that higher levels of transcendent experiences, experiences that Williams and Harvey (2001) describe in terms of moments of extreme happiness, of being in harmony with the whole world etc. come to those who are free to experience the 'organic wholeness' of nature (Scott, 1974).

In the quote that opened this chapter it was identified that experience is both individually and societally shaped (see Clegg & Baumeler, 2010). This quote originated in a study of liquid identity as it relates to consumer choice where Clegg and Baumeler (2010: 1719) establish that 'those individuals (we might say tourists) that are loosed from the bonds of concentrated surveillance ... are best able to chart their own imaginings' (Clegg & Baumeler, 2010: 1719). The parallel between tourist behaviours and broader consumer culture is we would suggest apt. Clegg and Baumeler (2010) note that 'being liquid depends on a continuum of mobility from the emotional mobility of the deepest core of the self through to the social mobility afforded by pragmatic affluence and the consumer culture'. Tourists represent to many the archetypal consumer group. Wearing and Wearing (2001) note that the success of a tourism based consumptive experience are often related to a tourist's consumption of signs and other forms of on and off site interpretation. While in a mass tourism context such consumption may take on purely commercial overtones, in a nature-based alternative tourism context like a national park there is the potential for the message of the tourism industry to instil positive changes in behaviour, promote long-term conservation and thus contribute to cultural and ecological sustainability (Weiler & Ham, 2002).

National Park Interpretation

In Chapter 1, the authors referred to the evolving agenda of national park agencies, noting ways in which the primacy afforded to nature conservation and human recreation has ebbed and flowed over the decades since Yellowstone was created in 1872. While Archer and Wearing (2001) have labelled the artificial demarcation of conservation and human usage interests as unhelpful for the integrated sustainable management of park areas, the fact remains that the effect of these competing histories has been that various stakeholder interests have striven to have their view of national park management recognised as authentic, as encapsulating principles of trustworthiness and accuracy. Interpretation, in its various on and off site forms, has been identified by King (2012) to be an essential component of the process of exposing a visitor to the essence of the protected area brand. While King *et al.* (2012) has gone on to suggest that education may play a positive role in allowing visitors to appreciate the ecological and cultural significance of a site, Reisenger and Steiner (2006) identify a range of tensions in equating any form of interpretation with authenticity. How after all can a 'substitute experience', a term for which interpretation is often associated, be considered authentic (Reisenger & Steiner, 2006)?

Freedman Tilden defined interpretation as 'an educational activity which aims to reveal meanings and relationships through the use of original objects by firsthand experience and by illustrative media, rather than simply to communicate factual information' (Tilden, 1977: 8–9). Since its inception, numerous studies have sought to equate the various available interpretation techniques (see Table 4.1) to the principles of sustainability and the management of nature based tourism in protected areas (e.g. Archer & Wearing, 2002;

Table 4.1 Common forms of interpretation

Location/Method of Delivery	Personal	Non-Personal
ON-SITE	Guided walks Guided tours Discovery programmes Presentations Ranger/Personnel	Visitor centres Exhibits Signs Interpretive trails Publications/brochures Slide shows Audio installations Various FM radio media
	Purpose: • To enrich the visitor experience of parks and other assets under the management of national parks • To assist people to develop a keen awareness, appreciation, and enjoyment of the value, features and issues of natural and wilderness areas • To educate visitors about appropriate behaviours to alter use patterns – attitude and value change	
OFF-SITE	Information nights Public meetings	Publications/Brochures Newspaper Articles Advertising/Marketing Posters/books
	Purpose: Pre-visit: • To inform prospective visitors of existence of site and its resources • To ensure visitors' expectations are realistic, that images portrayed are relevant and aligned with park management's views • To ensure that visitors have an understanding of the natural resource Post-visit: • to provide material to extend visitor's on-site experience	

Bramwell & Lane, 1993; Buckley, 2012; Kim *et al.*, 2011; Littlefair, 2003; Moscardo & Pearce, 1997; Orams, 1996; Tubb, 2003; Wearing & Archer, 2002; Wearing *et al.*, 2006). In this chapter, we will not attempt to re-trace these debates into the relative merits of interpretation as a tool for growing environmental awareness. Instead we wish to focus on Tilden's first principle of interpretation:

> Any interpretation that does not somehow relate what is being displayed or described to something within the personality or experience of the visitor will be sterile. (Tilden, 1977: 11)

Here we would revisit Tilden (1977: 11) who states 'the visitor's chief interest is in whatever touches his personality, his experience and his ideals'. We will use these words as a launching pad to consider ways in which on site forms of trails based interpretation may be linked to the various forms of peak and consumer experience that exist within a park locale. Too often, Quan and Wang (2004) note, the marketing of tourism has tended to focus on the operational aspects of a consumer's experience, focusing on issues of service quality. The plethora of tourism marketing textbooks in circulation at the present time is testament of this fact, focusing as they typically do on a range of operational issues including: understanding visitor behaviour, market segmentation, demand analysis, pricing strategies, the consumer mix etc. Quan and Wang (2004) counter this trend by calling for a reconceptualisation of the relationship between the social science and the marketing/management approach to studying experience.

The model, which Quan and Wang (2004) propose, was developed in a food tourism context for the journal *Tourism Management*. The central tenant of the model is a rebuke of what the authors' conceived to be a too simplistic demarcation of tourism experience into sociological and industry based consumptive elements. By focusing on the totality of experience, including the relationship between touristic experiences (i.e. peak, consumer and the everyday), Quan and Wang (2004) argue that it then becomes possible to see how single experiences may be either peak or consumer focused depending on the context. Two conceptual statements underpin the point of interchangeability (Quan & Wang, 2004: 300):

(1) the dimension of the peak touristic experience is, and should be, conceptually differentiated from the dimension of the supporting consumer experience, and;
(2) the dimension of the peak touristic experience and the supporting consumer experience can be interchangeable under certain conditions.

In applying Quan and Wang's (2004) model to a nature based tourism protected area context, the present authors have realised that while each of these statements holds true in its own right there are also challenges in their application when one remembers that the management of national parks is not an abstract notion for those involved in its formation. In Quan and Wang's (2004) model, food consumption is always seen from the perspective of the consumer with the tourism setting providing a blank canvas for touristic interpretation. To illustrate this point they give the example of a beach attraction. Like national parks, beaches serve as a common experience setting for tourists in many parts of the world. Quan and Wang (2004) pose the scenario a young man who has a romantic encounter with a female tourist while on holiday. While the young man may originally have seen the beach itself as the facilitator of his transformative or restorative peak experience, the process of engaging with a fellow traveller transforms the role of the beach to simply a facilitator of a supporting consumptive experience. The peak experience for the man becomes his romantic interlude. There is nothing essentially contradictory in such a conclusion. It is reflective of a broader appreciation that the tourism experience is an essentially postmodern and subjective phenomenon (Uriely, 2005). Where we would argue that challenges may develop is with the assumption that other tourism stakeholders are always going to be content with their region being portrayed in a manner that is enticing to the tourists. Archer and Wearing (2002) note that public sector agencies, such as the National Parks Service, Parks Canada etc., whilst being interested in the potential financial returns from tourism, have responsibilities that extend to the needs of a diverse stakeholder mix, which encompasses a range of community, industry, conservation agency and other interests. Park market segments include a diversity of stakeholders who may have conflicting values and expectations.[3] The park manager needs to be able to juggle these potentially conflicting responsibilities. Our discussion of the role of interpretation in the marketing of national parks begins with the tourist experience of national park trails used as and example; we then go on to examine ways that experience may be facilitated using management frameworks that are able to encompass wider cultural changes in society in Chapter 5.

Peak and Consumer Experiences of Nature on National Park Trails

In 1916, the *National Parks Service Act* established the dual conservation/human usage mandates of America's national parks system. This piece of legislation was the direct precursor to the establishment of a system of national historic trails, which initially included the Oregon Trail, Mormon Pioneer Trail, Lewis and Clark Trail and the Iditarod Trail (Alaska) (Runte, 1997). Three forms of trails currently exist as part of the current National Parks Service's trails system; historic, scenic and recreational. Each of these trail types has as its underlying focus 'the provision of simple pleasures within the reach of ordinary citizens' (Bureau of Outdoor Recreation in Krumpe & Lucas, 1986: 151). The close relationship between trails and visitor experiences has been recognised since the United States National Parks Service instigated the *National Trails System Act* in 1968. Under this act, a national system of recreation, scenic and historic trails were instigated, in part, 'to provide for the ever-increasing outdoor recreation needs of an expanding population' (National Parks Service, 2012b).

In Canada, trails are managed under the *Canadian National Parks Act*, the British Columbia *Parks Act* and a range of other legislative instruments. Vehicular trails such as the thematic Trail of the Great Bear provide Canadian tourism authorities with a unique opportunity to market the migratory routes of Canada's iconic brown bear populations. Whilst not denying its conservation value, authors such as Buckley (2003: 217) have gone as far as to suggest that the *Trail of the Great Bear* is essentially just a marketing 'scheme that links grizzly bear habitat and a wide range of tourist attractions along a scenic corridor from Yellowstone National Park .... to Jasper National Park in Alberta Canada'.

Robert Bednar, writing in the work *Observation Points the Visual Poetics of National Parks*, notes that 'trails in national parks are not simply the means for experiencing the national parks, but the medium through which the national parks present themselves as natural landscapes' (Bednar, 2012: 3). National parks are a people's resource in the sense that in addition to providing unique nature based experiences for onsite visitors, they also have a national significance as shrines and statements of a 'nation's special respect for its unique national resources' (Doremus, 1999: 438). The idea that national parks hold a special place in the imaginations of many in society marks them as potentially sites of transcendent peak experience.

Tilden (1977: 11) noted that a visitor's chief interest 'is in whatever touches his personality, his experience and his ideals'. At the present time, there is something of a dearth of academic literature on the experiences of trail users in national parks. This is regrettable in the sense that national park trails provide a mechanism for accessing some of the most extraordinary and isolated environments on the planet. A notable exception is the recently published work from Timothy and Boyd (2015) entitled *Tourism and Trails: Cultural, Ecological and Management Issues* that was recently published by Channel View Publications (Timothy & Boyd, 2015). The need to travel or dromo-mania is an all-encompassing psychological condition and trails, such as the Appalachian Trail in the Eastern United States, provide one of the primary mechanisms whereby 'ordinary people' can step out of their comfort zone and achieve personal greatness through the fulfilment of their own life's ambitions. As the travel writer Bill Bryson noted on the jacket cover of his work *A Walk in the Woods* (Bryson, 1998) regarding his walking of the Appalachian Trail; 'facing savage weather, merciless insects, unreliable maps and a fickle companion ... Bryson gamely struggled through the wilderness to achieve a lifetime's ambition – not to die outdoors'.

Transformative experiences of the type Bryson describes can be characterised as peak experiences. Peak experiences have been described by Abraham Maslow as a 'rebirth', as moments of emotion and cognition when an individual is affected by short intense moments of mystical revelation (1968). Originally seen in the context of peak experience of religion, Maslow (1962) has adopted a number of positions on the characteristics of these transcendent moments, characteristics that enrich our understanding of the theory's applicability to the study of wilderness based tourism. Above all else, Maslow (1962) identifies peak experiences to be absolute, the pinnacle of one's being, the 'fulfilment of our longing and the yearning'. McDonald *et al.* (2009) have drawn on these ideas when they described peak experiences of wilderness as being characterised by feelings of oneness and connections with nature. Recent scholarship has demonstrated the applicability of the concept to a range of common tourist activities including sky diving (Lipscombe, 1999), wild animal encounters (Curtin, 2006; DeMares & Krycka, 1998) and backpacking (Ryan *et al.*, 2003). By striving for unique forms of transcendent engagement with tourism's natural setting, it becomes possible in these and other contexts to achieve what the 19th century sociologist Thorstein Veblen described as creative consumption where tourists may develop a unique identity, formed on the basis a self-imposed social differentiation. Bott (2009) has described mountaineering in terms of a quest for identity that is founded on individual narratives of risk taking. The social kudos that is derived from completing treks to isolated locations of the world including Mount Everest, Angel Falls (Venezuela) and the like have been characterised by Laing and Crouch (2005) in terms of their designation as sites of discovery where the tourist moves beyond the tourist bubble and becomes a frontier trailblazer.

Trails throughout the Appalachian region, which stretches for over 2100 miles from Georgia to Maine in the eastern United States, forms an important part of the region's tourism marketing initiatives. Along with sites including the Great Smoky Mountains National Park the region is often marketed for its timeless beauty and the opportunities it offers detachment from the daily grind of one's day-to-day life. Such opportunities are not confined to United States or Canadian parks. The opportunities for travellers to avail themselves of a brief contact with a lost world in Tikal national park in Guatemala, or to observe first-hand the power of nature that helped give rise to Charles Darwin's Theory of Evolution in the Torres Del Paine National Park in Chile, enable tourists to intensify his or her self-identity, and in the case of the aforementioned celebrity traveller Michael Palin, the opportunity for an intensification of the everyday experience of one's journey:

> As we drive deeper in the [Torres Del Paine] park the patterns of light and shade change constantly so that from every new angle the peaks seem to alter their shape and size, one stepping grandly forward for a moment,

another shrinking modestly into the background. Dazzling clear blue lakes offer the chance to see this stunning landscape twice.

It's four o'clock and the light is beginning to fade as we reach the small hosteria of Lago Grey where we shall spend the night. From the shore in front of our windows the lake stretches north to the base of a glacier from which slabs of blue ice have calved and drifted down the lake towards us. Eroded by the wind and rain the lie beached on the banks of gravel, like abandoned carnival floats.

Few souls ventured far into the park at this time of year and we have the hosteria to ourselves. Sitting by the wood burning stove, playing dominoes and drinking seven year scotch with seven thousand year old glacier ice. Sometimes work is almost bearable. (Palin, 1997: 221)

With these words, Palin (1997) illustrates a core theme in Quan and Wang's model of the totality of experience; 'if the attractions that constitute the major motivation to travel are disappointing, then, even the high quality of other consumer services such as accommodation cannot fully compensate for this deficiency and regret'. Michael Palin, in a 2011 interview for the Telegraph newspaper in London, identifies his motivation to travel as being nothing more or less than a genuine curiosity about the world (Ross, 2012). This curiosity has led to a number of major travel journeys. As he describes in relation to his formative years as a student in Sheffield, locations such as Nottingham were not simply locations on a map to be travelled to, instead, the presence in Nottingham of Nottingham Castle laid a cultural/ historical allure in the mind of a young boy of the need to step outside one's comfort zone and explore (Ross, 2012).

Returning to the Appalachian case, there is similar evidence of an allure being marketed to visitors, which is intentionally juxtaposed against the everyday. One marketing advert that is particularly relevant for our discussion reads; 'Remember life before soccer schedules and video games? Get reacquainted with what really counts, in Wild and Wonderful West Virginia' (Fritsch & Johannsen, 2004: 89). The broader context of this television advertising campaign from 2002 portrays images of a family bicycling down a country road next to a creek (Fritsch & Johannsen, 2004). The act of bicycling is not in itself significant for the present discussion, except in the way that it portrays the family in question as predisposed to the merits of a nature based holiday for which national parks are well suited to provide. Of greater interest here is that way that an apparently benign activity of bicycling can be marketed through a process of extension and intensification as something that people who enjoy the outdoors can complete for personal fulfilment.

The country road that is referenced in the Appalachian marketing case represents only one of a number of transport routes that commonly exist within national parks. Some, like the Trans-Canada Highway near Banff, function primarily as locations for supporting consumer experiences. In such locales, tourists engage with a range of accommodation, retail and other tourism services as they move between urban environments such as Calgary, through various accommodation centres, and on to popular tourism localities such as Castle Mountain, Mount Temple and Spirit Island. In the course of navigating the highway, tourists are exposed to a range of experiences such as the opportunity to observe the flowing waters of the Bow River. Whilst forming part of what Leiper (1990b) described as the tourist transit region, and thus not within the scope of traditional tourist satisfaction studies, Neal and Gursoy (2008) have demonstrated that satisfaction with experience within the tourism transit region, in this case a transit route through a national park, will play a major role in determining a tourist's overall level of satisfaction with their total travel experience (see also Cutler et al., 2014).

A study by Kyle et al. (2003) identified a correlation between one's bond to the Appalachian Trail and the opportunities that the trail affords for pleasurable experiences and self-expression. Iconic walking trails are not alone in their ability to promote such personal connections for visitors. A recent National Geographic special edition entitled *The Greatest Parks of the World* painted a similarly positive impression of major access roads to Banff National Park:

> It's impossible not to hold your breath as you travel down Trans-Canada 1 into the soaring heart of Banff. Stretching some 300 miles into the Canadian Rockies, there is something magical about the dramatic sweep of mountain peaks shaped by glaciers and icefields, and the water tumbling down them to form swift running rivers and glacial lakes. Surrounded by such majesty, it isn't difficult to imagine the delight railway workers must have felt when they first stumbled upon a natural hot spring here in 1883, paving the way for the millions of visitors who have been dazzled by this park ever since. (Anon, 2014: 15)

Earlier in this chapter we referred to the work of the novelist and wilderness defender Edward Abbey, where he bemoaned the increasing reliance on automobile usage in national parks as a threat to their characterisation as sacred places. Herremans and Reid (2006: 164) go onto state that Edward Abbey felt that cars prevented visitors from really seeing anything intently; 'it is better to experience a small area of the park intensely than to see the entire park superficially'. The idea that national parks offer the opportunity for a profound experience of nature, and the potential for such experiences to be compromised through the inclusion of artificial stimuli into a natural setting is a common theme in much of the literature on ecotourism. The oft cited founder of the term ecotourism Ceballos-Lascurain termed this new form of tourism as that which 'involves travelling to relatively undisturbed or uncontaminated natural areas with the specific object of studying, admiring and enjoying the scenery and its wild plants and animals' (Lascurain,

1988: 13). The idea that tourism may contaminate the natural environment has spurned a seemingly never ending body of literature on tourism's impacts (Wearing & Neil, 2009). In a national park context, a number of scholars have charted the relationship between automobiles and park management (Herremans & Reid, 2006; Louter, 2009; White, 2006; Whittaker *et al.*, 2012).

For more than half a century, automobiles have served both as an enabler of tourist experiences with nature and one of the biggest challenges for land use managers looking to preserve the natural resource upon which parks derive most of their tourism value (Sheller, 2004). Any attempt to separate the competing forces of environment and society is complicated by Urry's (2000: 202) observation that nature is intrinsically connected with 'social practices and their characteristic modes of cultural representation'. To illustrate this point, McManus and Pritchard (2000) incorporated John Brack's iconic painting *The Car* into the monograph *Land of Discontent*, which traces development and forces of change in rural Australia. The painting had originally been created in 1955, and portrays a family driving through a rural setting with the occupants admiring the scenery while the father drives. Painted as it was in an age where car sales in Australia were on the increase following the Second World War, the configuration of the traveller's relationship to their physical environment in the painting is a reflection of a particular set of temporal, spatial and power based elements (see Jokinen & Veijola, 1997). While the idea of a self-drive holiday is becoming increasingly accepted as a transportation and marketing option for national park visitors and managers such as the NSW National Parks and Wildlife Service, the growth of this form of tourism has tremendous implications for the carrying capacity of protected areas, as is shown in this continuation of the earlier quote from Sax:

> ... Tourism in the parks today, by contrast, is often little more than an extension of the city and its lifestyle transposed onto a scenic background. At its extreme Yosemite Valley or at the South Rim of the Grand Canyon, for example, one finds all the artefacts of urban life; traffic jams, supermarkets, taverns, fashionable shops, prepared entertainments, and the unending drone of motors. The recreational vehicle user comes encased in a rolling version of his home, complete with television for amusement when the scenery ceases to engage him. (Sax, 1980: 11–12)

The implication of these ideas is that the development of modern mass tourism is promoting a national park experience where travel is simply an extension of the home with all its congestion related and other consequences (Fredman & Hörnsten, 2004; Hallo & Manning, 2009; McCool & Christensen, 1996). The International Union for the Conservation of Nature has identified that there are currently more than 7000 individual national parks throughout the world. Each park is characterised by the presence of walking and vehicular trails that are broadly reflective of the park's geographical reality. By way of example, the Mercantour National Park in France includes walks along cobble streets past medieval forts and villages including St Martin-Vesubie, as well as more remote, higher altitude and demanding treks including the five day Grande Randonnée. Different types of trails and their corresponding support infrastructure will appeal to different types of experience seekers. Csikszentmihalyi (1991) proposes that flow experiences are defined 'as involving a sense of control—or more precisely, as lacking the sense of worry about losing control that is typical in many situations of normal life'. When applied to the act of hiking, one of the most common trails based activities, in a national park setting, peak experiences for a solo hiker can be said to occur when the objective or perceived challenges of the hike are balanced with the skills of the hiker (Coble et al., 2003).

Since 2010, Australian based protected area agencies have developed and managed national park based trails according to the criteria laid down under the *Australian Walking Track Grading System*. This national initiative, which grades tracks on the basis of length, gradient, requisite level of experience required to complete etc. has been designed in part to provide a tourism product, which can be easily aligned to the interests and skill sets of park visitors (Department of Sustainability and the Environment, n.d.). The idea that there is a correlation between experience and access has been noted by the Professor Emeritus Dr John Marsh from Trent University as being important supply characteristics for the marketing of trail based tourism. Drawing on the notion of the '4As of tourism marketing, Marsh (2004) identifies the development of successful products as being predicated on the availability of information on tourist demand for trails and the provision of advertising, accommodation and attractions to support this demand.

Over the last twenty years, a range of studies have been undertaken to understand the determinants of positive trail based experiences (e.g. Beeton, 1999, 2006; Bradford & McIntyre, 2007; Cathores et al., 2001; Cessford, 2003; Dorwart et al., 2007; Hearne & Salinas, 2002; Lynn & Brown, 2003; McCool & Cole, 2000; McCool & Christensen, 1996). An important characteristic of these studies has been the management approaches that can be adopted to ensure the experiences of visitors are fulfilled in a manner that is reflective of park conservation agendas. Trail based natural and cultural features are not present simply to serve as the plaything of visitors. To see park management in such a light is to downplay the relational elements of the tourist space. Wearing et al. (2010) have written that 'tourism is first and foremost about a series of direct and mediated relationships with, and in, the context of space/place' (2010: 10). When such relationships are predicated solely on the needs of the tourist, we see the perpetuation of unequal power relations between visitor and host, as well as justification for traditional marketing agendas focused on disseminating on the perpetuation of an image which encapsulates an experience, which has value to the tourist (Marzano & Scott, 2005). Massey (2005) has argued that representations of space, of which tourism marketing is but one type, are limiting in the sense that they provide a closed view of the world. What is also needed is an appreciation of the relational elements of space (Massey, 2005). 'What is depicted or not depicted in destination image advertising, and on whose authority it is selected, involves a more complex question of what comprises the destination and who has the power to define its identity' (Fesenmaier & MacKay, 1996: 37).

Traditionally, groups such as the United States National Parks Service have defined marketing as 'the development of products/services which are consistent with client needs, pricing, promoting and distributing' (National Parks Service, 1984: 3 in Wearing & Neil, 2009: 174). The central premise of this book as outlined in Chapter 1 is the presence of a symbiotic relationship between the economic imperative of a sustainable park based tourism industry, and the maintenance of the sociocultural and environmental elements of a park's conservation agenda. In this chapter, we have sought to delve deeper into the processes of experience formation in national parks. Understanding such experiences is vital for the sustainable management of park resources in that, as Moscardo and Pearce (1986 in Tubb, 2003) note, visitors have to be motived and encouraged to engage in learning. It is not enough Tubb (2003) notes for park managers to simply have an ideological agenda and to demand that visitors adjust their behaviour to suit. After all, as Cheong and Miller (2000) have noted, tourists, as with locals and brokers, form a tripartite system of power agents in the management of tourism environments. In the next chapter, we will consider in greater detail this issue of stakeholder power. National park authorities, indigenous populations and other stakeholder groups are often tagged as custodians of some of the most significant natural resources on the planet. Where does this legitimacy come from? In the next chapter we will advance a notion that legitimacy in fact comes from culturally derived power, which itself is framed in relation to the contested and evolving discourse of 'place'.

Case Study 4: An ephemeral experience of John Muir

In this chapter, we have described tourist ephemeral experiences as those experiences that are truly transformational, built on personal interaction with nature. Just as ephemeral or vernal pools come and go with the elements, so too are ephemeral experiences short lived and transitory. The intense individuality of many of the themes discussed in this chapter means that we will end with a case study, not one which focuses on a particular park environment or tourism operation, but instead with a personal reflection/experience from the founder of the modern conservation movement, John Muir.

The work from which the following reflections are taken was first published in 1911. *My First Summer in the Sierra* recounted a year spent by Muir in the Californian Wilderness, in what would later be named the Yosemite Valley. The following excerpt is taken from the chapter 'The Yosemite':

July 20. —Fine calm morning; air tense and clear; not the slightest breeze astir; everything shining, the rocks with wet crystals, the plants with dew, each receiving its portion of irised dewdrops and sunshine like living creatures getting their breakfast, their dew manna coming down from the starry sky like swarms of smaller stars. How wondrous fine are the particles in showers of dew, thousands required for a single drop, growing in the dark as silently as the grass! What pains are taken to keep this wilderness in health, —showers of snow, showers of rain, showers of dew, floods of light, floods of invisible vapour, clouds, winds, all sorts of weather, interaction of plant on plant, animal on animal, etc., beyond thought! How fine Nature's methods! How deeply with beauty is beauty overlaid! the ground covered with crystals, the crystals with mosses and lichens and low-spreading grasses and flowers, these with larger plants leaf over leaf with ever-changing colour and form, the broad palms of the firs outspread over these, the azure dome over all like a bell-flower, and star above star.

Yonder stands the South Dome, its crown high above our camp, though its base is four thousand feet below us; a most noble rock, it seems full of thought, clothed with living light, no sense of dead stone about it, all spiritualized, neither heavy looking nor light, steadfast in serene strength like a god.

Our shepherd is a queer character and hard to place in this wilderness. His bed is a hollow made in red dry-rot punky dust beside a log which forms a portion of the south wall of the corral. Here he lies with his wonderful everlasting clothing on, wrapped in a red blanket, breathing not only the dust of the decayed wood but also that of the corral, as if determined to take ammoniacal snuff all night after chewing tobacco all day. Following the sheep he carries a heavy six-shooter swung from his belt on one side and his luncheon on the other. The ancient cloth in which the meat, fresh from the frying-pan, is tied serves as a filter through which the clear fat and gravy juices drip down on his right hip and leg in clustering stalactites. This oleaginous formation is soon broken up, however, and diffused and rubbed evenly into his scanty apparel, by sitting down, rolling over, crossing his legs while resting on logs, etc., making shirt and trousers water-tight and shiny. His trousers, in particular, have become so adhesive with the mixed fat and resin that pine needles, thin flakes and fibres of bark, hair, mica scales and minute grains of quartz, hornblende, etc., feathers, seed wings, moth and butterfly wings, legs and antenna of innumerable insects, or even whole insects such as the small beetles, moths and mosquitoes, with flower

(continued)

Case Study 4: An Ephemeral Experience of John Muir (*continued*)

petals, pollen dust and indeed bits of all plants, animals, and minerals of the region adhere to them and are safely imbedded, so that though far from being a naturalist he collects fragmentary specimens of everything and becomes richer than he knows. His specimens are kept passably fresh, too, by the purity of the air and the resiny bituminous beds into which they are pressed. Man is a microcosm, at least our shepherd is, or rather his trousers. These precious overalls are never taken off, and nobody knows how old they are, though one may guess by their thickness and concentric structure. Instead of wearing thin they wear thick, and in their stratification have no small geological significance.

Besides herding the sheep, Billy is the butcher, while I have agreed to wash the few iron and tin utensils and make the bread. Then, these small duties done, by the time the sun is fairly above the mountain-tops I am beyond the flock, free to rove and revel in the wilderness all the big immortal days.

Sketching on the North Dome. It commands views of nearly all the valley besides a few of the high mountains. I would fain draw everything in sight, —rock, tree, and leaf. But little can I do beyond mere outlines, —marks with meanings like words, readable only to myself, —yet I sharpen my pencils and work on as if others might possibly be benefited. Whether these picture sheets are to vanish like fallen leaves or go to friends like letters, matters not much; for little can they tell to those who have not themselves seen similar wildness, and like a language have learned it. No pain here, no dull empty hours, no fear of the past, no fear of the future. These blessed mountains are so compactly filled with God's beauty, no petty personal hope or experience has room to be. Drinking this champagne water is pure pleasure, so is breathing the living air, and every movement of limbs is pleasure, while the whole body seems to feel beauty when exposed to it as it feels the camp-fire or sunshine, entering not by the eyes alone, but equally through all one's flesh like radiant heat, making a passionate ecstatic pleasure glow not explainable. One's body then seems homogeneous throughout, sound as a crystal.

Perched like a fly on this Yosemite dome, I gaze and sketch and bask, oftentimes settling down into dumb admiration without definite hope of ever learning much, yet with the longing, unresting effort that lies at the door of hope, humbly prostrate before the vast display of God's power, and eager to offer self-denial and renunciation with eternal toil to learn any lesson in the divine manuscript.

Source: Muir (2007: 92).

Notes

(1) In Australia, botanic gardens represent a category of protected area under the Australian Constitution, along with other classifications including national parks and indigenous protected areas (Department of Foreign Afairs and Trade, 2012).
(2) A peak advocacy group for the tourism, transport and infrastructure sectors in Australia.
(3) We base our approach on what Rittel and Webber (1973) have suggested as 'wicked'; that is, problems that 'defy efforts to delineate their boundaries and to identify their causes, and thus expose their problematic nature' (p. 167).

5 The Multifaceted Rural, Power and the Marketing of Culture through Interpretation

Introduction

In the previous chapter, it was suggested that park managers need to actively engage with the diversity of the tourist experience if they are to develop effective park interpretation strategies. In the current chapter, we will take this discussion one step further and ask from where do national park managers derive the legitimacy to advance particular messages in their interpretation strategies. Interpretation, at its most basic level, involves an exchange of ideas between interpretation framers and recipients. Central to such exchange is the reconciliation of values as they are used to interpret the destination image. Writing in the *Dictionary of Human Geography*, Dubow (2009: 369) describes the theoretical notion of an 'image', which we would argue is a construct which is at the heart of all tourism marketing as both 'a medium through which the world is most persuasively relayed to our understanding ... [and] as a graphic language that invisibly encodes whole systems of value – a history, a geography, a morality – an epistemology'. The idea that one stakeholder would persuasively seek to impose their value positions on another draws parallels between the concept of marketing and the theoretical notion of power.

Power has been described by Hauggard and Clegg (2009) as a concept that is both elusive and ubiquitous to any understanding of society. Evolving essentially for as long as there has been consideration of the nature of society and social order, numerous scholars including Machiavelli, Dahl, Lukes, Foucault and Clegg have attempted to conceptualise the various systemic, coercive, manipulative and other related characteristics of the concept of power (see Clegg, 1989; Dahl, 1957; Foucault, 1977, 1982; Lukes, 1974; Machiavelli, 1998). At its core, tourism is a field that can be understood effectively through sociological discourses, such as power, on account of the ability of said discourses to shed light on debated and values driven concepts such as authenticity and the tourist gaze (Cohen & Cohen, 2012). In recent years, a number of works including *Tourism, Power and Space* (Church & Coles, 2006) have provided detailed analyses of the evolving interplay of concepts of power and tourism. While a full review of this history is beyond the scope of the present chapter, what is of interest here is the intersection of notions of culture and power. Specifically we will explore how the concept of the 'rural' lends certain stakeholders in the national park marketing arena culturally formed legitimacy to advance a particular framework for marketing a destination image to visitors through park based tourism interpretation mechanisms.

The material in this chapter will be drawn from a number of separate, but ultimately mutually reinforcing, research traditions. The first is theoretical commentary on the nature of power as a mechanism of cultural persuasion. On this we will follow the lead of Fredrick Engelstad who in the *SAGE Handbook of Power* defined power as a 'set of actions upon other actions' (Foucault, 1983: 220 in Engelstad, 2009: 211). Engelstad's reasoning in the selection of this definition was that it allows one's focus to not be on what power is, but rather to be on the pragmatic mechanisms whereby power is enacted in a situational context (2009). If we take the idea from Engelstad (2009) that power 'works on, in and through actor's beliefs about the worlds they imagine and in which they operate' (Hauggard & Clegg, 2009: 13); 'power as practice' if you will; this then leads us to the second body of scholarship, which focuses on the evolving culturally defined context of national parks.

Since the very earliest days of the national park movement, park environments have been just as much a cultural construct as a physical entity. Published histories of the national parks movement have placed considerable attention on the idea that parks reflect a particular form of cultural nationalism. While the circumstances in which discourses of power vary from park context to park context, a range of studies have been published that have considered power relations between native populations and early park visitors (Carruthers, 1995; Denzin, 2005; Meskell, 2005; Neumann, 1995). In Denzin's study 'Indians in the Park', he seeks to highlight the way in which a romanticised (Hollywoodised) perception of Native Americans allows them to simultaneously be seen as both 'within and outside white culture' (Denzin, 2005: 13) as it is perceived in Yellowstone National Park. The notion that certain parts of the Yellowstone space can be figuratively excised from a nation's cultural heritage brings us to the third body of scholarship; the contested and multifaceted rural.

The rural is a concept that is synonymous with the culture of many regions of the world. 'The American West' and the 'Australian Outback' for example, are important touchpads for understanding the evolving history of many peoples and regions. In addition to presenting a basis for contemporary tourism marketing, such terms encapsulate many ideals to which wider cultures seek to aspire. The problem is, however, that such rural landscapes are seldom value free. The have been and will continue to be contested on the basis of the way that individuals and communities perceive the importance of different variables of sustainability. McManus has thus defined regional sustainability in the following terms:

> The sustainable region should have a strong regional identity, which is always a process of 'becoming'. This regional identity should be based on the interrelationships between ecological/sociocultural and economic processes, and supported by institutional arrangements that at least do not counteract these relationships. (McManus, 2008: 1277)

The analysis of the various social, economic and ecological components of rural space requires the development of models for understanding the totality of rural space. With this in mind, the authors have chosen to base much of the discussion in this chapter around Halfacree's Three-Fold Model of rural place (Halfacree, 2006, 2007) and Frisvoll's (2012) subsequent conceptual extension, which extended Halfacree's original model to include three hubs of entangled stakeholder defined power relations. Frisvoll's extended Halfacreen model is a valuable extension to debates in the sense that it draws attention to the pluralistic nature of power in rural localities. As Frisvoll (2014) noted; 'power as entanglements asserts that the only way power is epistemologically discernible/available is through studying the social practices, as power is embedded within action'. What it does not show currently, we would argue, in sufficient detail is where individual stakeholders draw their legitimacy from to advance specific agendas in a national park marketing context. This chapter will argue that such legitimacy may come from the alignment of stakeholder agendas to culture and contested notions of rural place. Our particular focus is on the culturally defined legitimacy of park based interpretation.

Cultural Legitimacy of Interpretation in a Multifaceted Rural Setting

When Freeman Tilden (1977) first wrote his book *Interpreting Our Heritage*, six so called principles of interpretation were proposed:

(1) Any interpretation that does not somehow relate what is being displayed or being described to something within the personality or experience of the visitor will be sterile.

(2) Information, as such, is not interpretation. Interpretation is revelation based upon information but they are entirely different things. However, all interpretation includes information.
(3) Interpretation is an art which combines many arts whether the materials presented are scientific, historical or architectural. Any art is in some degree teachable.
(4) The chief aim of interpretation is not instruction, but provocation.
(5) Interpretation should aim to present a whole rather than a part and must address itself to the whole man rather than any phase.
(6) Interpretation addressed to children should not be a dilution of the presentation to adults, but should follow a fundamentally different approach. To be at its best it will require a separate programme.

In the previous chapter we focused on principle 1 as we discussed the tourist experience. We now turn our attention to items 3 and 4 of this list, which deal in various ways with the notion of culture as power. Culture has been defined broadly as those quintessential 'meanings, norms and aesthetic/ ritual practices' that define a society (Engelstad, 2009: 210). It is on the basis of cultural capital that Pierre Bourdieu (1984 in Rojek, 2005) notes that an individual is able to feel solidarity to the society in which they are situated. This is not to say, however, that culture is static and immune from challenge. Butler (2008) has defined performance arts as comparable with the quest for cultural critique and commentary in the social science. Tilden (1977) similarly draws a direct connection between artistic expressions, noting that art allows one to tell stories that are imbued with the personally framed cultural richness that are not to be found in a simple inventory of irrefutable scientifically defined facts.

Differing interpretations of culture and society are the source of wicked problems, which the authors considered in Chapter 3. While technically unsolvable, stakeholder debate on the correct way to tackle wicked problems is inevitable with different stakeholder groups seeking to steer debate in directions that support their own vested self-interest. Such provocations are an important component of interpretation as defined by Tilden. Whilst focused on the imparting of fact, interpretation also has a higher level objective; to 'stimulate the reader or hearer toward a desire to widen his [or her] horizon of interests and knowledge' (Tilden, 1977: 33). Tilden's explanation of the manner in which interpretation occurs is much idealised with frequent phrases reflecting notions of visitors as 'wonderfully well-mannered and pathetically eager for guidance toward the larger aspects of life' (Tilden, 1977: 36). While this may be a very characteristic way of describing many national park visitors, it is potentially diminishing the complex culture power issues that underpin such social exchanges. National park visitors are not always empty vessels into which park managers and others can pour the fruits of their enlightened perspectives on conservation.

Rather, tourists, as with communities, park managers and others are social beings in their own right; beings whose perceptions and expectations of their planned experiences will be governed by their own liquid (see Bauman, 2013) interpretations of a range of social, environmental and economic forces in rural areas.

To be sustainable, national park-based tourism and park managers must engage proactively with the unknown (white space) that is often characteristic of rural place. In 2013, *Organization Studies* published a special edition on white spaces of organisation; white spaces being those currently unknown aspects of an organisation's spatial reality (O'Doherty et al., 2013). The aim of this special edition was to promote discussion amongst organisational theorists of an emerging problematic in organisation theorising. For many years there has been a preoccupation with the idea that organisations are run on routines, assembling their identity through the skilful reproduction and translation of these routines (see Reed, 2006). Tourism is very much characteristic of such trends, characterised as it is by the development of highly industrialised systems in the period post World War II with a complex array of supply and demand forces. The development of industrialised tourism systems does not, however, make tourism immune from the social forces that characterise its operational environment. Organisations, Clegg and Hardy (2006: 428) note, can increasingly be seen as 'sites of situated social action more or less open to explicitly organised and formal disciplinary knowledge ... and also to conversational practices embedded in the broad social fabric'. For this reason, organisations, including tourism, must engage with the unknown of their rural environment. Engagement provides real opportunities for innovation and to capitalise on the opportunities provided by change and uncertainty in one's environment (Drucker, 2014; Maletz & Nohria, 2001).

Many of the world's iconic national parks including Tikal in Guatemala, Yosemite in the American High Sierra Mountains and Mercantour in the French Alps are located in rural areas. Characteristics of the rural setting have often become an important component of marketing initiatives for such parks. The Peak District National Park in the United Kingdom, by way of example, has made the undulating beauty of its moorland plateaus a feature of marketing strategies targeting mountain bike riders and walkers. In addition the opportunity afforded to visitors to Peak District to engage with living monuments to the region's early medieval history through visits to sites including Haddon Hall, and to experience what it was like to live as a mill worker in Victorian England, sites such as the Bakewell Old House Museum provides evidence that rural life was something beyond picturesque vistas. Drawing on earlier work by Morgan and Pritchard, we are suggesting that the image of a region is not objective or transparent but rather 'are produced within sites of struggle' (1998: 6). A historic site is a physical structure, nothing more nothing less. That is until one realises that it is a lived locality, one that generations of residents have in various ways laid claim to over the time (see Tuan, 1977).

If one accepts the lived nature of the rural, it becomes difficult to characterise rural areas as a homogenous 'other', which is defined solely by urban dwellers (including destination marketing organisations) on the basis of a voyeuristic fascination with the less powerful, much as 'visitors to a human zoo' (Jackson, 1989: 73 in Lawrence, 1997: 2). Writing in the SAGE *Handbook of Tourism Studies,* Bernard Lane (2009) noted that the concept of the 'rural' is one that defies such positivist and rational formulations. While politicians and the media often characterise rural areas simply as being something that is not urban, or as that indeterminate region outside of capital cities (McManus & Pritchard, 2000), the reality is often far more complex. While it is true that many rural areas in countries including Australia and the United States are characterised by growing instances of rural disadvantage (Alston, 2004; Gibson & Argent, 2008; Pritchard & McManus, 2000; Stockdale, 2006; Taylor & Martin, 2001), other studies have sought to identify the role that traditional agricultural sectors continue to play in the development of regions and communities (McManus *et al.*, 2012).

Within any rural area there is variation both within and across generations. From a temporal perspective, the forces that enact on the rural are always in a state of flux. Gregory *et al.* write of 'the revivification of [interest in the rural in Britain on account of] a series of political and cultural concerns: the threat to the countryside and wildlife posed by urbanisation, the transformation of agriculture and the aggressive rise of agribusiness, the rise of new modes of recreation ...' (Gregory *et al.*, 2009: 659). The notion of a linear development of rural areas from the broad agrarian economies that characterised many countries economic outlook in the 18th century, through to the industrial revolution with its various subsequent technological and productivity 'improvements', is a classic method for describing the history of many rural societies. All societies it has to be said narrate; whether it is narration of the course of the history of a war, an institution or community; narration provides a lens onto the meanings that a society attaches to a set of lived experiences. A simple Google Scholar search around the search strings 'rural' and 'narration' reveals a plethora of papers that in different ways have used narrative as a mechanism to give a voice to different groups in a rural population, and demonstrate stakeholder defined meaning (e.g. Dorfman *et al.*, 2004; Jessop & Penny, 1998; Vanderbeck & Dunkley, 2003).

Similarly, narratives have proven to be an important part of national park marketing and experience making since the earliest days of the park movement. In an 1871 edition of the Monthly Literary magazine *Scribners*, Langford talks eloquently of a desire to fulfil a long wished for indulgence to see the upper valley of the Yellowstone and to record the results of these journeys:

> The stories told by trappers and mountaineers of the natural phenomena of that region were so strange and marvellous that, as long ago as 1866

I first contemplated the possibility of organising an expedition for the express purpose of exploring it. (Langford, 1871)

Written very much as a sequential narrative of his journeys and inspired by the narratives of other earlier pioneers that had gone before him, the writings of early park visitors such as Langford conform to the cultural expectations of their readers. As Wyckoff and Dilsaver somewhat disparagingly note:

Imaging the West was the armchair avocation of millions of Americans in the late nineteenth and early twentieth centuries. Popular fiction, landscape paintings and sketches, traveller's accounts, newspaper articles, and promotional materials defined the regional character of the American West for an ever larger and always curious national population. (Wyckoff & Dilsaver, 1997: 1)

The image of the American West that was so attractive to affluent urban populations drew on an increasingly romanticised perception of nature. Romanticism carries with it a series of meanings related to the fictitious, extravagant and fabulous that have made it a driving force for the development of tourism as a literary and cultural movement (Robinson, 2002). To sell a place requires us to accept that meaning is developed through language (Lichrou et al., 2008). While this is not always in a written form (see Robinson, 2002; Tussyadiah & Fesenmaier, 2008) narratives are essential for the study of tourism marketing specifically because:

Marketing is better 'understood as dialectic between material practices and symbolic meanings, because marketing works by assigning the material attributes of space symbolic and aesthetic value and these representations of narratives of people and place assume an exchange value as the objects of consumption'. (Lichrou et al., 2008: 11)

Beeton (2004) refers to the important role that romantic rural images have played in the development of rural based tourism industries. Simultaneously, however, she notes that in Australia, for example, the reality of the rural often did not live up to such idealised constructs. In part this may be due to the effects of natural events like floods and droughts over the just more than 200 years of European settlement in Australia (see Connell & McManus, 2011). It may also, however, be connected to the evolving industrial base that characterises many rural regions. Throughout Australia and the United States large rural areas are being opened up to unconventional mining practices (shale gas, coal seam gas etc.). In recent years, the impacts of these operations have spurred an ever increasing level of academic scholarship into the social and environmental impacts on local populations (Brasier et al., 2011; Jacquet, 2009; Lacey & Lamont, 2014; Lloyd et al., 2013; Mercer et al.,

2014; Schafft et al., 2013; Walton et al., 2013; Wearing et al., 2014). In discussing the development of coal seam gas operations in the Gloucester Region of New South Wales (Australia), Sherval and Hardiman (2014: 185) go as far as to suggest that 'powerful and competing discourses over land use threaten not only the sustainability of the region but the integrity of its sense of place, centred on community, rurality, agricultural production and confrontation of risk from mining'.

The truth or not of Sherval and Hardiman's observations on the sustainability of coal seam gas are best left for another time. Suffice to say at this point, however, that the coal seam gas discussion draws home the idea that in seeking to determine the legitimacy or not of different rural land uses, such as tourism and national parks, one is forced to grapple with vastly different understandings of 'rurality' (see Bell, 2006; Fabes et al., 1983; Halfacree, 1996; Little & Austin, 1996; McLaughlin, 1986; McManus et al., 2011). Power relations are everywhere in such discussions. McManus (2008: 1279) has identified that the Hunter Valley, of which Gloucester is a part, is not so much a clearly delineated spatial locality, but more as a space 'that is constructed through discursive conflicts, boundary delineations, and material practices of transforming nature into economically viable products'. King and Woolmington (1960) have written of the importance of the Hunter River and its various tributaries to the development of early agricultural, timber and mining operations; the absence of clearly identifiable administrative or bioregional criteria for defining the Hunter has meant that each of the various industries that inhabit the region including mining (open cut and coal seam gas), thoroughbred breeding and tourism have sought to package the surrounding physical space in a manner that is reflective of their own ideal of how humankind's relationship with landscape should be managed (see a thoroughbred example in McManus et al., 2012).

Returning to tourism and national parks, the key issue to flow out of this discussion of land uses in the Australian Hunter Valley becomes; who defines the cultural legitimacy of different stakeholders in a multi-use rural environment? On one level this is a fairly easy question to answer for national parks as it was on the basis of the passing of the Wilderness Act by Congress in 1964 that the United States Park Service was invested with responsibility to manage the various wilderness areas to 'secure for the American people of present and future generations the benefits of an enduring resource of wilderness' (United States Department of Agriculture, n.d.). The meaning of this brief has evolved over time, as is shown in the following extended quote from Manning:

> Wilderness has played a leading role in American history from the very beginning of settlement. Burdened with the cultural baggage of their European heritage, the Pilgrims stepped from the Mayflower in 1620 on to the shores of 'a hideous and desolate wilderness.' These religious zealots and their direct descendants thought the wildness of nature threatened not

only their physical safety but also their spiritual well-being. In the conservative tradition of Judeo-Christian teachings, wilderness was viewed as the antithesis of the Garden of Eden and other heavenly graces. Cotton Mather, the fiery puritan preacher of colonial America, held forth to his congregation that the American wilderness harboured 'Dragons,' 'Droves of Devils,' and 'Fiery Flying Serpents.' It was the Christian duty of each member of the congregation to clear away the evil wilderness.

Soon after the fringes of wilderness were cleared for settlement, American interest in nature turned exploitative. Nature was seen as a resource of raw materials to enhance the physical standards of life and to enable the fledgling nation to compete economically on world markets. Virgin timber was cut, wildlife harvested, minerals mined, water harnessed, and the soil plowed and planted. All of these efforts were conducted on a massive scale and often in a wasteful manner for the material resources of nature were seen as "superabundant."

By the end of the nineteenth century the natural environment of the United States had been altered dramatically and civilisation had spread across the continent. The census of 1890 confirmed that there was no longer an American frontier; much of the wildness had been removed from the American wilderness. This led to a more appreciative view of nature based on a romantic nostalgia. Along with the growing affluence of American society came the leisure to appreciate nature . . . but nature was disappearing.

Nature was taking on another important scarcity value as well. The raw materials provided by wilderness had been the source of much of America's prosperity. But these resources were now seen as finite and in danger of being depleted. The conceptual foundation of the Conservation Movement of this period was to use these resources more thoughtfully and wisely so as to extend their availability indefinitely. As a consequence, millions of acres of public land, once slated for disposal into private hands, were retained in government ownership to foster a stewardship ethic.

More recently conservation has grown to include preservation. The environmental movement born in the 1960s has popularized the science of ecology and the interrelationships among living things. Man's very survival is seen as ultimately dependent on maintaining environmental quality. One of the most effective methods of protecting the environment is seen as preserving large areas of nature as wilderness. (Manning, 1989: 25)

On face value, a reading of the quote from Manning (1989) could lead one to assume that the power relationships between human beings and wilderness have historically been framed in terms of evolving discourses of 'power [of human beings] over' nature. This traditional, Marxist inspired view of power (see Onyx *et al.*, 2007) equates with the idea that power in a rural context is held by a small number of dominant groups and institutions. When applied to a tourism marketing context, Marzano and Scott (2009) found evidence of such elitist, authoritarian power in the marketing of the destination image of the Gold Coast (Australia). Drawing on semi structured interviews with a range of representatives of Gold Coast Tourism it was found that six stakeholder groups including Theme Parks and Five Star Hotels exercised a dominant impact on the framing of a marketing brand for the Gold Coast Region. Whilst the results of this study present a useful case study of the process of image formation in a highly urbanised sea side environment; right at the end of the paper the authors make an observation on a previous study by Ritchie (1999) concerning the marketing of national parks, which has implications for the present work.

Marzano and Scott (2009: 63) assert that 'whilst Ritchie (1999) emphasises only collaboration in the value driven process of visioning a national park, the individual interests in embedded in a destination brand encourage the exercise of power'. This we would argue is a fairly simplistic interpretation of the form and purpose of the process Ritchie was describing. The principal reason for this is that, as Ritchie (1999) notes, the Banff National Park visioning process has not removed the influence of powerful stakeholders to craft the precise development of different land uses into the future. At the conclusion of Ritchie's work, reference is made to ways in which the visioning process has allowed tourism, park management and broader government interests the opportunity to craft specific agendas for different parts of the park environment. What we would suggest is of interest for Ritchie (1999), and indeed to ourselves in this book, is not the power relations that manifest the ongoing management of the park, but rather the way that stakeholder collaboration invests different stakeholder groups with a culturally defined legitimacy to manage parks to achieve a particular set of sustainability agendas. Onyx *et al.* (2007) define the antithesis of 'power over', 'power to' as enabling. By recognising that power outcomes are negotiated, complex and diffuse it is argued that it becomes possible to explore how case specific bonds and bridges are built within communities in a way that enables collective agency within society (Onyx *et al.*, 2007). To understand how this process of collaboration may manifest itself we now turn to Halfacree's Three-Fold Model of rural place.

Halfacree's Three-Fold Model of Rural Place and Frisvoll's Power Extension

In the 1990s, Keith Halfacree wrote a paper for the journal *Antipode* in which he sought to consider the implications of the United Kingdom's

Criminal Justice and Public Orders Act 1994 on gypsies. His particular area of concern was with the proposed changes that had been proposed to laws surrounding the criminalisation of trespass and the repeal of the gypsy site provision measures from the Caravan Sites Act 1968 (Halfacree, 1996). Over the years, much has been written of gypsies as a nomadic peoples and their historical and contemporary marginalisation from society (e.g. Clark & Cemlyn, 2005; Helleiner, 1995; Lloyd & Norris, 1998; Niner, 2004). The gypsy experience is of relevance for the present discussion on account of the fact that just as with the experience of gypsies in the United Kingdom in the 1990s, the position of nature tourism industries in protected areas is bound up in a conflict between what Halfacree (1996) describes as capitalist space versus absolute space. Capitalist space, Halfacree notes, is abstract. Abstract space is characterised by a focus on notions of production and the fragmentation of absolute space according to principles of 'crude economic reductionism' (Halfacree, 1996: 48).

While rural industries, such as tourism, necessarily involve some degree of commodification of rural landscapes, experiences and cultures (see Woods, 2010: Chapter 4), capitalist driven abstract space, Halfacree (1996) notes, is intrinsically bound up with the notion of exchange and thus cannot be divorced from the wider absolute space that surrounds it. Torelli and Shavitt (2010) define power as a basic force in all social relationships, and it is for this reason that later in this chapter we will consider ways in which culturally defined notions of place may serve to underpin power relations in tourism marketing. In a paper discussing the role of National Park Authorities (NPA) in the marketing and sustainable development of English National Parks, Sharpley and Pearce (2007: 570) made two observations regarding the development of cooperative approaches between park agencies and tourism interests:

(1) Generally, a holistic approach to managing national parks should be adopted. The current piecemeal approach to developing sustainable tourism and the lack of integration and varying influence of NPAs within partnerships revealed by the research is undoubtedly reducing the ability of the parks to meet their statutory purposes with a sustainable framework.
(2) Whilst seeking to maintain and build partnerships, NPAs should exploit the opportunity to communicate appropriate sustainable tourism messages. The challenges of maintaining effective collaboration or partnerships are well known, but efforts should be made to optimise the benefits of working in partnership with other stakeholders. There may be a need for appropriate training and advice to be provided to both NPA representatives and other partnership members.

On the first of these points, Sharpley and Pearce (2007) observed a very fragmented approach to the sustainable management of many parks, both within and external to park management organisations. National Parks include a wide variety of natural, cultural and other amenities that are essential to their marketability (see Eagles & McCool, 2002). For marketing to serve a broader sustainable development outcome and not to simply serve as a mechanism for advancing the interests of market segments with varying degrees of environment consciousness, the environment in which it is situated must be seen in its totality. Often cited as the original proponents of the term 'sustainable marketing', Sheth and Parvatiyar (1995a) define the purpose of sustainable marketing as being the reconciliation of ecological and economic factors through reinvented products and product systems. These often disparate voices form important components of Halfacree's Three-Fold Model of Tourism Space, which is the subject of the rest of this section. The model is reproduced in Figure 5.1 below.

In the course of developing a model to represent the totality of rural space, Halfacree drew heavily on earlier scholarship from the French philosopher Henri Lefebvre (see Halfacree, 2006, 2007; Woods, 2010), which has over the last few years been applied by authors in a range of studies into the framing of rural space and related management issues (e.g. Boyle et al., 2014; Heley & Jones, 2012; Jansson, 2010; Yarwood, 2012). Halfacree's expressed aim in the development of the model was to reconnect rural capitalist endeavours with the totality of space in which they are situated, a space which he suggests 'appears increasingly fragmented and partially and poorly known' (Halfacree, 2007: 127). This white space must, we would suggest, be understood by capitalist interests, if they are to develop sustainably with respect to their local context. As Lefebvre has previously suggested, space can no longer be seen as separate from society's modes of production (Heley & Jones, 2012). Instead there is a necessity to see space as a social product, one in which the 'abstract spaces of capitalism [must be examined critically in relation to the] sacred spaces of the religious societies that preceded it and the contradictory and differential spaces yet to come' (Hubbarb, 2009: 698). This form of contextual understanding is an important pre-requisite for establishing the legitimacy of public sector agencies (as well as we would suggest rural industries) to act in the public interest in rural environments.

Legitimacy has been defined as a generalised perception or assumption that the actions of an entity are desirable, proper, or appropriate within some socially constructed system of norms, values, beliefs and definitions (Suchman, 1995: 574). To achieve legitimacy, Suchman (1995) notes, requires that an organisation either conform to pre-existing societal expectations, manipulate those expectations or selectively match their own objectives with societal views by shifting to a new location of operation (Suchman, 1995). Such ends can only be met by considering an organisation's position in relation to an environment as a whole. As Gordon et al. (2009: 18) proposed in the context of a study of the NSW Police Force in Australia; 'when structures of dominancy and a mobilisation of bias exist simultaneously, then problematic structures of legitimacy are formed. They are problematic because such structures of legitimacy privilege the practices and perspectives of a select few in positions of dominance'. Such institutional forces are a central component of Halfacree's model (see Figure 5.1). Seeking, according to Halfacree (2006), to dominate the other two components of the model (physical space and rural people) under a regime of abstract space, the relative power of formal institutions is one of the key determinants of the manner in which agencies such as National Parks Authorities will seek to form partnerships with other stakeholders whilst simultaneously exploiting the opportunity to communicate messages one personally deems to be important (see Sharpley & Pearce, 2007).

When Halfacree's model is considered in the context of power, Frisvoll (2012) notes that two concepts stand out; 'trial by space' and 'structural

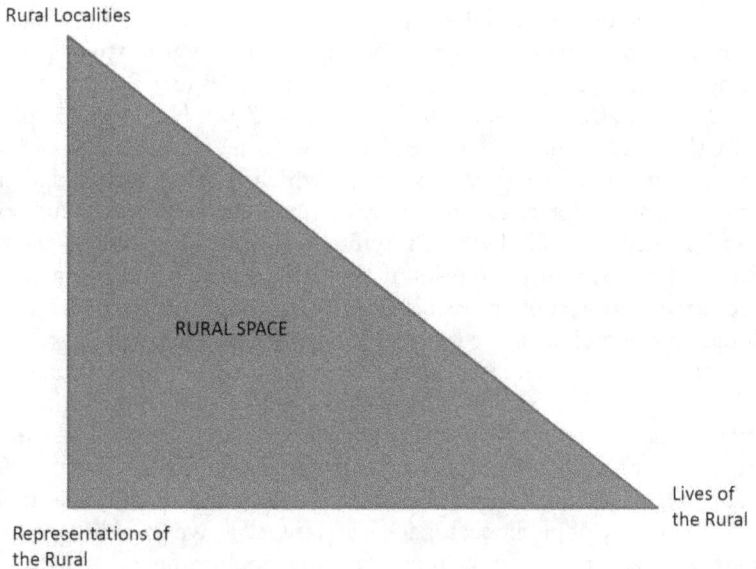

Figure 5.1 The three-fold model of rural space (after Halfacree, 2007)

1. **Rural localities** inscribed through relatively distinctive spatial practices, linked to production and/or consumption activities;
2. **Formal representations of the rural** such as those expressed by capitalist interests, cultural arbiters, planners or politicians;
3. **Everyday lives of the rural**, which are inevitably subjective and diverse, and with varying levels of coherence/fracture. They both take in and, to a greater or lesser extent, subvert the other categories.

(Halfacree, 2007: 127).

coherence'. Lefebvre (1991[1947]) introduced the concept of 'trial by space' in the context of the afore mentioned discussion of the distinction between abstract versus absolute space with the aim of arguing that no interpretation of what constitutes capitalist driven abstract space is ever absolute. Any form of production must constantly be re-assessed and evaluated on the basis of its social relations. The implications of such a notion to the interplay of tourism marketing and national park based interpretation are considerable. Tubb (2003: 476) has asserted that interpretation 'is capable of contributing to the goals of sustainable tourism development by achieving knowledge restructuring and resulting behavioural intentions from visitors'. If this is true, the obvious question that must be asked is why should such change be necessary? Why can't the interests of a capitalist driven market based system be in sync with the concerns of wider socio-cultural and environmental forces in the host region? In the next section, we will suggest that the answer to this question lies with a culturally defined interpretation of power, which itself is grounded in the notion of place.

Halfacree (2007) termed the level of agreement between different conceptualisations of the rural as 'structural coherence'. He noted that levels of coherence could be variously described as: congruent and unified, contradictory and disjointed or chaotic and incoherent. The heterogeneous nature of rural regions throughout the world with their characteristic interplay of conservation forces, primary industries and service industries lend themselves to a situation where one would assume that there would be incoherent rural spaces (Woods *et al.*, 2014). The fact, therefore, that an incoherent and diverse rural space can continue to have coherence in the minds of a population is said to point to the way in which over time different views have become prevailing, or to the way in which power is enacted. This brings us to Frisvoll's conceptual extension to Halfacree's model.

Frisvoll (2012) composed his conceptual extension (see Figure 5.2) of Halfacree's model out of concern for the fact that, in his view, the actions of stakeholders and their power relations were left largely invisible in the original Three-Fold Model of Rural Space. Drawing on the work of power theorists including Foucault and Sharp (2000), Frisvoll proposes a conceptualisation of power not based on 'blocks of institutional structures, with pre-established, fixed tasks (to dominate, to manipulate)' but rather as a social relation. Reminiscent of arguments put forward by Cheong and Miller (2000) in their oft cited work *Power and Tourism: A Foucaldian Observation*, power is seen by Frisvoll as omnipresent and represented in a tripartite system. Cheong and Miller (2000) articulated the components of this system as being tourists, brokers and locals, arguing for greater attention to be afforded to the role of brokers and locals as Foucaldian agents. Frisvoll (2012) takes a somewhat different approach arguing for the presence of three hubs of entangled power; a material hub, an immaterial hub and a personal hub.

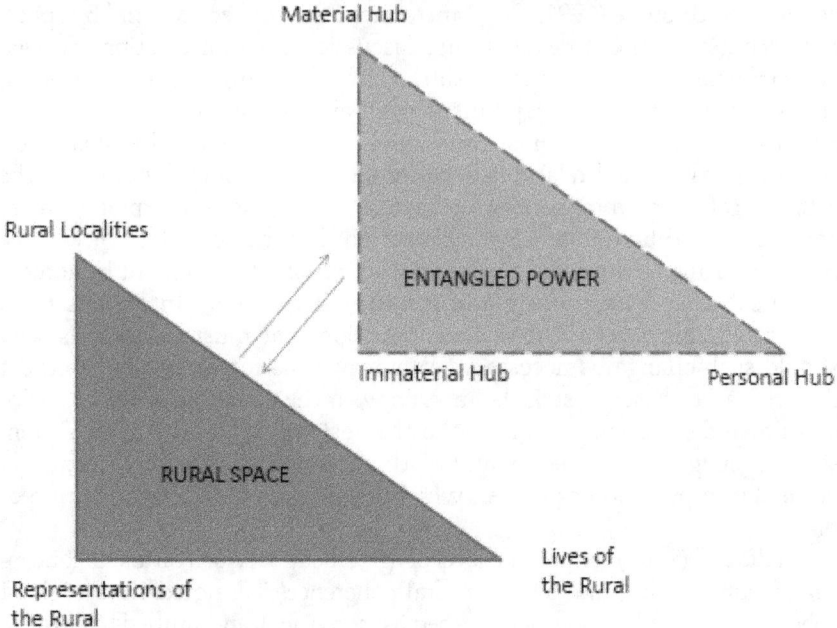

Figure 5.2 Untangling power in the rural place (after Frisvoll, 2012)

The material hub encompasses material elements of industry including 'property, its location, usufruct, money and means of violence' (Frisvoll, 2012: 449). While Hogenauer (2001) notes that as a public place, parks should be accessible to all; the reality is that parks are mixed use environments that are managed for a range of different stakeholder groups (International Union for Conservation of Nature, 2014). Park managers will seek to maximise experience using a range of infrastructure forms, including viewing platforms, trails etc. As Carter (2006) notes such experiences do not, in themselves, represent the totality of experiences available at a destination. They do, however, represent a clear identity statement from managers as to the types of visitor they wish to market to, along with a statement of who they believe should be excluded. The effect of such management decisions is the potential for conflict with stakeholders who may believe they have been marginalised from decision making processes. Where this occurs, responses have ranged from silent protests, petitioning of elected officials and at the extreme outright physical violence directed at trail users (see Hall, 2014: 142–151).

In Clegg's *Frameworks of Power,* episodic power represents the occasional exercising of power over other stakeholders (Clegg, 1989). The notion that this overt form of power will encourage resistance (see Davenport & Leitch, 2005) brings us to the second of Frisvoll's hubs of entangled power;

the personal hub. The personal hub in Frisvoll's (2012: 450) model refers to 'the personal side of actor's dealings in a rurality's trial by space. Examples could be actors' careers and/or career plans and family, as well as their follow through of implemented strategies (threats, violence), fondness of fighting and/ or perceptions of threat and gender. Other examples would be their attempts to secure perceived bases of existence and their desired way of life'. The theming of experiences represents an important component of strategic tourism marketing. In Chapter 4 we discussed the notion of authenticity from the tourist's perspective. By creating experiences that are meaningful to tourists, marketers can create an increased level of place attachment, which theoretically can also promote greater destination loyalty (Tsiotsou & Goldsmith, 2012). Simultaneously the linking of experience to a community's history and culture may lead to a strengthening of a community's sense of identity.

In a discussion of power discourses in participatory rural planning, Johansen and Chandler (2015) note that different rural contexts will be susceptible in different ways to different mechanisms of power. If one examines the history of parks in the United States, the initial joint management of the resource by the Departments of War, Agriculture and the Interior led Horace Albright (2nd director of the National Parks Service) to comment that 'national parks were anybody's business and therefore nobody's business' (Shea, 2015). Confusion over management had led to the proliferation of poaching, cattle grazing and the like in the early years of the park movement. The effect of 'state power' to control such actions has been defined by Jessop (2009: 376-377) as dependant on the structural relations between the state and its contextualising political system, on the strategic ties among politicians and state officials and other political forces, and finally on the complex web of structural interdependencies and strategic networks that link the state system to its broader social environment. All of these forces were in evidence in the processes whereby, through the work of pioneers including Stephen Mather, the publicist Robert Sterling Yard and others, the National Parks Service was established in 1916. Albright had noted that public support was necessary to have legislation passed to establish a parks agency and for that reason the role of Sterling was crucial in developing marketing strategies to increase visitation. At the time Tranel and Hall (2003) note there was wide spread public support, not only for the maintenance of the grand parks including Yosemite in the West of the country, but also for further expansion of the parks throughout the United States. The high level of community support created a fertile ground for iconic marketing strategies including the See America First campaign. However, unintendedly at the time the focus on linking visitor rates to the success of the park movement spurned the growth of the dual park mandate debates and many of the conservation – industry conflicts we have explored in this book.

The third power hub in Frisvoll's (2012) is the immaterial hub. This hub is identified as including in a western context 'the judicial side (laws, bylaws and regulations) of actor's social relations, as well as actor's network relations and normative convictions' (i.e. the informal guidelines incorporated into a community's socio-historical fabric) (Frisvoll, 2012: 449). Knight (2014) uses the term legal pluralism to describe the intersection of state defined law and non-state norms articulated on the basis of societal expectations. It is important, he notes, to see the dual effect of these two forces as non-state norms provide many of the opportunities for resistance against institutionalised forms of power. All national parks are subject to an array of regulatory controls brought down by their various management bodies. These formal regulations include but are not limited to: zoning plans, sustainability guidelines, camping permits, fossicking permits, fishing licences etc. Tourism marketing is heavily influenced by such forms of power on account of their ability to control the level of contact that tourists may desire to have with various natural and social features of a park. At the same time, as power exercised through formal regulation is important; so too is the power exercised by local people. Cheong and Miller (2000) define local people as one of a suite of agents of power that have the ability to influence the experiences and activities of tourists in a Foucauldian conceptualisation of power. Resident values are often steeped in a need to simultaneously preserve the culture and heritage of the park setting whilst also preserving their community feel and also maintaining a 'proper' relationship with the economic imperative of business development (Eyre & Jamal, 2006).

Cultural Legitimacy of the Interpretive Message – Challenges for Park Managers

Frisvoll (2012) developed his conceptual extension of Halfacree's Three-Fold Model of rural space with the specific aim of giving greater focus to the fault lines by which certain rural actors may exercise agency over others. By defining power in terms of entanglements, Frisvoll (2012) was able to successfully give attention to the unsettled nature of the relations between different stakeholders. In the previous section we have endeavoured to briefly illustrate, in line with the approach employed by Frisvoll (2012), some of the different immaterial, personal and material forms of power as practice that exist in national parks. It is through the reconciliation of these various forms of stakeholder enacted power that a rural area's trial by space will be resolved and a certain level of structural coherence will or won't be determined (Frisvoll, 2012). What is less clear from Frisvoll's (2012) model is the role of the line of effect from Halfacree's production of rural space triad to Frisvoll's entangled power triad (highlighted in Figure 5.3). How do the formal representations of rural space and rurality in Halfacree triad lend legitimacy to any particular stakeholder's beliefs and subsequently actions?

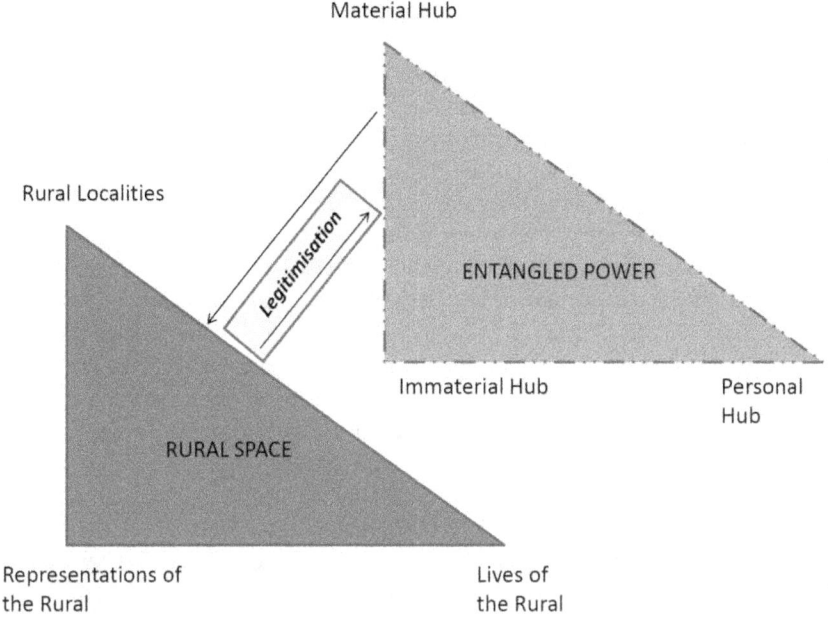

Figure 5.3 Rural place legitimisation and a three-fold architecture of entangled rural power

Why should it be necessary to consider the issue of stakeholder legitimacy as it relates to the management of rural park environments? Why can we not simply define parks as places where a set of social relations based around environmental, tourism and other stakeholder interests will strive to accomplish their goals independent of the influences of their neighbours? Such questions have important implications for the study of tourism marketing in the sense that there is a commonly recognised symbiotic relationship between tourism demand and supply forces. Ryan (2002) notes that continuous tourist demand for a place changes the nature of that place over time. As the initial demand is met local stakeholders must then constantly seek to re-asses their ability to supply resources to meet future demand. Depending on the availability of resources stakeholders can then choose to achieve a sustainability outcome by encouraging or discouraging market demand using a variety of mainstream or alternative marketing approaches (see Chapter 2). The ability of such sustainable outcomes to be realised depends in part on the level of social responsibility exhibited by different stakeholders in the park space. Being a socially responsible actor in a national park environment requires a combination of concerns including: ethical awareness where a set of moral obligations are recognised as legitimate; a focus on long-term mindsets rather than short-term advantage; a desire to achieve mutual benefits with others; and a belief that the autonomy of one's own firm and the autonomy of other stakeholders needs to be maintained (Spratlen, 1973 in Ryan, 2002).

When notions of societal responsibility are extended to power, Ryan (2002) equates notions of 'power over' with a level of 'responsibility for'. This idea of prescribed responsibility is important for the present discussion in the sense that, as Göhler (2009: 31) notes; 'power is not only the realisation of options to act; it is [the presence of] these options [to begin with]'. National park managers and tourism interests have a range of legal and or societal responsibilities prescribed to them. The 1916 *Organic Act* outlined the following corporate agenda for the fledging National Parks Service:

> to conserve the scenery and the natural and historic objects and the wild life therein and to provide for the enjoyment of the same in such manner and by such means as will leave them unimpaired for the enjoyment of future generations. (National Parks Service, n.d.-a)

In Chapter 1, the authors described the United States National Parks service and other protected area managers in terms of a noble lineage that can be traced back to the early environmental pioneers including John Muir and Gifford Pinchot. While we do not in any way retract from this view, it is appropriate to acknowledge tension in the perception held of such agencies by other stakeholders in the rural parks space (see Bennett & Dearden, 2014; Vodouhê et al., 2010; Walpole & Goodwin, 2001). The effects of this tension are neatly summed up in the title of the Sixth Biennial Scientific Conference on the Greater Yellowstone Ecosystem where it was asked; Yellowstone Lake: Hotbed of Chaos or Reservoir of Resilience? In the forward to the conference proceedings John Varley, Director of the Yellowstone Centre for Resources, makes the following observations on the relationship between the science of park management and wider community views:

> Since the establishment of Yellowstone National Park, its riches have largely been protected through the efforts of generation after generation of park managers and friends. The park's status as a World Heritage Site and a Biosphere Reserve affirm its international recognition as a unique place worthy of preservation. Its relatively unimpaired condition as a naturally functioning ecosystem makes it an ideal place to do research, even while its important standing in the world makes it a place charged with political and emotional controversy.

> Many of us see good science as the best antidote to controversy, as so, the purpose of the greater Yellowstone conference series, instituted in 1991, is to encourage the awareness and application of wide-ranging, high-calibre scientific work on the region's natural and cultural resources. There continues to be so much interest in Yellowstone science and issues

that a biennial series, with the active involvement of professional societies and other institutions, provides a perfect forum for the hundreds of researchers doing work here. (Anderson & Harmon, 2002)

For park managers to be successful in their aim to encourage greater faith in the appropriateness of managing parks according to scientific principles, they must, from a power perspective, encourage the subordinate to accept the primacy of the dominant (Ap, 1992). This is a challenging proposition when one considers the broad set of perspectives, each with its own internal logic that are held by different stakeholders in the marketing system. Not being mindful of these various perspectives can lead to the 'picking and choosing of taboos, sanctions, and other supposedly ecologically useful behaviours without meeting a complex culture in its own terms' (Hay-Edie, 2003: 91, 92).

We would suggest that, if planned carefully, interpretation has the ability to thread this balancing act of meeting environmental and human usage park values simultaneously (see also Vaske et al., 2000). In order to build a level of trust (one of the key constructs of relationship marketing, which was discussed in Chapter 2) in the eyes of conservation and tourism interests, it is vital that the framers of interpretive messages appreciate that whilst national parks are for many defined as service scapes; service scapes are themselves defined on the basis of a range of social rules, conventions and personal meanings (Arnould et al., 1998). Engelstad (2009) noted the importance of direct communication to the impartation of cultural meaning. While such communication may include normative commitments, there are also appeals that go to the heart of the recipient's self-esteem, identity and sense of belonging (Engelstad, 2009). For appeals to be successful the holder of power must understand the nature of their audience.

Backhaus (2003: 154) describes tourists as 'semioticians looking for relevant signs in their destinations'. Selby et al. (2008) talk of the textual model, developed initially by linguistic pioneers such as de Saussure as a mechanism whereby signs are employed to express meaning. Signs, they note, involve both the mechanism conveying the message and the message that it signifies (Selby et al., 2008). If we take it that 'tourists are, in effect, amateur semioticians, seeking out landscapes' (Selby et al., 2008: 186) it becomes paramount to understand not only the constituent components of the tourist gaze (see Chapter 4), but also the interpretive mechanisms available to managers to meld tourist motivations with broader conservation agendas.

John Muir has stated that 'in every walk with nature one receives more than he seeks' (Lekies & Whitworth, 2011: 249). In order for parks agencies to continue to achieve this vision of value adding to the wilderness, one must engage with the whole narrative of the wilderness excursion (Arnould & Price, 1993). In the context of river trips Arnould and Price (1993) note the challenges for visitors in perceiving the true nature of the wilderness experience prior to their trip. Similarly they identify the ways in which outfitters and other members of the commercial side of tourism industry are often indifferent of the gaps between a client's assumptions and realities, often seeing a tourist's journey on the basis of a narrowly defined process of service provision. Feelings of peak ecstasy resulting from one's engagement with wilderness may develop on the basis of triggers that change a visitor in ways they never considered possible.

Drawing on the existential psychology writings of Heidegger et al. (2006), these authors note the importance of park managers seeing the world through the eyes of the tourist. Tourists, they note, will see the world as a complex series of relationships. While human beings are an empty space waiting to be filled, one must be careful not to mediate between the tourist and the world (Reisinger & Steiner, 2006). Instead there is a need to systematically plan to enrich visitor experiences at different levels of engagement. In the 2010 *Banff National Park Management Plan,* there is the idea of five types of engagement for visitor experiences, which include virtual experiences, drive through awareness, view form the edge, a step into the wild and Rocky Mountains Wilderness Adventure (Parks Canada, 2010). Each of the mentioned visitor segments holds opportunities both for financial reward and conservation awareness for managers and over recent years a number of agencies have pursued innovative interpretive approaches to tap into these visitor preferences. In the United States, the development of the Nature Valley Trail View has provided trail users, as well as the broader public the opportunity to experience a street view perspective of the Grand Canyon, Great Smoky Mountains, Sequoia and Yellowstone National Parks. The technology is modelled off Google Street view and the online interface for visitors provides not only visual access to hundreds of kilometres of national park trails, which serves as a form of pre visit marketing/communication but also provides up to date information on Nature Valley conservation works (see http://www.naturevalleytrailview.com). In Australia, Parks Victoria have taken the notion of visitor interaction one step further, employing Public Participation Global Information System technology in the management of the Greater Alpine Region. Brown and Weber (2011) describe the benefits of the technology, where visitors log their experiences, perceptions, environmental impacts and facility needs on an online portal. Brown and Weber (2011, NP) note that such strategies democratise the national park management process and 'help build and sustain trust in a park agency's planning processes and decisions'.

The United States National Park Service defined interpretation as the process of helping each park visitor find an opportunity to personally connect with a place (National Parks Service, 2012a). Over the last 50 or 60 years, the degree to which interpretation has received pride of place in protected area management agendas has tended to ebb and flow. From the golden age of the 1950s and 1960s, when the Parks Service in the United States pursued a rapid expansion of visitors centres and other interpretive mechanisms, through the subsequent budget cuts of the 1970s and periods of growing suspicion as to the alleged hijacking of traditional interpretive principles by entertainment based agendas. park managers have recently called for a return to the central principles of interpretation. Included within these principles are: the need for stakeholder involvement in interpretive planning; due consideration of the ways in which decisions on the content interpretation should be based on visitor expectations and other social trends, and the ways that the success or not of an interpretation strategy should be seen in the context of the communication of a park's story including 'the meanings, and the values associated with the resource themselves, and achieving the balance between resource protection and visitor use and enjoyment' (National Parks Service, 2000). The constructs inherent in relationship marketing such as communication, trust and cooperation need to be managed so this collaboration between the park managers and the stakeholders can be achieved.

Recent scholarship has demonstrated that this quest for trust and legitimacy is still a work in progress. In a study of the effectiveness of interpretation in Dartmoor National Park in the United Kingdom, Tubb (2003) observed a decline in visitor confidence in the ability of the local national park authority to protect the environment between a pre and post visit sample. While Tubb (2003) equates this with the poor placement of information on the authority in the interpretive venues; such a result is of concern in that National Park Authorities are increasingly taking on a role of a local sustainability champion (Sharpley & Pearce, 2007). Park authorities have the potential to galvanise a range of market and non-market forces to promote a holistic perception of the park place. When this is the case we can avoid a situation where the rural environment becomes a white space or 'a foreign land' (Perec, 1997: 168 [1974]) for tourism marketers. Success will, however, be dependent on the legitimacy of park managers in the eyes of neoliberal market and non-market stakeholder interests.

Case Study 5: North Yorkshire National Park – Mine or Moors?

The North Yorkshire National Park is a national park located on the English coast not far from the townships of Middlesbrough and Scarborough. Encompassing one of the largest areas of heather moorland in the United Kingdom, the park today covers an area of some 1436 square kilometres. The park is administered by the North York Moors National Park Authority under the provisions of the *National Parks and Access to Countryside Act* of 1949. The wide range of unique natural attractions in the area (Merlin falcons, rivers, forests etc.) and cultural relics dating back to the Iron Age has led to more than 3.7

(continued)

Case Study 5: North Yorkshire National Park – Mine or Moors? (*continued*)

million people visiting the region annually (North Yorkshire Dales National Park Authority, 2015). North Yorkshire National Park is characteristic of many of the debates over rural contestation that has been discussed in this chapter. Mordue (1999) has for instance written extensively on the issue of conflicting rural identities and the clash of traditional conceptualisations of quiet moorland communities with virtual identities characterised by the fictitious town of Aidensfield in the television series *Heartbeat* (see also Beeton, 2008; Busby & Klug, 2001; Mordue, 2001, 2009)

At the time of writing, the North Yorkshire National Park Authority has just given approval by a majority vote to a proposal from Sirius Minerals to build what has been described as the world's largest potash mine underneath the national park. The development, which is being seen as the largest United Kingdom based national park based infrastructure project since the opening of the Trawsfynydd nuclear power station development in Snowdonia National Park in 1968 (see Cherry, 1985; Curry, 1992; Spooner & Site, 2000; Woollam, 2004), has led to significant stakeholder contestation and a trial by space in the local area. Different aspects of Halfacree's conceptualisation of rural space are in evidence including: varying formal representations of the rural (mine operators, the West and North Yorkshire Chamber of Commerce, the Campaign to Protect Rural England and the National Trust). Outside of formal representations of the rural, the everyday lives of rural residents is also in evidence. Eighty-eight percent of the park's inhabitants and 99% of the communities in the villages of Redcar and Cleveland are said to be in favour of the mine development (Lean, 2015). Community members who stand to benefit economically from the development include the more than 300 farmers and other landowners who have signed royalty agreements with the mining company (Anon, 2015).

With respect to the legitimization of the North Yorkshire National Park Authority, the decision to grant approval to the mine on 1 July 2015 was significant. While it is not in dispute that the park authority was the final arbiter in the development process, a fascinating quote was provided by a member of the planning committee who noted that:

> We have the opportunity to provide a secure economic future for many people in this area and beyond and to attract investment we have so desperately needed for so long. (Bawden, 2015)

The primacy that the park authority seems to have afforded to economic imperatives stands in sharp contrast to many of the aims and objectives of park authorities that have been noted in the present book. The group Campaign for National Parks have labelled the 1 July decision 'a critical test of the protection provided to National Parks under national planning policy' (Jamasmie, 2015).

6 Tragedy of the Commons or Solution for the Commons

Textbooks on tourism marketing usually set out to canvas the basic processes of marketing delivery in service based economies. They discuss concepts including: the marketing mix; applications of marketing principles in the transport, accommodation and other sectors of the tourism system; the manner whereby the principal tools of marketing promotion such as brochures are employed across distribution channels to facilitate access; strategies for marketing campaigns etc. While undoubtedly useful concepts for practitioners to consider, they do not grapple with the fundamental dualism present in the sustainable management of national parks for both conservation and tourism uses. In the present book, we have aimed to deviate from this established approach by instead asking two simple and related questions; why is it that tourism marketing is seen by many solely as the quintessential exhibit of a neoliberalist based industry standing in direct opposition to environmental preservation? And, why can't tourism marketing instead be a tool that can be employed by national park managers to advance their dominant environmental preservation agenda, whilst also recognising the needs of their diverse customers and stakeholders?

Lafferty and Hovden (2003: 1) have written that one of the 'defining features of sustainable development [and we would argue sustainable marketing] is the emphasis on the integration of environmental objectives into non-environmental policy sectors'. Since the late 1890s, when John Muir first guided President Theodore Roosevelt, along with members of the California State Legislature through the Yosemite Valley to gain support for the establishment of Yosemite National Park from a range of competing interests including hunters and the Southern Pacific and the Yosemite Valley Railroad Company (Jones, 1963–1964), tourism interests have formed an important component in the development of a natural resource based capitalist system that would ultimately come for many to be their defining image of the western wilderness. In the United States alone, the national parks system currently 'supports $13.3 billion of local private sector economic activity and 267,000 local jobs' (Hardner & M'Kenney, 2006: 5).

The ability to sustain economic growth of this kind stems from the provision and maintenance of a comprehensive set of attraction attributes including: 'spectacular scenery, readily visible big game, wondrous geothermal features, nearly unsurpassed outdoor recreation opportunities and unique history' (Glick & Whelan, 1991: 59). Since the late 19th century, Banff National Park in Alberta Canada has, for instance, placed a premium on the idea that the provision of tourism opportunities is essential for the region's survival. By removing all competing industries (logging, agriculture etc.) from the area, policy makers effectively signalled their confidence in the ability of the Canadian wilderness to attract sufficient number of tourists to ensure the region's survival. The former CEO of the Canadian Pacific Railway (CPR), William Cornelius Van Horne, is often attributed with the observation that 'If we can't export the scenery, we'll import the tourists' (Fairmont Hotels, n.d.). To achieve this vision, national parks in the region developed alongside the rapidly expanding CPR and a series of lavish guest-houses from the Canadian Pacific Hotels group. In 2004, Banff National Park tourism industries contributed over CAN$800 million to the broader Alberta economy (Rettie et al., 2009).

However, for all their economic value, the various tourism industries that exist in national parks like Banff have for many years sat uneasily with the maintenance of the region's natural environment. Marketable commodities including the region's grizzly bear population have been identified as being negatively affected by tourism railway and highway infrastructure and the expansion of the Mount Norquay ski hill. Ryel and Grasse (1991) note that what makes a destination marketable are the features of its attractions spectrum and the infrastructure put in place to facilitate visitor access. Juggling these two related management exercises is challenging in the sense that both planning goals necessitate a complex interplay of utilitarian and conservation agendas. The consequences of a park agency or tourism sector not working in concert with the environmental and sociocultural surroundings would have the effect of simultaneously limiting the industry's growth potential but also its opportunities to become a socially responsible corporate citizen. To borrow an idea from Porter and Kramer (2006) in an article on the links between competitive advantage and corporate social responsibility for the *Harvard Business Review*, nature based tourism industries need the national park environment in its various physical, sociocultural, economic and other forms as much as said environments need tourism to add value to their long-term sustainable development. By encouraging visitors to enjoy and value the environment and culture of the area they are entering, it becomes possible for tourism services to make positive contributions to the local communities and others who inhabit a park locale.

So where does this leave us in relation to this book's key research questions? In considering how to answer these questions in a short conclusion we are faced with the inevitable temptation faced by all writers to simply summarise and explain the key themes of the work thus far with a view to telling you (the reader) what we have said (Cunliffe, 2014). Such an approach would we feel, at this point, test the readers' patience. It would also be potentially hubris on our part by presupposing that in the totality of the preceding chapters, we have necessarily addressed these issues to every reader's satisfaction. Instead we have chosen to first tell and then deconstruct a story. It is a story that we have already alluded to in passing in the earlier chapters of this book and one that most of the readership of this book would already be aware of, at least in passing. It is the story of the herdsmen and the pastoral field in Garrett Hardin's *Tragedy of the Commons*.

The story behind the story of the *Tragedy of the Commons* is well known. Garrett Hardin was American born ecologist who wrote a number of influential and often controversial works, calling into question social and institutional responses to population growth. The *Tragedy of the Commons*, published in the journal *Science* is perhaps his best known work. Written as a response to what Hardin considered to be the dangers of Adam Smith's advocacy of the free market as the solution to society's problems, *Tragedy of the Commons* posed an uncomfortable conundrum. Is it possible 'to exclude potential users from common pool resources that yield finite flows of benefits, [when it is as a result of this use that] those resources will be exhausted by rational, utility maximising individuals rather than conserved for the benefit of all' (Ostrom, 2008). In the years that have followed the publication of Hardin's influential treatise, various criticisms have been offered of his assumptions (Feeny et al., 1990; Gardiner, 2001; Neves-Graça, 2004). In the nearly five decades since the publication of Hardin's original treatise, notions of a tragedy of the commons have been advanced as a conceptual lens in a variety of environmental management fields including fisheries management (Berkes, 1985), forest management (Andersson & Agrawal, in press, corrected proof; Chhatre & Agrawal, 2009; Holmgren et al., 2010) and tourism management (Briassoulis, 2002; Neves-Graça, 2004; Stronza, 2010). As far back 1985, Cox noted that 'while academics are often too facile in labelling an article as "seminal" ... Hardin's 1968 article the Tragedy of the Commons deserves the accolade ... The term "tragedy of the commons" has slipped into common parlance at colleges and universities and is rapidly becoming common property'.

In this concluding chapter, our aim is not to establish whether national parks necessarily are or perhaps aren't characteristic of a tragedy of the commons, that is a debate worth having but is best left for another time. Instead we are using the story of the herdsmen as a metaphor for the story of human endeavour in national parks, human endeavour that has been characterised in part by the rapid growth of national park based ecotourism industries. The use of such a metaphor is not without justification. As Hardin noted in his original work:

> The National Parks present another instance of the working out of the tragedy of the commons. At present, they are open to all, without limit.

> The parks themselves are limited in extent—there is only one Yosemite Valley—whereas population seems to grow without limit. The values that visitors seek in the parks are steadily eroded.
>
> Plainly, we must soon cease to treat the parks as commons or they will be of no value to anyone. What shall we do? We have several options. We might sell them off as private property. We might keep them as public property, but allocate the right to enter of wealth, by the use of an auction system.
>
> It might be on the basis of merit, as defined by some agreed-upon standards. It might be by lottery. Or it might be on a first-come, first-served basis, administered to long queues. These, I think, are all the reasonable possibilities. They are all objectionable. But we must choose—or acquiesce in the destruction of the commons that we call our National Parks. (Hardin, 1968: 1244–1245)

With these words, the reader immediately sees Hardin expressing many of his own socially constructed views on the conundrum of sustainable national park management. Before we explore these views in detail, let us tell Hardin's story of the pastoral herdsmen, as it is this story that we will deconstruct.

> Picture a pasture open to all. It is to be expected that each herdsman will try to keep as many cattle as possible on the commons. Such an arrangement may work reasonably satisfactorily for centuries because tribal wars, poaching, and disease keep the numbers of both man and beast well below the carrying capacity of the land.
>
> Finally, however, comes the day of reckoning, that is, the day when the long-desired goal of social stability becomes a reality. At this point, the inherent logic of the commons remorselessly generates tragedy.
>
> As a rational being, each herdsman seeks to maximise his gain. Explicitly or implicitly, more or less consciously, he asks, 'What is the utility *to me* of adding one more animal to my herd?' This utility has one negative and one positive component.
>
> (1) The positive component is a function of the increment of one animal. Since the herdsman receives all the proceeds from the sale of the additional animal, the positive utility is nearly +1.
> (2) The negative component is a function of the additional overgrazing created by one more animal. Since, however, the effects of overgrazing are shared by all the herdsmen, the negative utility for any particular decision-making herdsman is only a fraction of –1.

Adding together the component partial utilities, the rational herdsman concludes that the only sensible course for him to pursue is to add another animal to his herd. And another; and another (sic) ... But this is the conclusion reached by each and every rational herdsman sharing a commons. Therein is the tragedy. Each man is locked into a system that compels him to increase his herd without limit—in a world that is limited. Ruin is the destination toward which all men rush, each pursuing his own best interest in a society that believes in the freedom of the commons. Freedom in a commons brings ruin to all.

The world is full of stories of human endeavour to interact with the natural world. Across all areas of life including: academia, movie making, the courts, the media, novels and the church etc. The stories that we tell define our place in society, they define our beliefs and our prejudices and are written much as a historical record juxtaposing the individual with the collective society. Carr and Davies (1961/2008) once noted that society and the individual are inseparable and that it is on the basis of the society that we are born into, that we will be moulded into an identifiable social unit, as opposed to a purely biological one. The effect of this idea for our present discussion of the tragedy of the commons as it relates to national parks is that we must start by recognising that the herdsmen who form the principal character in Hardin's story are not participating in open access or free for all regimes, but rather are participating in social and economic processes subject to the customs, rule systems and enforcement mechanisms that characterise their particular circumstance (Bridge, 2009).

In an award winning six part documentary series entitled *The National Parks: America's Best Idea,* it was noted that parks are first and foremost a story of people:

> people from every conceivable background – rich and poor; famous and unknown; soldiers and scientists; natives and newcomers; idealists, artists and entrepreneurs; people who were willing to devote themselves to saving some precious portion of the land they loved, and in doing so reminded their fellow citizens of the full meaning of democracy. (PBS, 2009)

It is people that make or break a good story. Writing for the Harvard Business Review, Nancy Duarte notes that the best stories will follow Aristotle's three part story structure characterised by a beginning, middle and end (Duarte, 2012). By creating a tension in the audience's mind, characterised by strong characters that the audience feels empathy with, great storytellers are able to pursue the possibility of a transformation, a shift from the status quo to the new bliss. The herdsmen in Hardin's work are powerful principally because in the opening sentences Hardin paints a picture of the herdsmen as afflicted by that most basic of human conditions, the desire to protect one's individual conditions. Throughout the present book, the authors have repeatedly emphasised the diversity of opinions that characterise the development of the parks movement that we know today. In doing so, we have been careful to try to limit the degree to which our own biases on best practice park management, although we do acknowledge instances where our own ideologies do become obvious. We invite the reader to disagree with our assertions as it is only through active stakeholder dialogue that tourism marketers will be able to reconcile the age old conundrum 'it's not easy being green' (Shultz & Holbrook, 1999).

What activities 'are truly green enough to serve the long-term interests of the environment and its inhabitants' (Shultz & Holbrook, 1999: 218) is an evolving question in the national parks movement. The answer, we would argue, comes from one's ability to reconcile a range of positivist scientific and socially constructed measures. In this work we have attempted to paint a vivid picture of the socially constructed environment in which national parks have developed. George Kelly once noted that a 'person's processes are psychologically channelized by the ways in which he anticipates events' (Kelly, 1963). In making this statement in relation to his renowned *Theory of Personal Constructs*, Kelly was seeking to invest ordinary people with the power to define the world through their own socially defined terms. On the basis of historical hindsight and ideological bias, readers will doubtless disagree with the motivations of many of the historical and contemporary park stakeholders defined in this book. Such disagreement is healthy and is a recognised characteristic of wicked problems, which the authors considered in Chapter 3.

Camillus (2008) argues that whilst wicked problems can't by definition be solved, they can be tamed. Taming a wicked problem for Camillus is a product of the successful implementation of four principles, which were succinctly articulated by Clegg *et al.* (2011a: 24–25):

(1) Stakeholder involvement is crucial. Strategy becomes a forum in which to work out what the challenges might look like, as well as in what order they should be tackled. Making sense of the situation and agreeing on the nature of the problem are paramount.
(2) While the strategic plans for coping with problems will change, the organisation's sense of purpose and identity should not.
(3) Focus on action. Because wicked problems are complex, we cannot think them through and then act on the results of our reasoning. Rather we have to experiment, put ideas forward, act on them and then adjust in the light of experience.
(4) Feedback is not the best way to learn; as the name suggests it feeds back onto something from the past. A feed forward orientation would scan the environment for weak signals. Who would have thought that the

rise of the internet would change the music industry? Feedback tells us that it did; feed forward could have told us that it would.

It is with these four points that we will finish by positioning the present book in relation to what we believe is a potentially positive role for marketing in the development of solutions to the tragedy, which is the management of the national park commons. Firstly, as we have already alluded to, it is with active engagement with stakeholders that the problem can be perceived. A major focus of the present work has been the aforementioned articulation of the socially constructed nature of the stakeholder voice in national park management. Our engagement with this issue has been at a higher level discussion of the process of national park development and the evolving characteristics of the ephemeral national park experience. Readers interested in the practicalities of bringing stakeholders together in a specific national park case study area are directed to an excellent piece on the Banff Bow Valley Round table by Eyre and Jamal (2006). An important characteristic of Eyre and Jamal's (2006) is the notion that there is a dual mandate for national park managers, conservation and human usage.

How national park managers reconcile the balancing of these often conflicting priorities will change over time. That being said, however, an evolving strategy direction for parks should not result in the purpose and identity of an organisation being lost. Throughout the present work, we have been at pains to establish park managers as an equal voice to tourism interests. Shultz and Holbrook (1999) note that solving commons dilemmas is not so much about organisation reducing its size, but rather different groups working collaboratively for a common goal. They note that such collaborative strategies may actually increase the size of an industry, but in a way that 'emphasises the collective pursuit of self-interest' (Shultz & Holbrook, 1999: 221). With this in mind, the authors have spent considerable time outlining opportunities for alternative marketing strategies (ecological marketing, relationship marketing etc.) to be used as a mechanism to encourage tourism growth but in a manner that contributes to the attainment of broader park management objectives. How this bringing together of agendas is achieved will be based on the specific circumstances of the park in question. While it is impossible to canvas all parks, the case studies are intended to serve as a mechanism for park managers to begin to consider how they could action the development of sustainable marketing initiatives in their own area of interest.

If we accept the validity of alternative marketing approaches to developing sustainable marketing strategies in national parks, we are left with how best to respond to Hardin's (1968) assertion that ruin is likely to be the inevitable consequence of growth in a world without limits. While we do not dispute Hardin's (1968) assertion that there is only one Yosemite Valley, we are of the firm view that sustainable development is not about absolute limits to growth but rather 'limits imposed by the present state of technological and social organisation' (World Commission on Environment and Development, 1987). Determining carrying capacity requires that one make trade-offs between the ecological, societal and economic components of a park ecosystem. Where one's priorities should be will be determined on the basis of a forward thinking philosophy where a manager will scan the totality of their situation for weaknesses and opportunities. It is our sincere hope that if the reader takes one thing away from the present works it is that the development of tourism in parks does not have to be perceived as at odds to the development of a sustainable park ecosystem. Instead, if they are framed correctly, tourism marketing will be a vehicle for national park sustainable development.

References

Achrol, R.S. and Kotler, P. (2012) Frontiers of the marketing paradigm in the third millennium. *Journal of the Academy of Marketing Science* 40 (1), 35–52.

Ajani, J. (2007) *The Forest Wars*. Melbourne: Melbourne University Press.

Allaby, M. (ed.) (1994) *The Concise Oxford Dictionary of Ecology*. Oxford: Oxford University Press.

Alston, M. (2004) 'You don't want to be a check-out chick all your life': The out-migration of young people from Australia's small rural towns. *Australian Journal of Social Issues* 39 (3), 299–313.

American Marketing Association (2013) Definition of Marketing. See https://www.ama.org/AboutAMA/Pages/Definition-of-Marketing.aspx

Anderson, R. and Harmon, D. (2002) 6th Biennial Scientific Conference on the Greater Yellowstone Ecosystem: Yellowstone Lake Hotbed of Chaos or Reservoir of Resilience? See http://www.greateryellowstonescience.org/sites/default/files/references/6thConf_proceedings.pdf

Andersson, K. and Agrawal, A. (2015) Inequalities, institutions, and forest commons. *Global Environmental Change* (in press).

Anon (2009) Community. In D. Gregory, R.J. Johnston, G. Pratt, M. Watts and S. Whatmore (eds) *The Dictionary of Human Geography* (4th edn, pp. 103–104). Oxford: Blackwell Publishers.

Anon (2012) Dictionary of Sustainable Management: Ecological Marketing. See http://www.sustainabilitydictionary.com/

Anon (2013) Tourism is now Tanzania's Leading Economic Sector. *Africa Travel Magazine*. See http://www.africa-ata.org/tz_economy.htm

Anon (2014) Greatest Parks of the World. *National Geographic*.

Anon (2015) North York Moors potash mine gets £1.7bn go-ahead. *The Guardian*, 1 July. See http://www.theguardian.com/environment/2015/jun/30/north-york-moors-potash-mine-gets-17bn-go-ahead

Ansoff, H.I., Declerck, R.P. and Hayes, R.L. (1990) From strategic planning to strategic management (pp. 110–147). Physica-Verlag HD.

Ap, J. (1992) Residents' perceptions on tourism impacts. *Annals of Tourism Research* 19 (4), 665–690.

Archer, D. and Wearing, S. (2002) Interpretation and marketing as management tools in national parks: Insights from Australia. *Journal of Leisure Property* 2 (1), 29–39.

Armstrong, E. and Kern, C. (2011) Demarketing manages visitor demand in the Blue Mountains National Park. *Journal of Ecotourism* 10 (1), 21–37.

Armstrong, E.K. and Weiler, B. (2003) Improving the tourist experience: Evaluation of interpretation components of guided tours in national parks. Gold Coast, Queensland: Sustainable Tourism CRC.

Arnberger, A., Eder, R., Allex, B., Sterl, P. and Burns, R.C. (2012) Relationships between national-park affinity and attitudes towards protected area management of visitors to the Gesaeuse National Park, Austria. *Forest Policy and Economics* 19, 48–55.

Arnould, E.J. and Price, L.L. (1993) River magic: Extraordinary experience and the extended service encounter. *Journal of Consumer Research* 20, 24–45.

Arnould, E.J., Price, L.L. and Tierney, P. (1998) Communicative staging of the wilderness servicescape. *Service Industries Journal* 18 (3), 90–115.

Arrowsmith, C. and Inbakaran, R. (2002) Estimating environmental resiliency for the Grampians National Park, Victoria, Australia: A quantitative approach. *Tourism Management* 23 (3), 295–309.

Ash, J. and Turner, L. (1976) *The Golden Hordes: International Tourism and the Pleasure Periphery.* New York: St Martin's Press.

Audrey, G. and Geoff, S. (2007) Integrating sustainable tourism and marketing management: Can National Parks provide the framework for strategic change? *Strategic Change* 16 (5), 191.

Australian Broadcasting Corporation (2007) Lake Pedder. See http://www.abc.net.au/time/this.htm

Backhaus, N. (2003) 'Non-place jungle': The construction of authenticity in National parks of Malaysia. *Indonesia and the Malay World* 31 (89), 151–160.

Balabanis, G., Mueller, R. and Melewar, T. (2002) The relationship between consumer ethnocentrism and human values. *Journal of Global Marketing* 15 (3–4), 7–37.

Ballantyne, R., Packer, J. and Hughes, K. (2009) Tourists' support for conservation messages and sustainable management practices in wildlife tourism experiences. *Tourism Management* 30 (5), 658–664.

Balmford, A., Green, J.M., Anderson, M., Beresford, J., Huang, C., Naidoo, R. and Manica, A. (2015) Walk on the wild side: Estimating the global magnitude of visits to protected areas. *PLoS Biol* 13 (2), e1002074.

Bandyopadhyay, R. and Morais, D. (2005) Representative dissonance: India's self and western image. *Annals of Tourism Research* 32 (4), 1006–1021.

Barnes, T. (2009) Neo-liberalism. In R.J. Johnston, D. Gregory, G. Pratt, M. Watts and S. Whatmore (eds) *The Dictionary of Human Geography* (5th edn, pp. 497–498). Oxford: Blackwell Publishers.

Bartlemus, P. (2000) Sustainable development: Paradigm or Paranoia. *International Journal of Sustainable Development* 3 (4), 358–369.

Bauman, Z. (2013) *Liquid Modernity.* Hoboken, NJ: John Wiley & Sons.

Bawden, T. (2015) North York Moors: 'Test case' national park mining project gets go-ahead. *The Independent*, 30 June. See http://www.independent.co.uk/news/uk/home-news/north-york-moors-test-case-national-park-mining-project-gets-goahead-10356430.html

Becken, S. and Job, H. (2014) Protected areas in an era of global–local change. *Journal of Sustainable Tourism* 22 (4), 507–527.

Beder, S. (1996) *The Nature of Sustainable Development* (2nd edn). Newham, Australia: Scribe Publications.

Bednar, R. (2012) Being here, looking there: Mediating vistas in the national parks of the contemporary American west. In R. Patin (ed.) *Observation Points: The Visual Poetics of National Parks* (pp. 1–28). Minnesota: University of Minnesota Press.

Beeton, S. (1999) Hoofing it – One four or two feet? Managing multi-use trails and sites. *Current Issues in Tourism* 2 (2), 211–225.

Beeton, S. (2003) Swimming against the tide—integrating marketing with environmental management via demarketing. *Journal of Hospitality and Tourism Management* 10 (2), 95 (13).

Beeton, S. (2004) Rural tourism in Australia – has the gaze altered? Tracking rural images through film and tourism promotion. *International Journal of Tourism Research* 6 (3), 125–135.

Beeton, S. (2006) Sustainable tourism in practice: Trails and tourism. Critical management issue of multiuse trails. *Tourism and Hospitality Planning & Development* 3 (1), 1–21.

Beeton, S. (2008) From the screen to the field: The influence of film on tourism and recreation. *Tourism Recreation Research* 33 (1), 39–47.

Beeton, S. and Benfield, R. (2002) Demand control: The case for demarketing as a visitor and environmental management tool. *Journal of Sustainable Tourism* 10 (6), 497–513.

Beh, A. and Bruyere, B.L. (2007) Segmentation by visitor motivation in three Kenyan national reserves. *Tourism Management* 28 (6), 1464–1471.

Bell, D. (2006) Variations on the rural idyll. *Handbook of Rural Studies*, 149–160. Earthscan: London.

Bell, S. and Morse, S. (2008) *Sustainability Indicators: Measuring the Immesurable* (2nd edn). London: Earthscan Publications Limited.

Belz, F.-M. and Peattie, K. (2009) *Sustainability Marketing: A Global Perspective*. Chichester: Wiley.

Benfield, R. (2000) Good Things Come to Those Who Wait – Demarketing Sissinghurst Castle Garden, Kent for Sustainable Mass Tourism. Paper presented at the TTRA Annual Conference Proceedings.

Bennett, N.J. and Dearden, P. (2014) Why local people do not support conservation: Community perceptions of marine protected area livelihood impacts, governance and management in Thailand. *Marine Policy* 44, 107–116.

Bergin-Seers, S. and Mair, J. (2009) Emerging green tourists in Australia: Their behaviours and attitudes. *Tourism and Hospitality Research* 9 (2), 109–119.

Berkes, F. (1985) Fishermen and 'the tragedy of the commons'. *Environmental Conservation* 12 (3), 199–206.

Berry, L.L. (1995) Relationship marketing of services – growing interest, emerging perspectives. *Journal of the Academy of Marketing Science* 23 (4), 236–245.

Bitner, M.J. (1995) Building service relationships: It's all about promises. *Journal of the Academy of Marketing Science* 23 (4), 246–251.

Blamey, R.K. and Braithwaite, V.A. (1997) A social values segmentation of the potential ecotourism market. *Journal of Sustainable Tourism* 5 (1), 29–45.

Boorstin, D. (1964) *A Guide to Pseudo-events in America*. New York: Harper and Row.

Borden, N.H. (1964) The concept of the marketing mix. *Journal of Advertising Research* 4 (2), 2–7.

Borrie, W.T., McCool, S.F. and Stankey, G.H. (1998) Protected area planning principles and strategies. In K. Lindberg, M.E. Wood and D. Engeldrum (eds) *Ecotourism: A Guide for Planners and Managers* (vol. 2, pp. 133–154). North Bennington, VT: The Ecotourism Society.

Botanic Gardens Conservation International (n.d.) Botanic Gardens Definition. See http://www.bgci.org/resources/1528/

Boyle, P., Halfacree, K.H. and Robinson, V. (2014) *Exploring Contemporary Migration*. London: Routledge.

Bradford, L. and McIntyre, N. (2007) Off the beaten track: Messages as a means of reducing social trail use at St. Lawrence Islands National Park. *Journal of Park and Recreation Administration* 25 (1), 1–21.

Bramwell, B. and Lane, B. (1993) Interpretation and sustainable tourism: The potential and the pitfalls. *Journal of Sustainable Tourism* 1 (2), 71–80.

Bramwell, B. and Lane, B. (2000) Introduction. In B. Bramwell and B. Lane (eds) *Tourism Collaboration and Partnerships: Policy Practice and Sustainability* (pp. 1–23). Clevedon: Channel View Publications.

Brasier, K.J., Filteau, M.R., McLaughlin, D.K., Jacquet, J., Stedman, R.C., Kelsey, T.W. and Goetz, S.J. (2011) Residents' perceptions of community and environmental impacts from development of natural gas in the Marcellus Shale: A comparison of Pennsylvania and New York cases. *Journal of Rural Social Sciences* 26 (1), 32–61.

Briassoulis, H. (2002) Sustainable tourism and the question of the commons. *Annals of Tourism Research* 29 (4), 1065–1085.

Bridge, G. (2009) Tragedy of the commons. In R.J. Johnston, D. Gregory, G. Pratt, M. Watts and S. Whatmore (eds) *The Dictionary of Human Geography* (5th edn, pp. 766–767). Oxford: Blackwell Publishers.

Broder, O., Collins, M., Holmgren, V. and Macdonald, A. (eds) (2006) *And They're Still Falling*. Charnwood, ACT: Ginninderra Press.

Brown, G. and Weber, D. (2011) Public participation GIS: A new method for national park planning. *Landscape and Urban Planning* 102 (1), 1–15.

Brydon-Miller, M., Kral, M., Maguire, P., Noffke, S. and Sabhlok, A. (2011) Jazz and the banyan tree: Roots and riffs on participatory action research. In N. Denzin and Y. Lincoln (eds) *Handbook of Qualitative Research* (pp. 387–400). California: SAGE.

Bryson, B. (1998) *A Walk in the Woods*. New York: Random House.

Buck, R.C. (1977) The ubiquitous tourist brochure explorations in its intended and unintended use. *Annals of Tourism Research* 4 (4), 195–207.

Buckley, R. (2003) Tourism and land management: Practice and politics. In R. Buckley, C. Pickering and D.B. Weaver (eds) *Nature Based Tourism, Environment and Land Management* (pp. 1–6). Oxon: CABI Publishing.

Buckley, R. (2012) Sustainable tourism: Research and reality. *Annals of Tourism Research* 39 (2), 528–546.

Budowski, G. (1976) Tourism and environmental conservation: Conflict, coexistence, or symbiosis? *Environmental Conservation* 3 (1), 27–31.

Buhalis, D. (2000) Marketing the competitive destination of the future. *Tourism Management* 21 (1), 97–116.

Busby, G. and Klug, J. (2001) Movie-induced tourism: The challenge of measurement and other issues. *Journal of Vacation Marketing* 7 (4), 316–332.

Büscher, B., Sullivan, S., Neves, K., Igoe, J. and Brockington, D. (2012) Towards a synthesized critique of neoliberal biodiversity conservation. *Capitalism Nature Socialism* 23 (2), 4–30.

Bushell, R. and Eagles, P.F. (2007) *Tourism and Protected Areas: Benefits Beyond Boundaries: The Vth IUCN World Parks Congress*. Oxon: CABI Publishing.

Butler, S. (2008) *Performance, Art and Ethnography*. Paper presented at the Forum Qualitative Sozialforschung/Forum: Qualitative Social Research.

Camillus, J.C. (2008) Strategy as a wicked problem. *Harvard Business Review* 86 (5), 98.

Campbell, S. (1996) Green cities, growing cities, just cities?: Urban planning and the contradictions of sustainable development. *Journal of the American Planning Association* 62 (3), 296–312.

Carr, E.H. and Davies, R.W. (1961/2008) *What is History?* [R.W. Davies (ed.)] Penguin Books: Melbourne.

Carruthers, J. (1995) *The Kruger National Park: A Social and Political History*. Scotsville: University of Natal Press.

Carter, C. (2006) Adventure tourism: Will to power. In A. Church and T. Coles (eds) *Tourism, Power and Space* (pp. 63–82). London: Routledge.

Carter, C. (2013) The age of strategy: Strategy, organizations and society. *Business History* 55 (7), 1047–1057.

Carter, C., Clegg, S.R. and Kornberger, M. (2008a) Strategy as practice. *Strategic Organization* 6 (1), 83–99.

Carter, C., Clegg, S.R. and Kornberger, M. (2008b) *A Very Short, Fairly Interesting and Reasonably Cheap Book about Studying Strategy*. Newcastle: Sage.

Cathores, P., Vaske, J. and Donnelly, M. (2001) Social values versus interpersonal conflict among hikers and mountain bike riders. *Leisure Sciences* 23 (47–61).

Ceballos-Lascurain, H. (1988) The future of ecotourism. *Mexico Journal, January* 27, 13–14.

Cessford, G. (2003) Perception and reality of conflict: Walkers and mountainbikers on the Queen Charlotte Track in New Zealand. *Journal for Nature Conservation* 11 (4), 310–316.

Chandler, A.D. (1990) *Strategy and Structure: Chapters in the History of the Industrial Enterprise* (vol. 120). MA: MIT Press.

Cheong, S.-M. and Miller, M.L. (2000) Power and tourism: A Foucauldian observation. *Annals of Tourism Research* 27 (2), 371–390.

Cherry, G.E. (1985) Scenic heritage and national parks lobbies and legislation in England and Wales. *Leisure Studies* 4 (2), 127–139.

Chhatre, A. and Agrawal, A. (2009) Trade-offs and synergies between carbon storage and livelihood benefits from forest commons. *Proceedings of the National Academy of Sciences* 106 (42), 17667–17670.

Chiesura, A. (2004) The role of urban parks for the sustainable city. *Landscape and Urban Planning* 68 (1), 129–138.

Christensen, C. (2013) *The Innovator's Dilemma: When New Technologies Cause Great Firms to Fail*. MA: Harvard Business Review Press.

Church, A. and Coles, T. (eds) (2006) *Tourism, Power and Space*. London: Routledge.

Clark, C. and Cemlyn, S. (2005) *The Social Exclusion of Gypsy and Traveller Children*.

Clarke, J., Hawkins, R. and Waligo, V. (2013) Sustainability and marketing for responsible tourism. In S. McCabe (ed.) *The Routledge Handbook of Tourism Marketing* (pp. 41–53). London: Routledge.

Clarke, T. and Clegg, S. (2000) Management paradigms for the new millennium. *International Journal of Management Reviews* 2 (1), 45–64.

Clegg, S. and Baumeler, C. (2010) Essai: From Iron cages to liquid modernity in organisation analysis. *Organisational Studies* 31 (12), 1713–1733.

Clegg, S. and Hardy, C. (2006) Representation & reflexivity. In S. Clegg, C. Hardy, T. Lawrence and W. Nord (eds) *The SAGE Handbook of Organisation Studies* (pp. 425–444). London: Sage.

Clegg, S.R. (1989) *Frameworks of Power*. London: Sage.

Clegg, S.R., Carter, C., Kornberger, M. and Schweitzer, J. (2011a) *Strategy: Theory and Practice*. London: Sage.

Clegg, S.R., Kornberger, M. and Pitsis, T. (2011b) *Managing and Organizations: An Introduction to Theory and Practice*. London: Sage.

Clements, M.A. (1989) Selecting tourist traffic by demarketing. *Tourism Management* 10 (2), 89–94.

Coble, T.G., Selin, S.W. and Erickson, B.B. (2003) Hiking alone: Understanding fear, negotiation strategies and leisure experience. *Journal of Leisure Research* 35 (1), 1–22.

Cochrane, J. (2006) Indonesian national parks: Understanding leisure users. *Annals of Tourism Research* 33 (4), 979–997.

Cohen, E. (1979) A phenomenology of tourist experience. *Sociology* 13, 179–201.

Cohen, E. (1988) Authenticity and commoditization in tourism. *Annals of Tourism Research* 15 (3), 371–386.

Cohen, E. and Cohen, S.A. (2012) Current sociological theories and issues in tourism. *Annals of Tourism Research* 39 (4), 2177–2202.

Colchester, M. (2004) Conservation policy and indigenous peoples. *Environmental Science & Policy* 7 (3), 145–153.

Connell, J. and McManus, P. (2011) *Rural Revival*. Surrey: Ashgate.

Conrad, J. (1995) *Heart of Darkness*. See http://www.gutenberg.org/ebooks/219

Crompton, J. (1979) Motivations for pleasure vacations. *Annals of Tourism Research* 6 (4), 408–424.

Crompton, J. (1983) Selecting target markets – A key to effective marketing. *Journal of Park and Recreation Administration* 1 (1), 7–26.

Crompton, J.L. (1978) An assessment of the image of Mexico as a destination and the influence of geographical location upon that image. *Journal of Travel Research* 18, 18–23.

Cronon, W. (1996) The trouble with wilderness: Or, getting back to the wrong nature. *Environmental History* 1 (1), 7–28.

Csikszentmihalyi, M. and Csikzentmihaly, M. (1991) *Flow: The Psychology of Optimal Experience* (vol. 41). New York: HarperPerennial.

Cunliffe, A.L. (2014) *A Very Short, Fairly Interesting and Reasonably Cheap Book about Management*. London: Sage.

Cunningham, P., Huijbensb, E. and Wearing, S. (2011) From whaling to whale watching: Examining sustainability and cultural rhetoric. *Journal of Sustainable Tourism* 20 (1), 143–161.

Curry, N. (1992) Controlling development in the national parks of England and Wales. *Town Planning Review* 63 (2), 107.

Curtin, S. (2006) Swimming with dolphins: A phenomelogical exploration of tourist recollections. *International Journal of Tourism Research* 8, 301–315.

Dahl, R.A. (1957) The concept of power. *Behavioral Science* 2 (3), 201–215.

Darcy, S., Griffin, T., Crilley, G. and Schweinsberg, S. (2010) Helping park managers use their visitor information. Gold Coast: CRC for Sustainable Tourism Pty Ltd.

Dargavel, J. (2004) The fight for the forests in retrospect and prospect. *Australasian Journal of Environmental Management* 11 (3), 237–244.

Davenport, S. and Leitch, S. (2005) Circuits of power in practice: Strategic ambiguity as delegation of authority. *Organization Studies* 26 (11), 1603–1623.

Deffner, A. and Metaxas, T. (2009) Marketing the national marine park image in Greece. *Anatolia* 20 (2), 307–329.

Deloitte Economics (2013) Super-growth sectors worth $250b to build Australia's 'lucky country': Deloitte report. See http://www.deloitte.com/view/en_au/au/514b317cfb1 81410VgnVCM3000003456f70aRCRD.htm

DeLuca, K. and Demo, A. (2001) Imagining nature and erasing class and race: Carleton Watkins, John Muir, and the construction of wilderness. *Environmental History* 6 (4), 541–560.

DeMares, R. and Krycka, K. (1998) Wild-animal-triggered peak experiences: Transpersonal aspects. *Journal of Transpersonal Psychology* 30, 161–177.

Denzin, N.K. (2005) Indians in the park. *Qualitative Research* 5 (1), 9–33.

Department of Foreign Afairs and Trade (2012) Australia's protected areas.

Department of Sustainability and the Environment (n.d.) Users guide to the Australian Walking Track Grading System. See http://parks.dpaw.wa.gov.au/sites/default/files/docs/activities/users-guide-walks-classification-standards.pdf

Deutsch, J. and Liebermann, Y. (1985) Effects of a public advertising campaign on consumer behavior in a demarketing situation. *International Journal of Research in Marketing* 2 (4), 287–290.

Devine, M.A. (2012) A nationwide look at inclusion: Gains and gaps. *Journal of Park and Recreation Administration* 30 (2).

Dickman, S. (1999) *Tourism and Hospitality Marketing*. Oxford: Oxford University Press.

Diesendorf, M. (2000) Sustainability and sustainable development. In D. Dunphy, J. Benveniste, A. Griffiths and P. Sutton (eds) *Sustainability: The Corporate Challenge of the 21st Century* (pp. 19–37). St Leonards (Australia): Allen & Unwin.

Dinan, P.S. (2000) Social marketing and sustainable tourism – Is there a match? *International Journal of Tourism Research* 2 (1), 1–14.

Director of National Parks (2007) Kakadu National Park Management Plan 2007–2014. See http://www.environment.gov.au/system/files/resources/b2a20560-df55-4487-8426-21b4cd4c110f/files/management-plan.pdf

Doremus, H. (1999) Nature, knowledge and profit: The Yellowstone bioprospecting controversy and the core purposes of America's national parks. *Ecology LQ* 26, 401.

Dorfman, L.T., Murty, S.A., Evans, R.J., Ingram, J.G. and Power, J.R. (2004) History and identity in the narratives of rural elders. *Journal of Aging Studies* 18 (2), 187–203.

Dorwart, C. (2007) *Exploring Visitor's Perceptions of the Trail Environment and their Effects on Experiences in the Great Smoky Mountain National Park*. NC: North Carolina State University.

Dorwart, C., Moore, R. and Yu-Fai, L. (2007) *Visitor employed photography: Its potential and use in evaluating visitors' perceptions of resource impacts in trail and park settings*. Paper presented at the Proceedings of the 2006 Northeastern Recreation Research Symposium (Gen. Tech. Rep. NRS-P-14), Bolton Landing, NY.

Dovers, S. (2003) Are forests different as a policy challenge? In D. Lindenmayer and J.F. Franklin (eds) *Towards Forest Sustainability* (pp. 15–29, 215–231). Washington, D.C.: Island Press.

Dredge, D. and Jenkins, J. (2007) *Tourism Planning and Policy*. Milton, Queensland: John Wiley and Sons Australia, Ltd.

Drucker, P. (2014) *Innovation and Entrepreneurship*. London: Routledge.

Drucker, P.F. (1958) Marketing and economic development. *The Journal of Marketing* 252–259.

Duarte, N. (2012) Structure your presentation like a story. See https://hbr.org/2012/10/structure-your-presentation-li

Dubow, J. (2009) Image. In R.J. Johnston, D. Gregory, G. Pratt, M. Watts and S. Whatmore (eds) *The Dictionary of Human Geography* (5th edn, p. 369). Oxford: Blackwell Publishers.

Duffy, R. and Moore, L. (2010) Neoliberalising nature? Elephant-Back tourism in Thailand and Botswana. *Antipode* 42 (3), 742–766.

Dye, R. (2000) The buzz on buzz. *Harvard Business Review* (November–December), 139–146.

Eagles, P. (2002) Editorial (Special Edition on Tourism and Protected Areas). *PARKS* 12 (1), 1–2.

Eagles, P. and McCool, S. (2002) *Tourism in National Parks and Protected Areas: Planning and Management*. Oxon: CABI Publishing.

Eagles, P.F. (2002) Trends in park tourism: Economics, finance and management. *Journal of Sustainable Tourism* 10 (2), 132–153.

Eagles, P.F. (2014) Research priorities in park tourism. *Journal of Sustainable Tourism* 22 (4), 528–549.

Echtner, C. and Ritchie, J. (2003) The meaning and measurement of destination image. *Journal of Tourism Studies* 14 (1), 37–48.

Endersby, J. (2000) A garden enclosed: Botanical barter in Sydney, 1818–39. *The British Journal for the History of Science* 33 (3), 313–334.

Engelstad, F. (2009) Culture and power. *The SAGE Handbook of Power* (p. 210). London: Sage.

Evans, N. (2009) Tourism: A strategic business perspective. In T. Jamal and M. Robinson (eds) *The SAGE Handbook of Tourism Studies* (pp. 215–234). Los Angeles: SAGE.

Eyre, M. and Jamal, T. (2006) Adressing tourism conflicts in Banff National Park: The Banff Bow Valley Round Table Process. In I. Herremans (ed.) *Cases in Sustainable Tourism: Resource Guides for an Experiential Learning Environment* (pp. 187–200). New York: The Haworth Hospitality Press.

Fabes, R., Worsley, L. and Howard, M. (1983) *The Myth of the Rural Idyll*. Leicester: Child Poverty Action Group.

Fairmont Hotels. (n.d.) About Fairmont Hotels & Resorts. See http://www.fairmontheritageplace.com/heritageplace/LearnMore/AboutFairmontHotels/

Feeny, D., Berkes, F., McCay, B.J. and Acheson, J.M. (1990) The tragedy of the commons: Twenty-two years later. *Human Ecology* 18 (1), 1–19.

Feinstein, D. (2006) Senator feinstein warns against proposed revisions to National Park service management policies. See http://www.feinstein.senate.gov/public/index.cfm/press-releases?ID=792a0162-7e9c-9af9-75de-6ff377def008

Fesenmaier, D. and MacKay, K. (1996) Deconstructing destination image construction. *Tourism Review* 51 (2), 37–43.

Foucault, M. (1977) *Discipline and Punish: The Birth of the Prison*. New York: Vintage.

Foucault, M. (1982) The subject and power. *Critical Inquiry* 8 (4), 777–795.

Frank, J. (2008) Marketing the mountains: An environmental history of tourism in Rocky Mountain National Park. PhD thesis, University of Kansas. See http://proquest.umi.com/pqdlink?did=1686096121&Fmt=7&clientId=20928&RQT=309&VName=PQD

Fredman, P. and Hörnsten, L. (2004) *Social Capacity and Visitor Satisfaction in National Park Tourism*. Paper presented at the Proceedings from the 12th Nordic Symposium in Tourism and Hospitality Research, Stavanger, Norway.

Frisby, W., Thibault, L. and Kikulis, L. (2004) The organisational dynamics of undermanaged partnerships in leisure service departments. *Leisure Studies* 23 (2), 109–126.

Frisvoll, S. (2012) Power in the production of spaces transformed by tourism. *Journal of Rural Studies* 28, 447–457.

Frisvoll, S. (2014) Beyond the idyll: Contested spaces of rural tourism: The negotiation, commodification and consumption of conflicting ruralities. PhD thesis, Department of Geography, Norwegian University of Science and Technology.

Fritsch, A.J. and Johannsen, K. (2004) *Ecotourism in Appalachia: Marketing the Mountains*. KY: University Press of Kentucky.

Frost, W. and Hall, C.M. (2009) *Tourism and National Parks: International Perspectives on Development, Histories and Change* (vol. 14). London: Routledge.

Gardiner, S.M. (2001) The real tragedy of the commons. *Philosophy & Public Affairs* 30 (4), 387–416.

Gibson, C. and Argent, N. (2008) Getting on, getting up and getting out? Broadening perspectives on rural youth migration. *Geographical Research* 46 (2), 135–138.

Gill, N. (1999) The ambiguities of wilderness. In E. Stratford (ed.) *Australian Cultural Geographies* (pp. 48–68). Oxford: Oxford University Press.

Gilliam, A. (1979) *Voices for the Earth. A Treasury of the Sierra Club Bulletin 1893–1977*. Sierra Club, San Franciso, California.

Gilmore, A. and Simmons, G. (2007) Integrating sustainable tourism and marketing management: Can national parks provide the framework for strategic change? *Strategic Change* 16, 191–200.

Ginn, F. (2009) Colonial transformations: Nature, progress and science in the Christchurch Botanic Gardens. *New Zealand Geographer* 65, 35–47.

Glick, D. and Whelan, T. (1991) Tourism in Greater Yellowstone: Maximizing the good, minimizing the bad, eliminating the ugly. In T. Whelan (ed.) *Nature Tourism: Managing for the Environment* (pp. 58–74). Washington, D.C.: Island Press.

Göhler, G. (2009) Power to and power over. *The SAGE Handbook of Power* (pp. 27–39). London: Sage.

Gordon, R., Kornberger, M. and Clegg, S.R. (2009) Power, rationality and legitimacy in public organizations. *Public Administration* 87 (1), 15–34.

Graham, T. (2002) Survey of aquatic macroinvertebrates and amphibians at Wupatki National Monument, Arizona, USA: An evaluation of selected factors affecting species richness in ephemeral pools. *Hydrobiologia* 486 (1), 215–224.

Gregory, D., Little, J. and Watts, M. (2009) Rural geography. In R.J. Johnston, D. Gregory, G. Pratt, M. Watts and S. Whatmore (eds) *The Dictionary of Human Geography* (5th edn, pp. 659–660). Oxford: Blackwell Publishers.

Griffin, T., Moore, S., Crilley, G., Darcy, S. and Schweinsberg, S. (2010a) Protected area management: Collection and use of visitor data. *Volume 1: Summary and recommendations*. Goldcoast: CRC for Sustainable Tourism Pty Ltd.

Griffin, T., Moore, S., Crilley, G., Darcy, S. and Schweinsberg, S. (2010b) Protected area management: Collection and use of visitor data. *Volume 2: State agency overviews*. Goldcoast: CRC for Sustainable Tourism Pty Ltd.

Griffin, T. and Vacaflores, M. (2004) Project paper one: The visitor experience. *A Natural Partnership: Making National Parks a Tourism Priority*: TTF Australia Tourism and Transport Forum.
Groff, C. (1998) Demarketing in park and recreation management. *Managing Leisure* 3, 128–135.
Hackley, C., Skalen, P. and Stenfors, S. (2008) Marketing as practice. *Scandinavian Journal of Management* 27 (2), 189–195.
Halfacree, K. (1996) Out of place in the country: Travellers and the 'rural idyll'. *Antipode* 28 (1), 42–72.
Halfacree, K. (2006) Rural space: Constructing a three-fold architecture. In P. Cloke, T. Marsden and P. Mooney (eds) *Handbook of Rural Studies* (pp. 44–62). London: Sage.
Halfacree, K. (2007) Trial by space for a 'radical rural': Introducing alternative localities, representations and lives. *Journal of Rural Studies* 23 (2), 125–141.
Hall, C. (1988) The 'worthless lands hypothesis' and Australia's national parks and reserves. *Australia's ever changing forests. Australian Defence Force Academy, Canberra*, 441–459.
Hall, C.M. (2014) *Tourism and Social Marketing*. London: Routledge.
Hallo, J.C. and Manning, R.E. (2009) Transportation and recreation: A case study of visitors driving for pleasure at Acadia National Park. *Journal of Transport Geography* 17 (6), 491–499.
Hardin, G. (1968) The tragedy of the commons. *Science* 162 (3859), 1243–1248.
Harpers Ferry Center National Park Service (2005) The National Parks: Shaping the system. See http://www.nps.gov/parkhistory/online_books/shaping/index.htm
Harvey, D. (2005) *A Brief History of Neoliberalism*. Oxford: Oxford University Press.
Hauggard, M. and Clegg, S. (2009) Introduction: Why power is the central concept of the social sciences. In S. Clegg and M. Hauggard (eds) *The SAGE Handbook of Power* (pp. 1–24). Los Angeles: Sage.
Hay-Edie, T. (2003) The cultural values of protected areas. In D. Harmon and A. Putney (eds) *The Full Value of Parks: From Economics to the Intangible* (pp. 91–102). Lanham: Rowman and Littlefield Publishers.
Haynes, C.D. (2009) Defined by contradiction: The social construction of joint management in Kakadu National Park. Unpublished PhD thesis, Charles Darwin University, Darwin.
Hearne, R. and Salinas, Z. (2002) The use of choice experiments in the analysis of tourist preferences for ecotourism development in Costa Rica. *Journal of Environmental Management* 65 (2), 153–163.
Heath, E. and Wall, G. (1991) *Marketing Tourism Destinations: A Strategic Planning Approach*. London: John Wiley & Sons, Inc.
Heley, J. and Jones, L. (2012) Relational rurals: Some thoughts on relating things and theory in rural studies. *Journal of Rural Studies* 28 (3), 208–217.
Helleiner, J. (1995) Gypsies, Celts and tinkers: Colonial antecedents of anti-traveller racism in Ireland. *Ethnic and Racial Studies* 18 (3), 532–554.
Henty, C. (1988) *For the People's Pleasure: Australia's Botanic Gardens*. Richmond Victoria: Greenhouse Publications.
Herremans, I. and Reid, R. (2006) Yosemite National Park: Parks Without Private Vehicles. In I. Herremans (ed.) *Cases in Sustainable Tourism: An Experiential Approach to Descision Making* (pp. 161–174). London: Haworth Hospitality Press.
Hickey, J.E. and Brown, M.J. (2003) Towards ecological forestry in Tasmania. In D. Lindenmayer and J.F. Franklin (eds) *Towards Forest Sustainability* (pp. 31–46, 215–231). Washington, D.C.: Island Press.
Himalayan Tourism (2012) Welcome. See http://www.himalayantourism.com/
Himley, M. (2008) Geographies of environmental governance: The nexus of nature and neoliberalism. *Geography Compass* 2 (2), 433–451.

Hogenauer, A. (2001) *Marketing the National Parks – Oxymoron or Opportunity?* Paper presented at the NERR 2001 conference in Bolton Landing, NY. See www.nrs.fs.fed.us/pubs/gtr/gtr_ne289/gtr_ne289_053.pdf

Holden, A. (2003) Investigating trekkers' attitudes to the environment of Annapurna, Nepal. *Tourism Management* 24 (3), 341–344.

Holden, A. (2007) *Environment and Tourism*. London: Routledge.

Holden, A. and Sparrowhawk, J. (2002) Understanding the motivations of ecotourists: The case of Trekkers in Annapurna Nepal. *International Journal of Tourism Research* 4 (435–446).

Holloway, J. (2004) *Marketing for Tourism*. New York: Financial Times/Prentice Hall, an imprint of Pearson Education.

Holmgren, E., Keskitalo, E.C.H. and Lidestav, G. (2010) Swedish forest commons – A matter of governance? *Forest Policy and Economics* 12 (6), 423–431.

Howitt, R. (2002) Local and non-specialist participation in impact assessment. See http://www.es.mq.edu.au/~rhowitt/SIA_00E9.htm (accessed 20 March 2006).

Howitt, R. and Suchet-Pearson, S. (2006) Rethinking the building blocks: Ontological pluralism and the idea of 'management'. *Geografiska Annaler: Series B, Human Geography* 88 (3), 323–335.

Hubbarb, P. (2009) Social space. In R.J. Johnston, D. Gregory, G. Pratt, M. Watts and S. Whatmore (eds) *The Dictionary of Human Geography* (5th edn, pp. 697–698). Oxford: Blackwell Publishers.

Hudson, M. (2004) The archaeology of money: Debt versus barter theories of money's origins. *Credit and State Theories of Money. The Contributions of A. Mitchell Innes.* See http://arno.daastol.com/books/wray/Wray,%20Credit%20and%20State%20Theory%20of%20Money%20(2004)a.pdf#page=93

Hudson, S. and Ritchie, J. (2009) Branding a memorable destination experience. The case of 'Brand Canada'. *International Journal of Tourism Research* 11 (2), 217–228.

Hughes, G. (1995) Authenticity in tourism. *Annals of Tourism Research* 22 (4), 781–803.

Hunter, C. (1997) Sustainable tourism as an adaptive paradigm. *Annals of Tourism Research* 24 (4), 850–867.

Inglis, J., Whitelaw, P. and Pearlman, M. (2005) *Best Practice in Strategic Park Management Towards an Integrated Park Model*. Goldcoast: CRC for Sustainable Tourism.

Inoue, Y. and Lee, S. (2011) Effects of different dimensions of corporate social responsibility on corporate financial performance in tourism-related industries. *Tourism Management* 32 (4), 790–804.

International Union for Conservation of Nature (2014) Protected Areas Category II. See http://www.iucn.org/about/work/programmes/gpap_home/gpap_quality/gpap_pacategories/gpap_pacategory2/

Jacobides, M.G. (2010) Strategy tools for a shifting landscape. *Harvard Business Review* 88 (1), 76–84.

Jacquet, J. (2009) Energy boomtowns & natural gas: Implications for Marcellus Shale local governments & rural communities. NERCRD Rural Development.

Jamasmie, C. (2015) Opposition to Sirius Minerals $3bn potash project in national park builds up. See http://www.mining.com/opposition-to-sirius-minerals-3bn-potash-project-in-national-park-builds-up/

James, S. (2007) Constructing the climb: Visitor decision-making at Uluru. *Geographical Research* 45 (4), 398–407.

Jansson, A. (2010) Mediatization, spatial coherence and social sustainability: The role of digital media networks in a Swedish countryside community. *Culture Unbound: Journal of Current Cultural Research* 2 (2), 177–192.

Jarzabkowski, P. and Paul Spee, A. (2009) Strategy-as-practice: A review and future directions for the field. *International Journal of Management Reviews* 11 (1), 69–95.

Jessop, B. (2009) The state and power. *The SAGE Handbook of Power* (pp. 367–382). London: Sage.

Jessop, T. and Penny, A. (1998) A study of teacher voice and vision in the narratives of rural South African and Gambian primary school teachers. *International Journal of Educational Development* 18 (5), 393–403.

Johansen, P. and Chandler, T. (2015) Mechanisms of power in participatory rural planning. *Journal of Rural Studies* 40, 12–20.

Johnson, C.E. (2012) Getting there: Yosemite and the politics of transportation planning in the National Parks. *Society News, Notes & Mail* 29 (3), 351–361.

Johnson, N. (2009) Authenticity. In R.J. Johnston, D. Gregory, G. Pratt, M. Watts and S. Whatmore (eds) *The Dictionary of Human Geography* (5th edn, pp. 40). Oxford: Blackwell Publishers.

Johnston, A. (2000) Indigenous peoples and ecotourism: Bringing indigenous knowledge and rights into the sustainability equation. *Tourism Recreation Research* 25 (2), 89–96.

Johnston, R. (2009) Wilderness. In R.J. Johnston, D. Gregory, G. Pratt and M. Watts (eds) *The Dictionary of Human Geography* (5th edn, pp. 810–811). Oxford: Wiley Blackwell.

Jokinen, E. and Veijola, S. (1997) The disoriented tourist: The figuration of the tourist in contemporary cultural critique. In C. Rojek and J. Urry (eds) *Touring Cultures: Transformations of Travel and Theory* (pp. 23–51). London: Routkedge.

Jones, H. (1963–1964) *John Muir and the Sierra Club: The Battle for Yosemite*. San Francsco: Sierra Club.

Jones, P., Comfort, D. and Hillier, D. (2009) Marketing sustainable consumption within stores: A case study of the UK's leading food retailers. *Sustainability* 1 (4), 815–826.

Jones, S. and Lalley, J.S. (2013) Assessing the compatibility of ecotourism and hunting through the attitudes and choices of ecotourists. *African Journal for Physical Health Education, Recreation and Dance: Tourism Research Issues in Southern Africa: Supplement* 3 19, 266–275.

Jun, J., Kyle, G.T. and Mowen, A.J. (2009) Market segmentation using perceived constraints. *Journal of Park and Recreation Administration* 26 (1), 35–55.

Katja Neves-Graça, H. (2004) Revisiting the tragedy of the commons: Ecological dilemmas of whale watching in the azores. *Human Organization* 63 (3), 289–300.

Keating, P. (2014) Gardens trust must head the call of nature. *Sydney Morning Herald*, 9 April, 18–19.

Keenan, R. (2014) Abbott's half right: Our national parks are good but not perfect *The Conversation*. See http://theconversation.com/abbotts-half-right-our-national-parks-are-good-but-not-perfect-24029

Keiter, R.B. (2013) *To Conserve Unimpaired: The Evolution of the National Park Idea*. Washington DC: Island Press.

Kelly, G. (1963) *A Theory of Personality: The Psychology of Personal Constructs*. New York: The Norton Library W.W. Norton and Company Inc.

Kerlinger, F. and Lee, H.B. (2000) *Foundations of Behavioral Research*. New York: Harcourt.

Kern, C.L. (2006) Demarketing as a tool for managing visitor demand in national parks: An Australian case study. Unpublished MA in Tourism thesis, University of Canberra, Canberra.

Kilbourne, W.E., Beckmann, S.C. and Thelen, E. (2002) The role of the dominant social paradigm in environmental attitudes: A multinational examination. *Journal of Business Research* 55 (3), 193–204.

Kim, A.K., Airey, D. and Szivas, E. (2011) The multiple assessment of interpretation effectiveness: Promoting visitors' environmental attitudes and behavior. *Journal of Travel Research* 50 (3), 321–334.

Kim, H. and Jamal, T. (2007) Touristic quest for existential authenticity. *Annals of Tourism Research* 34 (1), 181–201.

King, H. and Woolmington, E. (1960) The role of the river in the development of settlement in the Lower Hunter Valley. *Australian Geographer* 8 (1), 3–16.

King, L. and Prideaux, B. (2010) Special interest tourists collecting places and destinations: A case study of Australian World Heritage sites. *Journal of Vacation Marketing* 16 (3), 235–247.

King, L.M. and Halpenny, E.A. (2014) Communicating the World Heritage brand: Visitor awareness of UNESCO's World Heritage symbol and the implications for sites, stakeholders and sustainable management. *Journal of Sustainable Tourism* 22 (5), 768–786.

Kirkpatrick, C. and Lee, N. (1997) *Sustainable Development in a Developing World: Integrating Socio-economic Appraisal and Environmental Assessment*. Northampton, MA: Edward Elgar Publishing.

Knight, F. (2014) *Law, Power and Culture: Supporting Change From Within*. London: Palgrave Macmillan.

Kopas, P. (2007) *Taking the Air: Ideas and Changes in Canada's National Parks*. Vancouver: UBC Press.

Kotler, P. (2011) Reinventing marketing to manage the environmental imperative. *Journal of Marketing* 75 (4), 132–135.

Kotler, P. and Armstrong, G. (2013) *Principles of Marketing 15th Global Edition*. London: Pearson.

Kotler, P., Berger, R. and Bickhoff, N. (2010) *The Quintessence of Strategic Management*. Berlin Heidelberg: Springer-Verlag.

Kotler, P. and Keller, K. (2007) *A Framework for Marketing Management* (3rd edn). New Jersey: Pearson – Prentice Hall.

Kotler, P. and Levy, S.J. (1971) Demarketing, yes, demarketing. [Article]. *Harvard Business Review* 49 (6), 74–80.

Kotter, J.P. and Rathgeber, H. (2006) *Our Iceberg is Melting: Changing and Succeeding under any Conditions*. London: Macmillan.

Krajnc, D. and Glavic, P. (2005) A model for integrated assessment of sustainable development. *Resources, Conservation and Recycling* 43 (2), 189–208.

Krippendorf, J. (1987) Ecological approach to tourism marketing. *Tourism Management* 8 (2), 174–176.

Krumpe, E. and Lucas, R. (1986) *Research on Recreation Trails and Trail Users a Literature Review for the President's Commission on America's Outdoors*. Washington, DC: US Government Printing Office.

Kuhn, T.S. (2012) *The Structure of Scientific Revolutions*. IL: University of Chicago Press.

Kyle, G., Graefe, A., Manning, R. and Bacon, J. (2003) An examination of the relationship between leisure activity involvement and place attachment among hikers along the Appalachian Trail. *Journal of Leisure Research* 35 (3), 249–273.

Lacey, J. and Lamont, J. (2014) Using social contract to inform social licence to operate: An application in the Australian coal seam gas industry. *Journal of Cleaner Production* 84, 831–839.

Lafferty, W. and Hovden, E. (2003) Environmental policy integration: Towards an analytical framework. *Environmental Politics* 12 (3), 1–22.

Lai, P.-H., Sorice, M.G., Nepal, S.K. and Cheng, C.-K. (2009) Integrating social marketing into sustainable resource management at Padre Island National Seashore: An attitude-based segmentation approach. *Environmental Management* 43 (6), 985–998.

Lai, P., Sorice, M., Nepal, S. and Cheng, C. (2009) Integrating social marketing into sustainable resource management at Padre Island National Seashore: An attitude-based segmentation approach. *Environmental Management* 43 (6), 985.

Laing, J.H. and Crouch, G.I. (2005) Extraordinary journeys: An exploratory cross-cultural study of tourists on the frontier. *Journal of Vacation Marketing* 11 (3), 209–223.

Lane, B., Jamal, T. and Robinson, M. (2009) Rural tourism: An overview. *The SAGE Handbook of Tourism Studies* (pp. 354–370). London: Sage.

Lane, M. (1999) Regional forest agreements: Resolving resource conflicts or managing resource politics? *Australian Geographical Studies* 37 (2), 142–153.

Langford, N. (1871) The wonders of the yellowstone. *Scribners Monthly: An Illustrated Magazine for the People*. See https://archive.org/stream/centuryillustrat02newyuoft#page/n7/mode/2up

Langton, M. (1996) What do we mean by wilderness?: Wilderness and terra nullius in Australian art [Address to The Sydney Institute on 12 October 1995]. *Sydney Papers* 8(1), 10.

Lannoy, N. (2012) Wilderness Ideologies in a Settler Colonial Society: A case study of the Everglades National Park. Unpublished MA in Arts Thesis, University of California, Los Angeles. 52p.

Law, G. (2001) *History of the Franklin River Campaign 1976–83*. Hobart: The Wilderness Society.

Lawrence, M. (1997) Heartlands or neglected geographies? Liminality, power, and the hyperreal rural. *Journal of Rural Studies* 13 (1), 1–17.

Lean, G. (2015) Will a mine be sunk into the moors?, *The Telegraph*. See from http://www.telegraph.co.uk/news/earth/greenpolitics/11702725/Will-a-mine-be-sunk-into-the-moors.html (accessed 27 June).

Lefebvre, H. (1991[1947]) *The Production of Space* (vol. 142). Oxford: Blackwell.

Leiper, N. (1990a) Partial industrialization of tourism systems. *Annals of Tourism Research* 17 (4), 600–605.

Leiper, N. (1990b) Tourism Systems: An Interdisciplinary Perspective Occassional Paper No. 2. Massey University: Department of Management Systems/Business Studies Faculty.

Leiper, N., Stear, L., Hing, N. and Firth, T. (2008) Partial industrialisation in tourism: A new model. *Current Issues in Tourism* 11 (3), 207–235.

Lekies, K.S. and Whitworth, B. (2011) Constructing the nature experience: A semiotic examination of signs on the trail. *The American Sociologist* 42 (2–3), 249–260.

Leopold, A. (1989) *A Sandcountry Almanac and Sketches Here and There*. New York: Oxford University Press.

Levenson, M. (1985) The value of facts in the heart of darkness. *Nineteenth-Century Fiction* 40, 261–280. Reprinted in R. Kimbrough (ed.) *Heart of Darkness An Authoritative Text, Backgrounds and Sources, Criticism* (3rd edn, pp. 391–405) New York: W.W. Norton, 1988.

Li, X.R. and Petrick, J.F. (2008) Tourism marketing in an era of paradigm shift. *Journal of Travel Research* 46 (3), 235–244.

Lichrou, M., O'Malley, L. and Patterson, M. (2008) Place-product or place narrative (s)? Perspectives in the marketing of tourism destinations. *Journal of Strategic Marketing* 16 (1), 27–39.

Lipscombe, N. (1999) The relevance of the peak experience to continued skydiving participation: A qualitative approach to assess motivations. *Leisure Studies* 18 (4), 267–288.

Little, J. and Austin, P. (1996) Women and the rural idyll. *Journal of Rural Studies* 12 (2), 101–111.

Littlefair, C. (2003) The Effectiveness of Interpretation in Reducing the Impacts of Visitors in National Parks. Griffith University: School of Environmental and Applied Sciences Faculty of Environmental Sciences.

Lloyd, D.J., Luke, H. and Boyd, W.E. (2013) Community perspectives of natural resource extraction: Coal-seam gas mining and social identity in Eastern Australia. *Coolabah* 10, 144.

Lloyd, G. and Norris, C. (1998) From difference to deviance: The exclusion of gypsy-traveller children from school in Scotland. *International Journal of Inclusive Education* 2 (4), 359–369.

Lohrey, A. (2002) Groundswell: The rise of the greens. *Quarterly Essay* (8), 1.
Louis, R.P. (2007) Can you hear us now? Voices from the margin: Using indigenous methodologies in geographic research. *Geographical Research* 45 (2), 130–139.
Louter, D. (2009) *Windshield Wilderness: Cars, Roads, and Nature in Washington's National Parks*. Washington DC: University of Washington Press.
Luke, T.W. (1997) Nature protection or nature projection: A cultural critique of the Sierra club. *Capitalism Nature Socialism* 8 (1), 37–63.
Lukes, S. (1974) *Power: A Radical View* (vol. 1). London: Macmillan.
Lumsdon, L. (1997) *Tourism Marketing*. Mumbai: International Thomson Business Press.
Lynn, N. and Brown, R. (2003) Effects of recreational use impacts on hiking experiences in natural areas. *Landscape and Urban Planning* 64 (1–2), 77–87.
Ma, X.-L., Ryan, C. and Bao, J.-G. (2009) Chinese national parks: Differences, resource use and tourism product portfolios. *Tourism Management* 30 (1), 21–30.
MacCannell, D. (1973) Staged authenticity: Arrangements of social space in tourist settings. *American Journal of Sociology* 79 (3), 589.
MacCannell, D. (1976) *The Tourist: A New Theory of the Leisure Class*. CA: University of California Press.
Machiavelli, N. (1998) *The Prince*. IL: University of Chicago Press.
Maletz, M.C. and Nohria, N. (2001) Managing in the whitespace. *Harvard Business Review* 79 (2), 102–111, 157.
Manning, R.E. (1989) The nature of America: Visions and revisions of wilderness. *Natural Resources Journal* 29 (1) 25–40.
Manoochehri, J. (2001) *Consumption Opportunities: Strategies for Change: A Report for Decision-makers*, Incumbent. See http://www.unep.ch/scoe/documents/en_SCO.pdf
Marsh, J. (2004) Trails and Tourism. Paper presented at the Proceedings of the Ontario Trails Council Annual Conference, Peterborough.
Marsh, T., Derose, K.P. and Cohen, D.A. (2012) Exploring park director roles in promoting community physical activity. *Journal of Physical Activity & Health* 9 (5), 731.
Martin, D. and Schouten, J. (2012) *Sustainable Marketing*. Boston: Prentice Hall.
Marzano, G. and Scott, N. (2005) Stakeholder Power in Destination Branding: A Methodological Discussion. Paper presented at the International Conference on Destination Branding and Marketing for Regional Tourism Development.
Maslow, A. (1962) Lessons from the Peak Experiences. *Journal of Humanistic Psychology* 2, 9–18.
Maslow, A. (1968) A theory of metamotivation: The biological rooting of the value life. *Psychology Today* 38–9, 58–61.
Massey, D. (2005) *For Space*. London: SAGE.
Mattsson, J. (2008) True marketing: A value based philosophy for strategic marketing. [Article]. *Journal of Strategic Marketing* 16 (3), 175–188. doi: 10.1080/09652540802117132
McBeth, M.K. and Shanahan, E.A. (2004) Public opinion for sale: The role of policy marketers in Greater Yellowstone policy conflict. *Policy Sciences* 37 (3–4), 319–338.
McCarville, R. and McCarville, R. (2002) *Improving Leisure Services through Marketing Action*. IL: Sagamore Publishing.
McCool, S. and Cole, D. (2000) Communicating Minimum Impact Behavior With Trailside Bulletin Boards: Visitor Characteristics Associated With Effectiveness. Paper presented at the Wilderness science in a time of change conference – Volume 4: Wilderness visitors, experiences, and visitor management, Missoula, MT.
McCool, S.F. and Christensen, N.A. (1996) Alleviating congestion in parks and recreation areas through direct management of visitor behavior. Crowding and congestion in the National Park System: Guidelines for management and research. *University of Minnesota Agriculture Experiment Station Publication*, 86–1996.
McElwee, P.D. (2012) Payments for environmental services as neoliberal market-based forest conservation in Vietnam: Panacea or problem? *Geoforum* 43 (3), 412–426.

McKercher, B., Weber, K. and du Cros, H. (2008) Rationalising inappropriate behaviour at contested sites. *Journal of Sustainable Tourism* 16 (4), 369–385.

McLaughlin, B. (1986) Rural policy in the 1980s: The revival of the rural idyll. *Journal of Rural Studies* 2 (2), 81–90.

McManus, P. (2000) Sustainable development. In R.J. Johnston, D. Gregory, G. Pratt and M. Watts (eds) *The Dictionary of Human Geography* (4th edn., pp. 812–816). Oxford: Blackwell Publishers.

McManus, P. (2008) Mines, wines and thoroughbreds: Towards regional sustainability in the Upper Hunter, Australia. *Regional Studies* 42 (9), 1275–1290.

McManus, P., Albrecht, G. and Graham, G. (2012) *The Global Horseracing Industry: Social, Economic, Environmental and Ethical Perspectives*. Abingdon: Routledge.

McManus, P., Albrecht, G. and Graham, R. (2011) Constructing thoroughbred breeding landscapes: Manufactured idylls in the upper hunter region of Australia. In S. Brunn (ed.) *Engineering Earth: The Impacts of Megaengineering Projects* (pp. 1323–1329). Dordrecht, The Netherlands: Springer Science+Business Media.

McManus, P. and Pritchard, B. (2000) Preface. In B. Pritchard and P. McManus (eds) *Land of Discontent: The Dynamics of Change in Rural and Regional Australia*. Sydney: University of NSW Press.

McManus, P., Walmsley, J., Argent, N., Baum, S., Bourke, L., Martin, J. and Sorensen, T. (2012) Rural community and rural resilience: What is important to farmers in keeping their country towns alive? *Journal of Rural Studies* 28 (1), 20–29.

Mercer, A., de Rijke, K. and Dressler, W. (2014) Silences in the boom: Coal seam gas, neoliberalizing discourse, and the future of regional Australia. *Ecology* 21, 222–348.

Meskell, L. (2005) Archaeological ethnography: Conversations around Kruger National Park. *Archaeologies* 1 (1), 81–100.

Middleton, V. (1998) *Sustainable Tourism: A Marketing Perspective*. London: Routledge.

Middleton, V. (2010) Sir William Edmund Haygate Colbourne (Billy) Butlin, 1899–1980. In R. Butler and R. Russell (eds) *Giants of Tourism* (pp. 32–44). Oxon: CABI.

Middleton, V. and Clarke, J. (2012) *Marketing in Travel and Tourism* (3rd edn). London: Routledge.

Middleton, V., Fyall, A., Morgan, M. and Ranchold, A. (2009) Marketing in travel and tourism (4th edn). Oxford: Butterworth-Heinemann.

Milbrath, L.W. (1989) *Envisioning a Sustainable Society: Learning our Way Out*. NY: Suny Press.

Miles-Watson, J. and Miles-Watson, S. (2011) Conflicts and connections in the landscape of the Manimahesh pilgrimige. *Preliminary Communication* 59 (3), 319–333.

Mill, R.C. and Morrison, A.M. (2002) *The Tourism System*: Kendall Hunt.

Miller, G.A. (2003) Consumerism in sustainable tourism: A survey of UK consumers. *Journal of Sustainable Tourism* 11 (1), 17–39.

Mitchell, R. and Carson, R. (1989) *Using Surveys to Value Public Goods: The Contingent Valuation Method*. Washington D.C.: Resources for the Future.

Mitchell, R.W., Wooliscroft, B. and Higham, J. (2010) Sustainable market orientation: A new approach to managing marketing strategy. *Journal of Macromarketing* 30 (2), 160–170.

Mitchell, R., Wooliscroft, B. and Higham, J.E. (2013) Applying sustainability in national park management: Balancing public and private interests using a sustainable market orientation model. *Journal of Sustainable Tourism* 21 (5), 695–715.

Montana Office of Tourism (2014) West Yellowstone Marketing Plan FY 14. See https://www.yumpu.com/en/document/view/27697396/west-yellowstone-chamber-cvb-marketing-plan-montana-office-of-

Mordue, T. (1999) Heartbeat country: Conflicting values, coinciding visions. *Environment and Planning A* 31 (4), 629–646.

Mordue, T. (2001) Performing and directing resident/tourist cultures in Heartbeat country. *Tourist Studies* 1 (3), 233–252.

Mordue, T. (2009) Television, tourism, and rural life. *Journal of Travel Research* 47 (3), 332–345.
Morgan, N. and Pritchard, A. (1998) *Tourism Promotion and Power: Creating Images, Creating Identities*. London: John Wiley & Sons Ltd.
Morgan, N., Pritchard, A. and Piggott, R. (2002) New Zealand, 100% pure. The creation of a powerful niche destination brand. *The Journal of Brand Management* 9 (4), 335–354.
Morgan, N.J., Pritchard, A. and Piggott, R. (2003) Destination branding and the role of the stakeholders: The case of New Zealand. *Journal of Vacation Marketing* 9 (3), 285–299.
Morrison, A. (2010) *Hospitality and Travel Marketing* (4th edn.). Australia: Delmar: Cengage Learning.
Moscardo, G. and Pearce, P. (1997) Interpretation and Sustainable Tourism in the Wet Tropics World Heritage Area: A Case Study of Skyrail Visitors. Townsville: Department of Tourism James Cook University.
Muir, J. (1894) The Mountains of California. See http://www.sierraclub.org/john_muir_exhibit/writings/the_mountains_of_california/
Muir, J. (2007) *My First Summer in the Sierra*. Edinburgh: Canongate.
Mules, T. (2005) Economic impacts of national park tourism on gateway communities: The case of Kosiuszko National Park. *Tourism Economics* 11 (2), 247–259.
Mullings, B. (2010) Neoliberalism. In B. Wharf (ed.) *Encyclopaedia of Geography*. London: Sage.
National Parks and Service (2015) Yellowstone's Vision for Sustainability. See http://www.nps.gov/yell/learn/management/upload/whole_doc.pdf
National Parks Service (2000) Comprehensive Interpretive Planning – National Parks Service Interpretation and Education Guideline. See http://www.nps.gov/hfc/pdf/ip/cip-guideline.pdf
National Parks Service (2012a) Interpretation ane Education. See http://www.nps.gov/learn/
National Parks Service (2012b) The National Trails System Act. See http://www.nps.gov/nts/legislation.html
National Parks Service (ND-a) Organic Act of 1916. See http://www.nps.gov/grba/learn/m anagement/organic-act-of-1916.htm
National Parks Service (ND-b) What are core values? See http://www.nps.gov/training/uc/whcv.htm
Neagu, O. (2011) Influencing the environmental behavior through the green marketing. The Case of Romania Paper presented at the 2011 International Conference on Financial Management and Economics, Hong Kong China.
Neal, J.D. and Gursoy, D. (2008) A multifaceted analysis of tourism satisfaction. *Journal of Travel Research* 47 (1), 53–62.
Neumann, R.P. (1995) Ways of seeing Africa: Colonial recasting of African society and landscape in Serengeti National Park. *Cultural Geographies* 2 (2), 149–169.
New South Wales Government (2003) North Head Quaratine Station Conservation and Adaptive Re-use Proposal (vol. 1, pp. 1–286). Deptartment of Environment and Planning.
Niner, P. (2004) Accommodating nomadism? An examination of accommodation options for Gypsies and Travellers in England. *Housing Studies* 19 (2), 141–159.
North Yorkshire Dales National Park Authority (2015) Visitors give £240 million boost to National Park economy. See http://www.yorkshiredales.org.uk/living-and-working/how-we-can-help/press-office/news/recent/visitors-give-240-million-boost-to-national-park-economy
Notzke, C. (2004) Indigenous tourism development in southern Alberta, Canada: Tentative engagement. *Journal of Sustainable Tourism* 12 (1), 29–54.
O'Neill, M., Riscinto-Kozub, K. and Hyfte, M. (2010) Defining visitor satisfaction in the context of camping oriented nature based tourism – the driving force of quality. *Journal of Vacation Marketing* 16 (2), 141–156.

O'Sullivan, E.L. (1991) *Marketing for Parks, Recreation, and Leisure*. Venture State College: PA.

O'Doherty, D., De Cock, C., Rehn, A. and Ashcraft, K.L. (2013) New sites/sights: Exploring the white spaces of organization. *Organization Studies* 34 (10), 1427–1444.

Oliver, C. (1990) Determinants of interorganizational relationships: Integration and future directions. *Academy of Management Review* 15 (2), 241–265.

Onyx, J., Edwards, M. and Bullen, P. (2007) The intersection of social capital and power: An application to rural communities. *Rural Society* 17 (3), 215–230.

Orams, M.B. (1996) Using interpretation to manage nature-based tourism. *Journal of Sustainable Tourism* 4 (2), 81–94.

Ord, C. (2013, May/June) Iconic Australasian Adventures. *Australian Geographic Outdoor Explore Adventure,* 20–21.

Ostrom, E. (2008) Tragedy of the commons. *The New Palgrave Dictionary of Economics* (pp. 360–362). London: Palgrave.

Palin, M. (1997) *Full Circle*. London: BBC Books.

Palin, M. (2011) Michael palin on geography: Presidential address and record of the RGS-IBG annual general meeting 2011. *The Geographical Journal* 177 (3), 275–278.

Palomino-Schalscha, M. (2012) Geographies of tourism and development. In C. Wilson (ed.) *The Routledge Handbook of Tourism Geographies* (pp. 187–193). Oxon: Routledge.

Parks Canada (2000) Unimpaired for future generations? Protecting ecological integrity with Canada's national parks *Vol.2, Report of the Panel on the Ecological Integrity of Canada's National Parks*. Ottawa, Ontario.

Parks Canada (2010) Banff National Park of Canada Management Plan. See http://www.pc.gc.ca/eng/pn-np/ab/banff/plan/gestion-management.aspx

Parks, C.S. (2014) Parks Online Resources for Teachers and Students (PORTS) Program. See http://www.ports.parks.ca.gov (accessed 17 April 2015).

PBS (2009) The National Parks: America's Best Idea. See http://www.pbs.org/nationalparks/

Pearce, P.L. and Moscardo, G. (1998) The role of interpretation in influencing visitor satisfaction: A rainforest case study. Paper presented at the CAUTHE 1998: Progress in tourism and hospitality research: Proceedings of the eighth Australian Tourism and Hospitality Research Conference, 11–14 February 1998, Gold Coast, Queensland, Australia.

Peaslee, R.M. (2011) One ring, many circles: The Hobbiton tour experience and a spatial approach to media power. *Tourist Studies* 11 (1), 37–53.

Peattie, K. (2001) Towards sustainability: The third age of green marketing. *The Marketing Review* 2 (2), 129–146.

Perec, G. (1997) *Species of Spaces and Other Pieces*. London: Penguin.

Pettigrew, C. and Lyons, M. (1979) Royal National Park: A history. *Parks and Wildlife* 2 (3–4), 15–30.

Pfeffer, J. and Salancik, G.R. (2003) *The External Control of Organizations: A Resource Dependence Perspective*. CA: Stanford University Press.

Pierce, J.P. and Gilpin, E.A. (1995) A historical analysis of tobacco marketing and the uptake of smoking by youth in the United States: 1890–1977. *Health Psychology* 14 (6), 500.

Pike, S. (2004) *Destination Marketing Organisations*. Oxford: Elsevier.

Pike, S. (2008) *Destination Marketing: An Integrated Marketing Communication Approach*. Amsterdam: Elsevier.

Pinchot, G. (1910) *The Fight for Conservation*. New York: Doubleday, Page & Company.

Polonsky, M.J. and Rosenberger III, P.J. (2001) Reevaluating green marketing: A strategic approach. *Business Horizons* 44 (5), 21–30.

Porter, M.E. (1987) *From Competitive Advantage to Corporate Strategy* (vol. 59). MA: Harvard Business Review.

Porter, M.E. (2008) The five competitive forces that shape strategy. *Harvard Business Review* 86 (1), 25–40.

Porter, M.E. and Kramer, M.R. (2006) The link between competitive advantage and corporate social responsibility. *Harvard Business Review* 84 (12), 78–92.
Power, M. (2003) *Rethinking Development Geographies*. London: Routledge.
Pritchard, B. and McManus, P. (2000) *Land of Discontent: The Dynamics of Change in Rural and Regional Australia*. Sydney: University of NSW Press.
Privette, G. (1983) Peak experience, peak performance, and flow: A comparative analysis of positive human experiences. *Journal of Personality and Social Psychology* 45 (6), 1361.
Putrill, J. (2013, April 27–28) Our national parks prove a marketer's nightmare, *Weekend Australian*.
Quan, H. (2000) Please don't visit: Crowds and overdevelopment are hurting our national parks. But what if Parks Canada were to try a little demarketing to encourage potential visitors to stay away? *Marketing Magazine* 105 (33), 14.
Quan, S. and Wang, N. (2004) Towards a structural model of the tourist experience: An illustration from food experiences in tourism. *Tourism Management* 25 (3), 297–305.
Quinlan Cutler, S., Carmichael, B. and Doherty, S. (2014) The Inca Trail experience: Does the journey matter? *Annals of Tourism Research* 45, 152–166.
Ramakrisha, P. (2003) Conserving the sacred: The protective impulse and the origins of modern protected areas. In D. Harmon and A. Putney (eds) *The Full Value of Parks: From Economics to the Intangible* (pp. 27–42). Lanham: Rowman and Littlefield.
Reed, M. (2006) 1.1 Organizational theorizing: A historically contested terrain. In S. Clegg, S. Hardy, T. Lawrence and W. Nord (eds) *The Sage Handbook of Organization Studies* (2nd ed., pp. 19–54). London: Sage.
Reed, M.G. (1997) Power relations and community-based tourism planning. *Annals of Tourism Research* 24 (3), 566–591.
Reggers, A., Schweinsberg, S. and Wearing, S. (2013) Understanding stakeholder values in co-management arrangements for protected area establishment on the Kokoda Track, Papua New Guinea. *Journal of Park and Recreation Administration* 31 (3), 45–60.
Reis, A.C., Thompson-Carr, A. and Lovelock, B. (2012) Parks and families: Addressing management facilitators and constraints to outdoor recreation participation. *Annals of Leisure Research* 15 (4), 315–334.
Reisinger, Y. and Steiner, C. (2006) Reconceptualising interpretation: The role of tour guides in authentic tourism. *Current Issues in Tourism* 9 (6), 481–498.
Reisinger, Y. and Steiner, C.J. (2006) Reconceptualizing object authenticity. *Annals of Tourism Research* 33 (1), 65–86.
Rettie, K., Clevenger, A. and Ford, A. (2009) Innovative approaches for managing conservation and use challenges in the National Parks: Insights from Canada. In T. Jamal and M. Robinson (eds) *The SAGE Handbook of Tourism Studies* (pp. 396–413). Los Angeles: Sage.
Ritchie, E., Laurence, B., Bradshaw, C., Watson, D., Johnston, E., Possingham, H. and McCarthy, M. (2013) Our national parks must be more than playgrounds of paddocks. See https://theconversation.com/our-national-parks-must-be-more-than-playgrounds-or-paddocks-14389
Ritchie, J.B. (1999) Crafting a value-driven vision for a national tourism treasure. *Tourism Management* 20 (3), 273–282.
Rittel, H.W. and Webber, M.M. (1973) Dilemmas in a general theory of planning. *Policy Sciences* 4 (2), 155–169.
Robinson, M. (2002) Between and beyond the pages: Literature-tourism relationships. In H.-A. Anderson and M. Robinson (eds) *Literature and Tourism* (pp. 39–79). London: Continuum.
Robinson, M. and Andersen, H. (2002) Reading between the lines: Literature and the creation of touristic spaces. In M. Robinson and H. Andersen (eds) *Literature and Tourism* (pp. 1–38). London: Continuum.

Rojek, C. (2005) *Leisure Theory: Principles and Practice*. New York: Palgrave.
Ross, B. (2012) Michael Palin: 'I'm just curious about the world'. See http://www.independent.co.uk/travel/news-and-advice/michael-palin-im-just-curious-about-the-world-8298290.html
Royal Botanic Gardens and Domain Trust (2014) Securing the Future: Draft master plan concepts. See http://www.rbgsyd.nsw.gov.au/__data/assets/pdf_file/0010/135937/212107_RBGDT_PublicBoards_V20_LR.pdf
Ruekert, R.W. (1992) Developing a market orientation: An organizational strategy perspective. *International Journal of Research in Marketing* 9 (3), 225–245.
Runnels, C. (2009) Defining the Alaska National Park experience: An exploration of adventure and authenticity as key components of an interpretive marketing strategy. PhD thesis, Austin State University. See http://proquest.umi.com/pqdlink?did=1907668591&Fmt=7&clientId=20928&RQT=309&VName=PQD
Runte, A. (1977) The national park idea: Origins and paradox of the American experience. *Forest & Conservation History* 21 (2), 64–75.
Runte, A. (1997) *National parks: The American Experience*. NE: U of Nebraska Press.
Runte, A. (2002) Why National Parks? See http://www.georgewright.org/192runte.pdf
Russell, D.W. and Russell, C.A. (2010) Experiential reciprocity: The role of direct experience in value perceptions. *Journal of Travel & Tourism Marketing* 27 (6), 624–634.
Ryan, C. (2002) Equity, management, power sharing and sustainability—issues of the 'new tourism'. *Tourism Management* 23 (1), 17–26.
Ryan, C., Trauer, B., Kave, J., Sharma, A. and Sharma, S. (2003) Backpackers-what is the peak experience? *Tourism Recreation Research* 28 (3), 93–98.
Ryel, R. and Grasse, T. (1991) Marketing ecotourism: Attracting the elusive ecotourist. In T. Whelan (ed.) *Nature Tourism: Managing for the Environment* (pp. 164–186). Washington, D.C.: Island Press.
Sax, J.L. (1980) *Mountains Without Handrails, Reflections on the National Parks*. MI: University of Michigan Press.
Schafft, K.A., Borlu, Y. and Glenna, L. (2013) The relationship between Marcellus Shale gas development in Pennsylvania and local perceptions of risk and opportunity. *Rural Sociology* 78 (2), 143–166.
Schwartz, S.H. (1994) Are there universal aspects in the structure and contents of human values? *Journal of Social Issues* 50 (4), 19–45.
Schweinsberg, S., Wearing, S. and Darcy, S. (2012) Understanding communities' views of nature in rural industry renewal: The transition from forestry to nature-based tourism in Eden, Australia. *Journal of Sustainable Tourism* 22 (2), 195–213.
Seaton, A.V. and Bennett, M.M. (1996) *The Marketing of Tourism Products: Concepts, Issues and Cases*. Mumbai: International Thomson Business Press.
Seelig, T. (2012) *inGenius: A Crash Course on Creativity*. London: Hay House, Inc.
Selby, M., Hayllar, B. and Griffin, T. (2008) The tourist experience of precincts. In B. Hayllar, T. Griffin and D. Edwards (eds) *City Spaces Tourist Places* (pp. 183–202). Amsterdam: Butterworth-Heinemann.
Sellars, R.W. (2009) *Preserving Nature in the National Parks: A History: With a New Preface and Epilogue*. NH: Yale University Press.
Sewell, W., Dearden, P. and Dumbrell, J. (1989) Wilderness decisionmaking and the role of environmental interest groups: A comparison of the Franklin Dam, Tasmania and South Moresby, British Columbia. *Natural Resources Journal* 29, 147–170.
Shaffer, M.S. (1996) 'See America First': Re-envisioning nation and region through Western Tourism. *The Pacific Historical Review* 75, 559–581.
Sharma, S. (1999) Trespass or symbiosis? Dissolving the boundaries between strategic marketing and strategic management. *Journal of Strategic Marketing* 7 (2), 73–88.
Sharp, J.P. (2000) *Entanglements of Power: Geographies of Domination/Resistance* (vol. 5). NY: Psychology Press.

Sharpe, G., Odegaard, C. and Sharpe, W. (1994) *A Comprehensive Introduction to Park Management*. United States: Sagamore Publishing.

Sharpley, R. and Pearce, T. (2007) Tourism, marketing and sustainable development in the English National Parks: The role of National Park authorities. *Journal of Sustainable Tourism* 15 (5), 557–573.

Shaw, G. and Williams, A.M. (2002) *Critical Issues in Tourism: A Geographical Perspective* (2nd edn). Oxford: Blackwell.

Shea, R. (2015) How Good Old American marketing saved the National Parks. See http://news.nationalgeographic.com/2015/03/150324-national-park-service-history-yellowstone-california-united-states/

Sheller, M. (2004) Automotive emotions feeling the car. *Theory, Culture & Society* 21 (4–5), 221–242.

Sherval, M. and Hardiman, K. (2014) Competing perceptions of the rural idyll: Responses to threats from coal seam gas development in Gloucester, NSW, Australia. *Australian Geographer* 45(2), 185–203.

Sheth, J.N. and Parvatiyar, A. (1995a) Ecological imperatives and the role of marketing. In J.P.-S Michael and T.M.W. Alma (eds) *Environmental Marketing: Strategies, Practice, Theory and Research* (pp. 3–20). New York: Haworth Press.

Sheth, J.N. and Parvatiyar, A. (1995b) The evolution of relationship marketing. *International Business Review* 4 (4), 397–418.

Shilbury, D., Westerbeek, H., Quick, S., Funk, D. and Karg, A. (2014) *Strategic Sport Marketing* (4th edn). Crows Nest, NSW: Allen and Unwin.

Shiu, E., Hassan, L.M. and Walsh, G. (2009) Demarketing tobacco through governmental policies–the 4Ps revisited. *Journal of Business Research* 62 (2), 269–278.

Shultis, J. (2003) Recreational Values of Protected Areas. In D. Harmon and A.D. Putney (eds) *The Full Value of Parks* (pp. 59–76). Lanham: Rowan & Littlefield Publishers Inc.

Shultz, C.J. and Holbrook, M.B. (1999) Marketing and the tragedy of the commons: A synthesis, commentary, and analysis for action. *Journal of Public Policy & Marketing* 18 (2), 218–229.

Sierra Club (2015) Who was John Muir? See http://vault.sierraclub.org/john_muir_exhibit/about/default.aspx

Singh, R. and Sharma, S. (2010) The Green Hiker attitude slowly picks up ast ManiMahesh. *Himalayan Highlights* (3), 2–4.

Skålén, P. and Hackley, C. (2011) Marketing-as-practice. Introduction to the special issue. *Scandinavian Journal of Management* 27 (2), 189–195.

Skyttner, L. (2001) *General Systems Theory: Ideas and Application*. Singapore: World Scientific.

Slattery, D. (2009) Bushwalking and Access: Byles, Dunphy and the Kosciusko Primitive Area debate 1943–6. Paper presented at the 'Outdoor education research and theory: Critical reflections, new directions', the Fourth International Outdoor Education Research Conference, La Trobe University, Beechworth, Victoria, Australia.

Smith, S.L. (1994) The tourism product. *Annals of Tourism Research* 21 (3), 582–595.

Spooner, K. and Site, T.D. (2000) Decommissioning of a UK nuclear power station in a national park—An owners perspective. Paper presented at the WM (Proc. Int. Conf. Tucson, 2000) WM Symposia Inc., Tucson, AZ.

Stanford, D.J. (2014) Reducing visitor car use in a protected area: A market segmentation approach to achieving behaviour change. *Journal of Sustainable Tourism* 22 (4), 666–683.

Stankey, G.H. (1989) Tourism and national parks; peril and potential. In P. Bateson, S. Nyman and D. Sheppard (eds) *National Parks and Tourism* (pp. 11–18). Hurstville: National Parks and Wildlife Service.

Steiner, C.J. and Reisinger, Y. (2006) Understanding existential authenticity. *Annals of Tourism Research* 33 (2), 299–318.

Stockdale, A. (2006) Migration: Pre-requisite for rural economic regeneration? *Journal of Rural Studies* 22 (3), 354–366.
Stronza, A. (2001) Anthropology of tourism: Forging new ground for ecotourism and other alternatives. *Annual Review of Anthropology*, 30, 261–283.
Stronza, A. (2010) Commons management and ecotourism: Ethnographic evidence from the Amazon. *International Journal of the Commons* 4 (1), 56–77.
Suchman, M.C. (1995) Managing legitimacy: Strategic and institutional approaches. *Academy of Management Review* 20 (3), 571–610.
Synergies Economic Consulting (2012) Measuring the contribution of the Outdoor Recreation Sector in Queensland A report prepared for the Queensland Outdoor Recreation Federation. See http://www.skillsalliance.com.au/wp-content/uploads/import_files/publications/other-publications-pdf/measuring_the_contribution_ofthe_queensland_outdoor_recreation_sector_final.pdf
Taylor, J.E. and Martin, P.L. (2001) Human capital: Migration and rural population change. *Handbook of Agricultural Economics* 1, 457–511.
Thapa, B. (2012) Why did they not visit? Examining structural constraints to visit Kafue National Park, Zambia. *Journal of Ecotourism* 11 (1), 74–83.
Thibault, L. and Harvey, J. (1997) Fostering interorganizational linkages in the Canadian sport delivery system. *Journal of Sport Management* 11, 45–68.
Tilden, F. (1977) *Interpreting our Heritage* (3rd edn). Chapel Hill: North Carolina Press.
Timothy, D. and Boyd, S. (2015) *Tourism and Trails: Cultural, Eological and Management Issues*. Bristol: Channel View Publications.
Timothy, D. and Tosun, C. (2003) Appropriate planning for tourism in destination communities: Participation, incremental growth and collaboration. In S. Singh, D. Timothy and R. Dowling (eds) *Tourism in Destination Communities* (pp. 181–204). Oxon: CAB International.
Torelli, C.J. and Shavitt, S. (2010) Culture and concepts of power. *Journal of Personality and Social Psychology* 99 (4), 703.
Tourism Australia (2005) The experience seeker. See http://www.tourism.australia.com/content/aussie_experiences/2007/experience_seekers.pdf
Tourism Australia (2012) Experience development strategies: Guidelines for Australia's National Landscape Steering Committees (2nd edn). See www.environment.gov.au/parks/.../experience-development.docx
Tourism Research Australia (2010) Indigenous tourism in Australia: Profiling the domestic market. See http://www.waitoc.com/wp-content/uploads/2011/06/Indigenous_Tourism_in_Australia_FINAL.pdf
Tower, J., Jago, L. and Deery, M. (2006) Relationship marketing and partnerships in not-for-profit sport in Australia. *Sport Marketing Quarterly* 15 (3), 167–180.
Tower, J., Jago, L. and Deery, M. (2010) Strategies for managing partnerships in community sport and recreation services. *Poster presentation at 2010 NRPA Conference*. Minneopolis, Minnesota: NAtional Recreation and Park Association.
Tranel, M. and Hall, A. (2003) Parks as battlegrounds: Managing conflicting values. In D. Harmon and A. Putney (eds) *The Full Value of Parks: From Economics to the Intangible* (pp. 253–268). Lanham: Rowman and Littlefield.
Travel Montana (2012) Yellowstone country montana: Marketing plan 2012–2013. See http://tourism.mt.gov/Portals/92/shared/docs/pdf/marketingPlans/Yellowstone%20Country%20FY13.pdf
Tsiotsou, R. and Goldsmith, R. (2012) *Strategic Marketing in Tourism Services*. United Kingdom: Emerald.
TTF Australia (2014) Royal Botanic Garden & Domain Masterplan. See http://www.ttf.org.au/Content/rbgdomain060414.aspx
TTF Australia: Tourism and Transport Forum (2007) Natural Tourism Partnerships Action Plan. Sydney: TTF Australia: Tourism and Transport Forum.

Tuan, Y.F. (1977) *Space and Place: The Perspective of Experience*. Minneapolis: University of Minnesota Press.
Tubb, K.N. (2003) An evaluation of the effectiveness of interpretation within Dartmoor National Park in reaching the goals of sustainable tourism development. *Journal of Sustainable Tourism* 11 (6), 476–498.
Tuohino, A. and Pitkänen, K. (2004) The transformation of a neutral lake landscape into a meaningful experience–Interpreting tourist photos. *Journal of Tourism and Cultural Change* 2 (2), 77–93.
Turnbull, D. (2007) Maps narratives and trails: Performativity, hodology and distributed knowledges in complex adaptive systems–an approach to emergent mapping. *Geographical Research* 45 (2), 140–149.
Turner, R.W. (2002) Market failures and the rationale for national parks. *The Journal of Economic Education* 33 (4), 347–356.
Tussyadiah, I.P. and Fesenmaier, D.R. (2008) Marketing places through first-person stories—an analysis of Pennsylvania Roadtripper Blog. *Journal of Travel & Tourism Marketing* 25 (3–4), 299–311.
UNESCO (2015) FAQ. See http://whc.unesco.org/en/faq/
United Nations (1993) Agenda 21: Programme of action for sustainable development: Rio Declaration on environment and development; Statement of Forest Principles: The final text of agreements negotiated by Governments at the United Nations Conference on Environment and Development (UNCED), 3–14 June 1992, Rio de Janeiro, Brazil. New York: United Nations Dept. of Public Information.
United Nations (2002) Report on the world summit on sustainable development Johannesburg, South Africa, 26 August–4 September. See http://daccessdds.un.org/doc/UNDOC/GEN/N02/636/93/PDF/N0263693.pdf?OpenElement (accessed 4 May 2006).
United States Department of Agriculture (n.d.) 1964 Wilderness act. See http://www.fs.usda.gov/detail/giffordpinchot/specialplaces/?cid=stelprdb5137139
University of Technology Sydney (2013) *Integrating Business Perspectives* (3rd edn.). Sydney: McGraw Hill.
Uriely, N. (2005) The tourist experience: Conceptual developments. *Annals of Tourism Research* 32 (1), 199–216.
Urry, J. (1990) *The Tourist Gaze*. London: Sage.
Urry, J. (1995) *Consuming Places*. London: Routledge.
Urry, J. (2000) *Sociology Beyond Societies: Mobilities for the Twenty-First Century*. NY Psychology Press.
Urry, J. (2002) *The Tourist Gaze* (2nd edn). London: Sage.
Van Dam, Y.K. and Apeldoorn, P.A. (1996) Sustainable marketing. *Journal of Macromarketing* 16 (2), 45–56.
Vanderbeck, R.M. and Dunkley, C.M. (2003) Young people's narratives of rural-urban difference. *Children's Geographies* 1 (2), 241–259.
Vargo, S.L. (2011) Market systems, stakeholders and value propositions: Toward a service-dominant logic-based theory of the market. *European Journal of Marketing* 45 (1–2), 217–222.
Veal, A., Darcy, S. and Lynch, R. (eds) (2013) *Australian Leisure*. Frenchs Forest: Pearson.
Veal, A.J. (2003) Tracking change: Leisure participation and policy in Australia, 1985–2002. *Annals of Leisure Research* 6 (3), 345–277.
Vodouhê, F.G., Coulibaly, O., Adégbidi, A. and Sinsin, B. (2010) Community perception of biodiversity conservation within protected areas in Benin. *Forest Policy and Economics* 12 (7), 505–512.
Wade, D.J. and Eagles, P.F. (2003) The use of importance–performance analysis and market segmentation for tourism management in parks and protected areas: An application to Tanzania's National Parks. *Journal of Ecotourism* 2 (3), 196–212.

Waitt, G., Lane, R. and Head, L. (2003) The boundaries of nature tourism. *Annals of Tourism Research* 30 (3), 523–545.

Walpole, M.J. and Goodwin, H.J. (2001) Local attitudes towards conservation and tourism around Komodo National Park, Indonesia. *Environmental Conservation* 28 (2), 160–166.

Walton, A.M., McCrea, R., Leonard, R. and Williams, R. (2013) Resilience in a changing community landscape of coal seam gas: Chinchilla in southern Queensland. *Journal of Economic & Social Policy* 15 (3), 4.

Wang, N. (1999) Rethinking authenticity in tourism experience. *Annals of Tourism Research* 26 (2), 349–370.

Watkins, T.H. (1990) Marketing Yosemite. *Wilderness* 54 (190), 22.

Wattchow, B. and Brown, M. (2011) *A Pedagogy of Place: Outdoor Recreation for a Changing World*. Clayton: Monash University.

Watts, M. (2009) Market. In R.J. Johnston, D. Gregory, G. Pratt, M. Watts and S. Whatmore (eds) *The Dictionary of Human Geography* (5th edn, pp. 439–443). Oxford: Blackwell Publishers.

Wearing, S. (2008a) Marketing national parks using ecotourism as a catalyst: Towards a theory and practice. In S. Babu, B. Mishra and B. Parida (eds) *Tourism Development Revisited: Concepts, Issues and Paradigms* (pp. 132–149). London: SAGE.

Wearing, S. (2008b) National parks, tourism and marketing. *Australasian Parks and Leisure, Summer* 11 (4), 29–34.

Wearing, S. and Archer, D. (2001) Towards a framework for sustainable marketing of protected areas. *Australian Parks and Leisure* 4 (1), 33–40.

Wearing, S. and Archer, D. (2002) Challenging interpretation to discover more inclusive. *World Leisure Journal* 44 (3), 43–53.

Wearing, S., Archer, D. and Beeton, S. (2001) *The Sustainable Marketing of Tourism in Protected Areas*. Gold Coast. CRC for Sustainable Tourism.

Wearing, S., Archer, D. and Beeton, S. (2007) *The Sustainable Marketing of Tourism in Protected Areas Moving Forward*. CRC for Sustainable Tourism Pty Ltd.

Wearing, S., Archer, D., Moscardo, G. and Schweinsberg, S. (2006) *Best Practice Interpretation Research for Sustainable Tourism: Framework for a New Research Agenda*. CRC for Sustainable Tourism Pty Ltd.

Wearing, S. and Darcy, S. (1999) Ecotourism options in coastal protected area management: A case study of North Head Quarantine Station, Australia. *Environmentalist* 18 (4), 239–249.

Wearing, S. and McDonald, M. (2002) The development of community-based tourism: Re-thinking the relationship between tour operators and development agents as intermediaries in rural and isolated area communities. *Journal of Sustainable Tourism* 10 (3), 191–206.

Wearing, S. and Neil, J. (2009) *Ecotourism: Impacts Potentials and Possibilities* (2nd edn). Oxford: Butterworth-Heinemann.

Wearing, S., Stevenson, D. and Young, T. (2010) *Tourist Cultures: Identity, Place and the Traveller*. Los Angeles: SAGE.

Wearing, S., van der Duim, R. and Schweinsberg, S. (2007) Equitable representation of local porters. Towards a sustainable Nepalese trekking industry. *Matkailututkimus* 3 (1), 72–93.

Wearing, S. and Wearing, B. (2001) Conceptualizing the selves of tourism. *Leisure Studies* 20 (2), 143–159.

Wearing, S.L., Schweinsberg, S., Lai, P.-H. and Lyons, K. (2014) A discussion of coal seam gas in Australia's hunter valley wine tourism region. *Australasian Parks and Leisure* 17 (2), 49.

Weaver, D. (2011) *Ecotourism* (2nd edn). Milton QLD: Wiley.

Weaver, D. and Lawton, L. (2014) *Tourism Management* (5th edn). Milton QLD: Wiley.

Weaver, D.B. and Lawton, L.J. (2002) Overnight ecotourist market segmentation in the Gold Coast hinterland of Australia. *Journal of Travel Research* 40 (3), 270–280.

Weiler, B. and Ham, S.H. (2002) Tour guide training: A model for sustainable capacity building in developing countries. *Journal of Sustainable Tourism* 10 (1), 52–69.

White, D.D. (2006) Visitor experiences and transportation systems in Yosemite National Park: Arizona school of community resources and development, Arizona State University. See http://www.academia.edu/5472429/Visitor_Experiences_and_Transportation_Systems_in_Yosemite_National_Park

White, D.D. (2007) An interpretive study of Yosemite National Park visitors' perspectives toward alternative transportation in Yosemite Valley. *Environmental Management* 39 (1), 50–62.

Whitelaw, P.A., King, B.E. and Tolkach, D. (2014) Protected areas, conservation and tourism–financing the sustainable dream. *Journal of Sustainable Tourism* 22 (4), 584–603.

Whittaker, D., Shelby, B., Meldrum, B., DeGroot, H. and Bacon, J. (2012) Transportation, recreation, and capacities in Yosemite National Park. *Society News, Notes & Mail* 29 (3), 338–350.

Whittington, R. (1996) Strategy as practice. *Long Range Planning* 29 (5), 731–735.

Whittington, R. (2007) Strategy practice and strategy process: Family differences and the sociological eye. *Organization Studies* 28 (10), 1575–1586.

Williams, K. and Harvey, D. (2001) Transcendent experience in forest environments. *Journal of Environmental Psychology* 21 (3), 249–260.

Wilton, J.J. and Nickerson, N.P. (2006) Collecting and using visitor spending data. *Journal of Travel Research* 45 (1), 17–25.

Witt, S.F. and Moutinho, L. (1994) *Tourism Marketing and Management Handbook*. Upper Saddle River: Prentice-Hall International.

Woodard, K. and Jones III, J. (2000) Ontology. In R.J. Johnston, D. Gregory, G. Pratt and M. Watts (eds) *The Dictionary of Human Geography* (4th edn, pp. 511–513). Oxford: Blackwell Publishers.

Woods, M. (2010) *Rural*. London: Routledge.

Woods, M., Flemmen, A.B. and Wollan, G. (2014) Beyond the Idyll: Contested spaces of rural tourism. *Norsk Geografisk Tidsskrift-Norwegian Journal of Geography* 68 (3), 202–204.

Woollam, P.B. (2004) Experience from the Trawsfynydd Public Inquiry. *Strategy Selection for the Decommissioning of Nuclear Facilities*, 217.

Worboys, G., Lockwood, M., Kothari, A., Feary, S. and Pulsford, I. (2015) Protected area governance and management. See http://press.anu.edu.au/wp-content/uploads/2015/02/WHOLE.pdf

World Commission on Environment and Development (1987) *Our Common Future*. Oxford: Oxford University Press.

World Commission on Environment and Development (1990) *Our Common Future* (Australian edn). Melbourne: Oxford University Press.

Wyckoff, W. and Dilsaver, L.M. (1997) Promotional imagery of Glacier National Park. *Geographical Review* 87 (1), 1–26.

Yarwood, R. (2012) One moor night: Emergencies, training and rural space. *Area* 44 (1), 22–28.

Yosemite and Maripossa Country Tourism Bureau (n.d.) Yosemite. See http://www.yosemiteexperience.com/yosemite/

Zanon, D., Hall, J., Lockstone-Binney, L. and Weber, D. (2014) Development of a whole agency approach to market segmentation in parks. *Journal of Leisure Research* 46 (5), 563–592.

Index

4Ps 31–32
5R Model of sustainable marketing 11–15, 34
Aerial drones 16
Australian Greens 13
Authenticity 68, 69, 76, 81
Authentic tourism experiences 69

Banff National Park 91, 107, 118, 123
Blue Mountains National Park 42
Botanic garden 80, 81
Brand Canada 20–21
Brand identity 13
Business environment 4, 50, 55–56, 61

Canada National Parks Act 88
Co-management theory 13
Community 82
Cooperative promotion 46–47, 48
Culture 101

Destination images 40, 41

Ecological sustainability 5, 7
Ecologically responsibility 36
Ecotourism 14, 56, 59
    Segments 76
Environment
    Conservation 7
Environment conservation
    Definition 15
Environmental change 5
Environmentally sustainable marketing 36
Ephemeral pools 65, 66
Experience
    Components 73
    Ephemeral experience 94–96
    National park experience 75, 77, 78
    Tourist experience 75
    Touristic experience 86
    Transcendent experience 84

Fortress conservation 71

Gesaeuse National Park 29
Green consumerism 35–36, 59
Green marketing 59

Halfacree's Three-Fold Model of Tourism Space 107–111
Himalaya 39–40
Himalayan Tourism 78, 79
Historic site 102
Human values 55

Image 98
Indigenous methodologies 83
Indigenous populations 75, 82, 83
Inter-organisational relationships (IORs) 44
International travellers 39
Interpretation 84–87, 98, 101, 111, 117–119

Kakadu 13
KPIs 32–33

Lake Pedder 60
Land ethic 69
Legitimacy 109

Mani Mahesh 70
Marketing
    Alternative marketing 2, 51, 128
    Complementary concepts 20
    Complementary approaches 33–34
    Definition 1, 6, 9, 94, 104

Demarketing 11, 16, 20, 41–43, 52, 72
Ecological marketing 35–38, 52
Environmental marketing 36
Innovation 3
Market segmentation 29, 30, 31
Marketing brands 66
Marketing in national parks 66–69
Orientation 2
Principles 52
Relationship marketing 44–51, 52, 119
Social marketing 38–42, 52, 55
Strategy 4, 26, 40, 60
Target markets 29, 30, 32, 33, 52
Tree model of marketing delivery 17–22, 51
Traditional marketing 20, 35, 40, 52
True marketing 11
Mass tourism 25, 37, 84, 92
Muir, John 2–3, 19, 71, 94–96

National Eco Certification Program 47
National park agencies 45
National Park Authorities (NPA) 108
National park managers 72
National park visitors 37, 101
National parks 2, 3, 7, 15, 16, 18, 36, 70, 76, 88, 91, 109, 124, 125
National Parks Service 116, 119
National Parks Service Act 87
National Trails System Act 88
Nature 92, 106
Nature-based tourism 2, 4, 58, 84
Neoliberalism 10, 27
Nepalese 41
North Head National Park 61–64
North Yorkshire National Park 119–121

Objectives 50

Park managers 2, 5, 44, 45, 82, 98, 112, 117
Parks Canada 42
Partnerships 42, 49, 58
Peak experiences 86–89
Pilgrimage environment 70
Phillip Island Nature Park 53
Pinchot, Gifford 3, 12, 13, 71
Planned tourism 58
Porter, Michael 56
Power 98, 100, 107, 108, 111
  Entangled power 111–115
  Episodic power 112

Power relations 105, 106
Process of innovation 3–4
Product development 93–94
Public goods 59
Public policy 59

Quarantine Station 61–64

Regional sustainability 56, 100
Rural areas 102, 103
Rural images 104

Serengeti National Park 14
Sierra Club 76, 77
Social paradigms 58
Societal responsibility 116
Sociocultural values 56
Stakeholders 7, 20, 26, 28, 30, 58
Strategy 4, 5, 10, 26, 56, 57
Structural coherence 110–111
Structures of power 21
Sustainability 8, 9, 26, 28, 81, 84, 102
Sustainable consumption 20
Sustainable development 1, 2, 60, 122
Sustainable marketing 2, 12, 26, 28, 36, 60, 109
Sustainable national park management 125
Sustainable plan 79
Sustainable relations 61
Sustainable tourism 1, 4, 8, 41

Tourism 29, 56, 79, 91, 92, 98, 102
Tourism agencies 75
Tourism bodies 49
Tourism industry 1, 40, 49, 73, 76
Tourism marketing 6, 8, 19, 26, 86, 107
Tourism platforms 21
Tourists 26, 72, 73, 75, 83, 84, 91, 117
Transportation 61
Tragedy of the Commons 124
Travel writing 77
Trekking 40
Trekkers 40, 41, 73
Trial by space 111

Uluru 36–37

Wicked problems 54, 127
Wilderness 73–75, 105–106
World Heritage 13, 47, 68

Yellowstone 5, 13, 22–24, 59, 71, 82, 116
Yosemite 3, 16, 37, 61, 74, 83, 122

For Product Safety Concerns and Information please contact our EU Authorised Representative:

Easy Access System Europe

Mustamäe tee 50

10621 Tallinn

Estonia

gpsr.requests@easproject.com